Modern Urban Poetry

MASTERPIECES OF
MODERN URDU POETRY

K.C. KANDA

NEW DAWN PRESS, INC.
UK • USA • INDIA

Dedicated
with loving regards to
Dr. J. S. Neki

NEW DAWN PRESS GROUP
Published by New Dawn Press Group

New Dawn Press, 2 Tintern Close, Slough, Berkshire, SL1-2TB, UK
e-mail: ndpuk@mail.newdawnpress.com

New Dawn Press, Inc., 244 South Randall Rd # 90, Elgin, IL 60123, USA
e-mail: sales@newdawnpress.com

New Dawn Press (An Imprint of Sterling Publishers (P) Ltd.)
A-59, Okhla Industrial Area, Phase-II, New Delhi-110020, India
e-mail: info@sterlingpublishers.com
www.sterlingpublishers.com

Masterpieces of Modern Urdu Poetry
Copyright © 1998, K.C. Kanda
ISBN 1 932705 44 9
Reprint 1999, 2004

PRINTED IN INDIA

PREFACE

This book is a complement to my earlier books: *Masterpieces of Urdu Ghazal* (1990), *Masterpieces of Urdu Rubaiyat* (1994), *Urdu Ghazal : An Anthology* (1994), *Masterpieces of Urdu Nazm* (1996), and *Mir Taqi Mir* (1997) — all of which are intended to introduce the reader, especially of the non-Urdu-knowing class, to the best specimens of Urdu poetry in its varied forms. While the aforesaid volumes concern themselves with the poetry of the classical poets, most of whom lived and wrote in the 18th and 19th centuries, the present book concentrates on modern poets whose main work was done around the fifties of the twentieth century, or who continue to occupy the centre-stage in India and Pakistan. The book contains 95 poems, *ghazals* as well as *nazms*, selected from the works of 33 poets, which include such famous names as : Firaq, Josh, N.M. Rashid, Meeraji, Sardar Jafri, Majid Amjad, Akhtar-ul-Iman, Nadeem Qasmi, Qateel Shifai, Kaifi Azmi, Nasir Kazmi, Ahmed Faraaz, Munir Niazi, Kishwar Naheed, and Parveen Shakir.

The poets are presented in a chronological order, and each poet is introduced with an authentic portrait and a biographical note. The Introduction to the book discusses the salient characteristics of modern Urdu poetry. The poems included in this volume have been carefully selected, keeping in view the richness and relevance of their thought and style. The language used for translation is simple, lucid and adequate, and I have tried to reflect in my translation, not only the sense and spirit, but also the harmony of the original.

The layout of the book is convenient and methodical. Each poem is first given in urdu calligraphics. This is followed, on the opposite page, by its English translation which, in turn, is succeeded by the romanised version of the text. The romanised

v

version should give a feel of the Urdu language even to those readers who are not conversant with Urdu in the Persian script. It should also prove helpful to the learners of Urdu.

I am grateful to all my friends who have given me advice and encouragement in the preparation of this book. On the top of this list stands Dr. J.S. Neki who gave me the initial stimulus to undertake the task of translation and enabled me, with steadfast encouragement, to take this task to completion. I am also grateful to Dr. Gopi Chand Narang, a renowned scholar and Professor of Urdu, who, as always, has helped me by lending me books from his personal library and by guiding me in the choice of poets and poems. Thanks are also due to my friends: Mr. Balraj Komal, Mr. Makhmoor Saeedi, Mr. Nazar Burney and Mr. Mahoob-ul-Rahman Farooqi, from whom I have received useful advice from time to time. I have no words to thank Mr. Munir Niazi of Pakistan, who, despite his advancing age and indisposition, has managed to send me his photograph and an autobiographical note written in his own hand. Finally, I am thankful to Mr. S.K. Ghai, Managing Director, Sterling Publishers, who has taken great interest in the publication of this volume.

K.C. Kanda

CONTENTS

INTRODUCTION

It is difficult to offer a precise definition of modern Urdu poetry or to draw a line between the old and new poetry for, quite often the two types overlap and co-exist in the same poet, making him now a romantic singer of the *ghazal* in the older mode, and now a defiant iconolast bent upon breaking the shibboleths of convention in matters of style and diction. And there are some modern poets like Firaq Gorakhpuri (1896-1982) and Nasir Kaazmi (1925-1972) who continue to show their allegiance to the traditional form of poetry, complete with "radif" and "qafia", though they have adapted the old form to the needs of their modern sensibility.

The seeds of the new poetry were sown way back in the last quarter of the 19th century, when, under the aegis of *Anjuman-e-Punjab*, founded in 1865, Mohammed Hussain Azad, Maulana Hali, Shibli Numani and others called upon the practising poets to come out of the stranglehold of the *ghazal*, stop harping on the outworn themes of love and romance, and harness their poetic energies in the service of society. In short, they exhorted them to follow the edict of "art for life's sake", rather than "art for art sake". Though Hali and Azad did not advocate a complete break with the tradition of "radif" and "qafia", they did object to he indiscriminate use of "poetic" diction and hackneyed imagery. Further, they discouraged the practice of "tarahi" mushairas, where the competing poets were asked to build heir poems on the metrical pattern of a model poetic line. Instead, they introduced a new type of mushaira called "munazima" where the participants were asked to write their poems on particular topics, rather than in a particular measure. By prescribing topics of general human interest such as Peace, Justice, Hope, Patriotism, Spring, Winter, etc., these leaders of poetic reform attempted to

1

bring Urdu poetry down from the sublime heights of love and mysticism to the lowland of the common man. Hali also wrote his famous critique of Urdu poetry : *Muqaddama-e-Shair-o-Shairy*, a document which, like Wordsworth's *Preface to the Lyrical Ballads*, underscored the flaws in the content and form of the convenional *ghazal*, especially when it is handled by uninspired poetasters in sheer imitaion of the masters.

Hali's attempt at reforming Urdu poetry, though it represents an important milestone on the path of poetic development, was not sufficiently forceful or well-orchestrated to change its course and direction. This task was done by the Progressive Writers' Association which was set up in London in 1935 under the leadership of Sajjad Zahir. This movement was, in fact, the outcome of the ferment of ideas and ideologies that had come into being in the Western world before the beginning of World War II—the ferment that had challenged the ruling concepts of imperialism, feudalism, and fascism and confronted them with the new creed of socialism and communism, conceived and developed in Soviet Russia. Just as the French Revolution of 1789 was an important inspirational force behind he Romantic Revival in England, the Red Revoltion of 1917, wih its emphasis on the collected might of the Proletariat, became a strong rallying point for the Progressive writers and inellectuals all over the world, including India, where the new ideals of social equality and equity found powerful expression in the works of poets like Faiz Ahmed Faiz, Ali Sardar Jafri, Kaifi Azmi, Sahir Ludhianvi, Makhdoom Mahiuddin and others. The aim of these writers was to exorcise through their poems the ghost of the past, rid poetry of its obsession wih the *ghazal*, and bring it in tune with the spirit of the times.

Consequently, the emphasis in new poetry shifts from the *ghazal* to the *nazm* which is handier of the two as an instrument of social and political communication. Most "progressive" poets turn to the *nazm* for the expression of their political and social ideals which expression was, in fact, a paramount concern of the writers of the Progressive Movement. Even a romantic poet like Majaz Lucknavi becomes, under the influence of this movement, a soldier of freedom and a crusader against bourgeois oppression.

2

In one of his popular verses he calls upon his sweetheart to change her mantle into a banner of revolution :

تِرے ماتھے کا یہ آنچل بہت ہی خوب ہے لیکن
تو اس آنچل کو اِک پرچم بنا لیتی تو اچھا تھا

The mantle falling on your brow presents a lovely sight,
Could you turn it to a banner, it would have been better still.

And a deeply committed poet like Sardar Jafri identifies himself completely with the cause of radical socialism. In a line reminiscent of Josh Malihabadi, he makes a public declaration of his faith in revolution :

بغاوت میرا مسلک، میرا مذہب نوجوانی ہے !   ("نوجوانی")

Youth is my religion, Revolution, my creed!

His poem, "Jang aur Inqilaab", ends on a similarly fiery note:

غم کے سینے میں خوشی کی آگ بھرنے دو ہمیں
خوں بھرے پرچم کے نیچے رقص کرنے دو ہمیں

Let's instil the fire of joy into the grieving hearts,
Let's dance beneath the banner dripping gory drops !

This kind of poetry, though it serves an important timely need and makes an instant appeal to the younger audiences, is liable to degenerate, in less accomplished hands, ino empty rhetoric. Sensing such an eventuality, Sajjad Zahir, himself a leading "progressive", cried halt to this type of "literary terrorism", and enjoined upon the younger writers to desist from such unrestrained dogmatism in the interest of art and sanity.

It may be noted in this context that the Progressive poets were not the first to use poetry as a vehicle of political and patriotic fervour. The ground for this kind of poetry had already been prepared by men like Chakbast, Hasrat Mohani, and, above all, by Josh Malihabadi, whose poems such as "Baghawat" and

3

"Zawaal-e-Jahanbanai" are memorable expressions of partiotic and revolutionary zeal. Nor can we forget the valuable contribution made by Dr. Mohammed Iqbal to the cause of Indian nationalism and freedom. His poems like "Naya Shivala", "Tarana-e-Hindi" and "Tasweer-e-Dard" are imperishable parts of our national heritage. Lines like the following :

نہ سمجھوگے تو مٹ جاؤگے اے ہندوستاں والو
تمھاری داستاں تک بھی نہ ہوگی داستانوں میں

Wake up, my countrymen ! or, you'll bewail,
None in the world so wide will even know your tale,

will continue to inspire the readers' heart and imagination generation after generation. That Iqbal was a Progressive even before the Progessive movement was born becomes evident when we read his poem, "Farman-e-Khuda. Farishton ke Naam", occurring in *Bal-e-Jibreel*. Here is a specimen :

اٹھو میری دنیا کے غریبوں کو جگادو
کاخِ امرا کے در و دیوار ہلادو
جس کھیت سے دہقاں کے میسر نہ ہو روزی
اُس کھیت کے ہر خوشہِ گندم کو جلادو

Go, rouse the earth's poor from their slumber deep,
Pull down the palaces, stately tall and steep;
Burn away the fields, and singe the stalks of wheat,
That do not feed the farmer, nor serve his basic needs !

But it was left to the poets of the Progressive Movement to propagate the ideals of Marxism and communism with a dedicated zeal. It goes to the credit of the "Progressives", that despite their ideological fervour they—at least the better ones among them—do not cease to be poets. By and large, they voice their political beliefs with artistic propriety, with the aid of symbol, suggestion and imagery, which, if they do not innovate or invent, they surely re-charge with a new meaning relevant to their theme.

4

The skilful manipulation of imagery to deepen its meaning and make it responsive to both romantic and political needs is a special feature of Faiz's poetry, and a secret of his strong appeal. Another point may also be noted. The "Progressive" poets, though they betray a strong political bias, do not snap their ties completely with the romantic tradition. Sardar Jafri can write wih equal ease a poem like "Niwala", as also a philosophic poem in the style of Wordsworth or Whitman—"Mera Safar"—, while in a poem like "Teen Sharabi", he can indulge his taste for convivial verse and social satire. So also is the case with Kaifi Azmi who has given us a beautiful love lyric like *Ek Lamha* besides writing politically eloquent poems. But this is true only of the genuine poets who are really inspired and talented. In the case of those who are less talented and more fanatical in their ideological commitment, political agenda sometimes overrides the considerations of art. In the hands of such poets, poetry is reduced to mere slogan-mongering or versification of trite political phenomenon, resulting in lines of the following type :

شہر میں بل کھا رہی ہے سُرخ فوج

سُوئے برلن جارہی ہے سُرخ فوج

Winding through the town goes the Red brigade.
Towards the ciy of Berlin flows the Red brigade.

This is not poetry but a rhythmical rendering of a politico-military situation which could as well be stated in prose. With such lines abounding in "Progressive" journals like *Shahrah*, the movement itself came under a cloud, and some of its senior and sensible members saw the futility of continuing the "Progressive" experiment in its existing form. Moreover, they felt stung by self-doubt for they were not sure how far il was right to clip thc wings of the Muse, and instruct the artist about what to write and what not to write. Sensing the need of the hour, men like Sajjad Zahir and Abdul Alim, who were among the leaders of the Progressive Movement, decided to disband the Association in the interest of the freedom of the artist.

5

But by this time, the movement had attained some of its desired objectives. It had successfully weaned the younger writers away from the mythical world of the rose and the nightingale, and had caused a public awareness of the burning issues of poverty, hunger and exploitation, and the need to fight them. Sahir's refusal to sing the songs of love :

ابھی نہ چھیڑ محبت کے گیت اے مطرب
ابھی حیات کا ماحول خوشگوار نہیں

Sing not, O lutanist, songs of youthful love,
Life doesn't as yet present a pleasant face;

Faiz's refusal to be obsessed with love :

اور بھی دکھ ہیں زمانے میں محبت کے سوا

There are other griefs besides the grief of love—Makhdoom's passionate desire to destroy the old world and create a new one in its place :

اِس زمیں موت پروردہ کو ڈھایا جائے گا
اک نئی دُنیا، نیا آدم بنایا جائے گا

This land by death husbanded will be razed to dust,
A new world, a new man, will replace this vale accursed.

Majaz Lucknavi's angry determination to root out the relics of the feudal past :

بڑھ کے اس اندر سبھا کا ساز و ساماں پھونک دوں
اس کا گلشن پھونک دوں، اُس کا شبستاں پھونک دوں

Let me burn all the trappings of this sensual meet.
I'll burn this nightly chamber, this garden retreat,

or, Sardar Jafri's plea to reject the old, superstitious beliefs and live in the light of reason :

6

آہ اے ناداں خیالی دیوتاؤں کو نہ پوج
بُہن میں بنتے ہیں جو ایسے خداؤں کو نہ پوج

Don't grovel, silly man, before the non-existent gods
Don't ye make obeisance to the idols false—,

all such exhortations are meant to warn the reader against the seductive sirens of past tradition, inimical to the growth of reason and intelligence.

The Progressive Movement couldn't break the fascination for the *ghazal*, but it did succeed in investing this form with a sense of purpose and direction, so that a poet like Faiz or Ahmed Faraaz could use it as a vehicle both of lyrical reflection and political comment :

مقام فیض کوئی راہ میں جچا ہی نہیں
جو کوئے یار سے نکلے تو سوئے دار چلے

I couldn't bring myself, O Faiz, to like any place en route,
Forced out of my love's lane, I made for the gallows straight.

In the matter of style and form, the Progressive Movement didn't prescribe any radical reform, though it enlarged the scope of the poet's freedom in such matters by allowing him to experiment with new modes and measures including blank-verse and free-verse, which forms were effectively employed by several poets including Faiz, Akhtar-ul-Imaan, Majid Amjad, N.M. Rashid, Kaifi Azmi and Sardar Jafri.

Contemporaneously with the Progressive Writers' Association, there had sprung into action another literary organisation, "Halqa-e-Arbaab-e-Zauq", whose members believed in the theory of "art for art sake", rather than "art for life's sake". In their view the Progressive Movement with its avowed political and economic agenda was not qualified to promote the growth of great art which is concerned as much with the political and practical needs of life, as with the spiritual, psychological, and emotional needs of man. Yet these two movements may be called complementary rather than contradictory, for the purpose of both was to serve the cause of art and life, though in their own separate ways. The members of the two literary associations used to meet on a friendly basis for exchange of views on art and literature. That the two groups read and admired each other's writings is proved by the fact that Nazar Mohammed Rashid, an important member of the *Halqa,* had written the Preface for Faiz's book: *Naqsh-e-Faryaadi,* while Krishan Chander, an eminent "progressive" had written the Introduction for Rashid's *Maawra.* Yet the members of the two groups followed their own literary principles. The "progressives" were, generally speaking, outward looking people, who sought their inspiration in Soviet political ideology, whereas the members of the "halqa" looked for inspiration in their own hearts and souls, and in their own surroundings. While the Progressive Writers' Association was guided by political motives, the *Halqa* was a purely literary club, whose aim was to encourage creative talent in Urdu, to protect the rights of Urdu poets and writers, and to develop a critical acumen among the readers and writers of poetry. Above all, the aim of this organisation was to promote the growth of pure poetry as distinguished from poetry adulterated wih political or pragmatic overtones.

While the "progressives" believed in giving a clear and unambiguous expression to their proletarian beliefs, wihout veiling their intent behind symbols and metaphors, the members of the "halqa" considered the symbolist technique as the best available mode of artistic utterance. We may recall that Sardar Jafri had criticised Faiz Ahmed Faiz for the ambiguity of his poetic expression. Picking his poem, "15h August", he had faulted with the expression, "woh sehar", "woh manzil", pointing out that with such vague phrases the poem could as well be appropriated by the followers of any other reactionary creed including those of the Muslim League or the Hindu Mahasabha. Faiz should have clearly stated that what he was waiting for was the dawn of socialist freedom. Thus with the "progressives", a clear and fearless propagation of the political philosophy sometimes acquired precedence over poetry.

The *Halqa-e-Arbaab-e-Zauq* was fortunate in having among its members several well-known poets including Meeraji, Nazar Mohammed Rashid, Yusuf Zafar, Qayoom Nazar, Majid Amjad and Ehsaan Daanish. Among these poets Meeraji occupied a pivotal position in this literary circle. He was the *"Pir-e-Mughan"*, the presiding deity of the tavern who directed the activities of this organisation and showed new paths to the budding Urdu poets. Together with N.M. Rashid, the author of the famous poetical collection, *Maawra*, Meeraji perfected and popularised the free-verse writing in Urdu poetry. In fact, both these poets had imbibed literary influences from abroad, in particular from the poetry of England and France, and transmitted the same wih necessary adjustments, to Urdu poetry. Though both of them were adepts in the classical form of poetry, free-verse poetry in conversational rhythm was their forte, which became a point of emulation for several younger poets. In addition, they ntroduced into their poems the dramatic element and the technique of internal dialogue, acquired, possibly, from the English masters of the dramatic monologue, and thus enhanced the richness and complexity of Urdu poetry. Meeraj's poem : "Mujhe Ghar Yaad Aata Hai", and Rashid's "Love Song of a Clerk", show the quality of the new poetry which was to win many admirers among the 20th century poets. Meeraji also experimented with the diction of Urdu poetry and tried to bring it nearer to the native soil by a judicious mixture of Urdu and Hindi words, and by using in his poetry pure Hindi imagery drawn from Hindu scriptures and mythology. That Meeraji is also at home in the traditional kind of rhymed verse, ethical and instructive, can be gauged from his poem, "Sindbaad Ki Waapsi", an excerpt from which given in this anthology strongly recalls Tennyson's "Ulysses".

Under the combined influence of the literary movements detailed above, and under the pressure of ideas flowing from he Western literary world, Urdu poetry of the latter half of the 20th century underwent a palpable change in its content and form. Turning away from the romanticism of the classical school, it became more earh-bound and more deeply concerned with the dilemmas of the ordinary man—a fragmented personality trying to come to terms wih a world where old altruistic values of truth

9

and morality sound hollow and meaningless. Akhtar-ul-Imaan's poem: "Sheeshe ka Aadmi", (the fragile man) beautifully suggests the predicament of such a man who both deeply desires and dreads to speak the truth and do the right, lest it disturbs his equation with the outside world. Much of the modern poetry is the poetry of protest against the prevailing scheme of things. Earlier it was the question of combating the alien rule, now it is the question of fighting the system ruled by corrupt politicians and greedy money bags. The poet, being a highly sensitive species, finds himself thrown in a wasteland, reminiscent of the *Wasteland* of T.S. Eliot. We have to read poems like Makhdoom's "Andhera" or Rashid's "Saba Weeraan", to get a taste of the nightmare world in which the modern man finds himself encaged. These dark and fearsome landscapes where there is "no trace of bud or leaf or grass" *(Saba Weeraan)*, may be treated as objective correlatives of the speaker's inner consciousness, torn with conflicts and tensions. This, incidentally, reminds us that the modern poet is keenly interested in exploring the dark recesses of the individual mind and unravelling its inner state with the aid of concrete, visual imagery

It is apparent that the type of sustained protest with which the modern poet is often concerned, can be more readily channelised through the medium of the *nazm* than the *ghazal*, for the *nazm* has a wider canvas and is less restricted by the laws of poetic composition. This accounts for the primacy enjoyed by the *nazm* over the *ghazal* in the present age. However, it would be wrong to infer that the *nazm* has completely supplanted the *ghazal*. Far from it. Nearly all the important poets, despite their avowed aversion to the *ghazal*, have fallen for its charm, and men like Nasir Kaazmi and Firaq Gorakhpuri have done exceedingly well in this genre, and both of them, it is significant, have taken their cue from the great classic : Mir Taqi Mir.

Similarly, the modern poet's defiance of the classical convention of "radif" and "qafia", and his adoption, insead, of the free-verse or blank-verse line as the measure of poetry, hasn't reduced the importance of the regularly rhyming verse which continues to have its admirers, despite the notable achievement

10

in the other direction, of men like Meeraji, Rashid, Balraj Komal, Majid Amjad, and a host of other poets.

Further, as the emphasis in modern poetry shifts from the "heroic" character to the ordinary man, the language of poetry too, accordingly, becomes a little more relaxed and earth-bound to suit the needs of the new protagonist. Shedding excessive ornament and urbanity, it acquires a speech-like flow, suited to the expression of everyday experiences. No word is now considered unpoetical if it can deliver the goods, and is in keeping with the character and situation. There is sometimes a deliberate attempt at coarsening rather than refining the language of poetry. the language of Akhtar-ul-Imaan in the line : "Paan ki peek hai yeh, Amman ne thooki hogi", might shock the sensibility of a reader used to the controlled and cultured language of classical poetry, but in the context where it is used, and in view of its thematic function, the line doesn't seem odd or out of place. There is also a trend exhibited by certain poets like Meeraji, Nasir Kaazmi, or Firaq Gorakhpuri, to use Hindi words in combination with the standard Urdu vocabulary which, again, might seem offensive to the sticklers of purity, but is conducive to the indigenisation of Urdu poetry. As already mentioned, another feature of modern poetry is the replacement of the lyrical with the dramatic mode so that a poem may be seen as a dialogue of the mind with itself, as in Akhtar-ul-Imaan's "Ek Larka". this dramatic mode is specially helpful in tapping the tensions hidden in the sub-conscious. We may recall that one of the books of Parveen Shakir is entitled : "Khud Kalaami" (self-communion).

The general mood of modern Urdu poetry, like the mood of a sensitive modern man is one of discontent and disillusion with the industrial and material world of today. This wide-pervasive ennui is reflected, sometimes directly and sometimes obliquely, in the representative poems of many modern poets, as can be seen in the following random selection of some of the popular verses :

ہمیں سے رنگ گلستاں، ہمیں سے رنگ بہار
ہمیں کو نظم گلستاں پہ اختیار نہیں

11

We make the garden bloom, we set the spring aglow,
Yet we have no control in the garden's governance.

(Sahir)

or,

زندگی کیا کسی مفلس کی قبا ہے جس میں
ہر گھڑی درد کے پیوند لگے جاتے ہیں

What's life but a poor man's cloak,
To frequent painful stitches exposed !

(Faiz)

or,

اس دَور میں زندگی بشر کی
بیمار کی رات ہو گئی ہے

Life in the present age,
Has become a sick man's night !

(Firaq)

or,

وہی کس میں سی، وہی بے حسی آج بھی ہر طرف کیوں ہے طاری؟

This listlessness, this helplessness,
Why should even now prevail ?

(Akhtar-ul-Imaan)

The euphoria caused by the advent of Indian independence
was too illusory to last, and the harsh realities of the human
situaion have fallen like a heavyweight on every sensitive heart.
Yet, it goes to the credit of our poets that they manage to find a
silver lining in every dark cloud, and don't allow their discontent

to sink into despair, or vanquish their faith in the essential goodness of life. That's why nearly every sad poem ends on a note of hope and consolation. Makhdoom's poem, "Andhera" (Darkness), in spite of carrying us through the nightmare world of blood and terror, closes on an optimistic note :

رات کے ماتھے پہ یہ آزردہ ستاروں کا ہجوم

صرف خورشیدِ درخشاں کے نکلنے تک ہے

The night besieged with faded stars
Will end with glorious rise of morn.

Akhtar-ul-Imaan, despite being constantly troubled by the ironies and inequities of life, refuses to succumb to despair :

آپ ہوں میں نہیں انساں سے مایوس ابھی

ابھی پھوٹے ہیں شگوفے ابھی گمن ہے بہار

شبنمی سبز لبادوں سے مہک آتی ہے

خاک و خوں توڑ ہی دیں گے کبھی دیرینہ خواب

You may be, I am not despaired of human race,
The buds are yet to open out, spring is yet to come of age,
The dewy verdant sheet of earh smells fresh and sweet,
Flesh and blood sure one day would their stupor shake.

One source of the modern poet's optimism even in the face of doubt and darkness lies in his unwavering faith in the power of love to lift the pall of gloom. It's significant that love is an all-permeating subject in modern poetry—as it has been in the poetry of the past. The speakers of several modern poems turn to their beloveds in their hour of weariness. Faiz Ahmed Faiz pours his woes into the ears of his beloved in his poem: "Chand Roz Aur Miri Jaan" or in "Mujh se Pehli si Mohabbat Miri Mehboob Na Maang". Sahir Ludhianvi leans on the shoulder of his beloved while commenting upon the feudal aspects of the Taj ; Meeraji, in his "Love Song of a Clerk", yearns for his beloved, whom, alas,

13

he cannot possess for want of wealth and rank, while N.M. Rashid in "Dareeche ke Qarib" shares with his beloved his disgust for centuries of sufferance and passivity. It is this link with the sweetheart, actual or imagined, that gives strength to the speakers in their time of depression. We may recall that Nida Fazli in his poem, "Faza Khamosh Hai", admits that he cannot complete the various good tasks proposed unless he is joined and supported by his beloved :

میں اتنے سارے کاموں کو اکیلا کر نہیں سکتا

All alone I cannot all these tasks perform.

And Kaifi Azmi in "Ek Lamha" tells us how the world is suddenly transformed to a paradisal place when for a moment he achieves perfect closeness with his love. All this underscores the modern poet's abiding faith in love which serves as an unfailing source of inspiration in his life and art.

Another and a more philosophic cause of the poet's attitude of hopeful serenity lies in his mature undersanding, like Meeraji of the lines quoted below, that dark and bright, good and evil are two sides of the coin of reality, and it is the tug-of-war between the two that makes life exciting and worthwhile. Man's desire to join the battle as a soldier of the good, strengthens his spirit, saves him from despair, and invests life with a purpose:

سفر یہ اُجالے اندھیرے کا چلتا رہا ہے تو چلتا رہے گا یہی
رسم ہے رہ کی ایک آیا، گیا، دوسرا آئے گا، رات ایسے گزر جائے گی

(جاتری)

This journey of light and dark will continue as heretofore, this is the custom of the road, one comes and goes, another follows, So the night doth pass

Long before Meeraji a similar thought was also expressed by Hali :

بُری اور بھلی سب گزر جائے گی

یہ کشتی یونہی پار اُتر جائے گی

ملے گا نہ کلیوں کو گل کا پتہ

ہر اِک پتھری یوں بکھر جائے گی

Times good and bad, both will pass away,
And the boat of life will touch the shore one day;
The flower-plucker will not find even a trace of rose,
Every petal, changed to dust, will be blown away.

Despite the similarity of thought in the two passages, there is a palpable difference in their tone, texture and style. The mood of the later poet is one of quiet resignation, with a mild tinge of ennui; the tone is of subdued soliloquy, not of bold assertion, the language is shorn of poetic metaphor and rhetorical flourish, and there is a deliberate avoidance of regular rhyming and end-stopped lines—the qualities which epitomise some of the salient characteristics of modern poetry.

Firaq Gorakhpuri
(1896-1982)

RAGHUPATI SAHAI FIRAQ (1896-1982)

Raghupati Sahai Firaq was born at Gorakhpur in Uttar Pradesh. His father, Munshi Gorakh Prasad, was an advocate by profession, but a poet by taste and temperament. Firaq thus grew up in an enlightened, literary environment which must have activated his innate artistic instincts. He was a distinguished student specially inerested in Urdu, Persian and English literature, in which last he had also obtained a Master's degree. He had a chequered career which included a short period of government service as Deputy Collector, several years of political and patriotic work in the Indian National Congress, and finally, a long career as a teacher of English at Allahabad University. Firaq married at the comparatively young age of 18, but it was an unhappy marriage, a constant cause of friction between husband and wife.

As a poet of the "ghazal" and "rubai", Firaq stands foremost among the 20th century writers. His poetry and personality were nurtured by several diverse influences. He was thoroughly familiar with the Urdu poetic tradition, and was specially impressed by the poetry of Mir and Momin; the was also influenced by English poetry, in particular by the poetry and poetics of he Romantics; and he had imbibed within him the spirit of the ancient Hindu thought and culture. Consequently, Firaq's poetry has acquired a unique flavour. It is remarkable for its sensuousness, for its frank commitment to physical beauty, for its sensitivity to human sorrow, and for its exploration of the mysteries of the night. Another mark of his distinction lies in bringing Urdu diction close to the Indian soil, by blending it with Hindi words, and indigenous imagery.

Firaq was honoured with the "Jnanpith Award" (1969) for his poetical collection, *Gul-e-Naghma*. He was also given the "Sahitya Akademy Award" in 1960.

فراق گورکھپوری

☆

رس میں ڈوبا ہوا لہراتا بدن کیا کہنا
کروٹیں لیتی ہوئی صبحِ چمن کیا کہنا

باغِ جنت پہ گھٹا جیسے برس کے کھل جائے
سوندھی سوندھی تری خوشبوئے بدن کیا کہنا

جیسے لہرائے کوئی شعلہ کمر کی یہ لچک
سر بسر آتشِ سیّال بدن کیا کہنا

قامتِ ناز لچکتی ہوئی اک قوسِ قزح
زلفِ شب رنگ کا چھایا ہوا گھن کیا کہنا

جس طرح جلوہَ فردوس ہواؤں سے چھنے
پیرہن میں تری رنگینیئ تن کیا کہنا

جلوہ و پردہ کا یہ رنگ دمِ نظارہ
جس طرح ادھ کھلے گھونگھٹ میں دلہن کیا کہنا

جگمگاہٹ یہ جبیں کی ہے کہ یُو پھٹتی ہے
مسکراہٹ ہے تری صبح چمن کیا کہنا

زلفِ شب گوں کی چمک، پیکرِ سیمیں کی دمک
دیپ مالا ہے سرِ گنگ و جمن کیا کہنا

18

Firaq Gorakhpuri

Honey-exuding limber body, how should I describe !
Shifting, turning garden dawn, ah, what a surprise !

Rain-sprinkled paradise in the after-glow of rains,
Ah, your figure fragrance-breathing, beyond description lies !

Undulating, slender waist, like a quivering flame,
Ah, your body's molten fire leaves us all tongue-tied.

The stately stature, rainbow-like, delicate in its swing and grace,
Shaded by the sable locks, what a captivating sight !

As the scenes of paradise by whiffs of breeze unveiled,
So glimmers your loveliness through your robes descried.

Ah, that tantalising pose, half-concealed and half-revealed,
Like a bride behind the veil, both bold and shy.

The beauteous forehead all aglow suggesting break of dawn,
The smile, like the garden morn, scattering deep delight.

The glossy tresses, night-black, radiant, argent frame,
Lo, the ganga and the jamuna celebrate the fest of lights !

Ras mein dooba hua lahraata badan kya kahna,
Karwaten leti hui subah-e-chaman, kya kahna !

Bagh-e-Jannat pe ghata jaise baras ke khul jaae,
Sondhi sondhi tiri khushboo-e-badan, kya kahna !

Jaise lahraae koi shola, kamar ki yeh lachak,
Sar ba-sar aatish-e-sayyaal badan kya kahna !

Qaamat-e-naaz lachakti hui ik qaus-e-qazah,
Zulf-e-shab rang ka chhaaya hua gahan kya kahna !

Jis tarah jalwa-e-firdaus hawaanon se chhine,
Pairaahan mein tire rangeeni-e-tan, kya kahna !

Jalwa-o-parda ku yeh rang dam e nazzara,
Jis tarah adh-khule ghoongat mein dulhan, kya kahna !

Jagmagaahat ye jabeen ki hai ke pau phat-ti hai,
Muskaraahat hai tiri subah-e-chaman kya kahna !

Zulf-e-shab-goon ki chamak, paikar-e-seemein ki damak,
Deep maala hai sar-e-gang-o-jaman, kya kahna !

19

فراق گورکھپوری ☆

یہ بکھوں کی نرم روی ، یہ ہوا ، یہ رات
یاد آ رہے ہیں عشق کو ٹوٹے تعلقات
مایوسیوں کی گود میں دم توڑتا ہے عشق
اب بھی کوئی بنالے تو بگڑی نہیں ہے بات
اک عمر کٹ گئی ہے ترے انتظار میں
ایسے بھی ہیں کہ کٹ نہ سکی جن سے ایک رات
ہم اہلِ انتظار کے آہٹ پہ کان تھے
ٹھنڈی ہوا تھی، غم تھا ترا ، ڈھلی چلی تھی رات
ہر سعی و ہر عمل میں محبت کا ہاتھ ہے
تعمیرِ زندگی کے سمجھ کچھ محرکات
اہلِ رضا میں شانِ بغاوت بھی ہو ذرا
اتنی بھی زندگی نہ ہو پابندِ رسمیات
ہم اہلِ غم نے رنگِ زمانہ بدل دیا
کوشش تو کی سبھی نے مگر بن پڑے کی بات
اٹھ بندگی سے مالکِ تقدیر بن کے دیکھ
کیا وسوسہ عذاب کا کیا کاوشِ نجات
مجھ کو تو غم نے فرصتِ غم بھی نہ دی فراق
دے فرصتِ حیات نہ جیسے غم نیات

20

Firaq Gorakhpuri

This soft, floating fragrance, this breeze, this night,
Remind me of the broken bonds, of passions unrealised.

Life is gasping for breath, with deep despair distressed,
Even now it can be saved if someone really tries.

I have spent my whole life waiting for your sight,
There are those who couldn't survive a single night.

We who are resigned to wait, were all intent to hear your steps,
The air was cool, deep the grief, the night was in its last stride.

It's love that works behind the world's momentous deeds,
You should also understand the secret of creative life.

Those submitting to His will should learn a little defiance too,
Life shouldn't for mere ritual be for ever sacrificed.

Abandon abject genuflection, be the master of your fate,
Shed the hope of salvation, the fear of doom defy.

Grief didn' permit me, Firaq, to ariculate my sorrow deep,
As the grief of life constricts the free flow of human life.

Yeh nikhaton ki narm ravi, yeh hawa, yeh raat,
Yadd aa rahe hain ishq ke toote ta-alluqaat.

Maayoosion ki god mein dam torta hai ishq,
Ab bhi koi bana le tau bigri nahin hai baat.

Ik umr kat gai hai tire intezaar mein,
Aise bhi hain ke kat na saki jin se ek raat.

Hum ahl-e-intezaar ke aahat pe kaan the,
Thandi hawa thi, ghum tha tira, dhal chali thi raat.

Har saie-o-har-amal mein mahabbat ka haath hai,
Taameer-e-Zindagi ke samajh kuchh muharakaat.

Ahl-e-raza mein shaan-e-baghaawut bhi ho zara,
Itni bhi zindagi na ho paaband-e-rasmiaat.

Uth bandgi se, maalik-e-taqdeer ban ke dekh,
Kya waswasa azaab ka, kya kaawish-e-nijaat.

Mujh ko tau ghum ne fursat-e-ghum bhi na di Firaq,
De fursat-e-hayaat na jaise ghum-e-hayaat.

21

فراقؔ گورکھپوری ☆

اے جذبِ نہاں اور کوئی ہے کہ وہی ہے
خلوت کدۂ دل میں اک آواز ہوئی ہے

کہہ دے تو ذرا سر ترے دامن میں چھالوں
اور یوں تو مقدر میں مرے بے وطنی ہے

وہ رنگ ہو یا بو ہو کہ بادِ سحری ہو
اے باغ جہاں جو بھی یہاں ہے سفری ہے

یہ بارشِ انوار یہ رنگینیٔ گفتار
گل باری و گل سیری و گل پیرہنی ہے

اے زندگی عشق میں سمجھا نہیں تجھ کو
جنّت بھی جہنم بھی یہ کیا بوالعجبی ہے

ہے نطق جسے چومنے کے واسطے بے تاب
سو بات کہ، اک بات تری بے سخنی ہے

موجیں ہیں مئے سرخ کی یا خطِ دہن ہیں
لب ہیں کہ کوئی شعلۂ برقِ عنبی ہے

جاگے ہیں فراقؔ آج غم ہجر میں تا صبح
آہستہ سے آجاؤ ابھی آنکھ لگی ہے

22

Firaq Gorakhpuri

Is it he or someone else, tell me, passion deep,
In the lonesome house of heart, I hear a voice speak.

May I, if you allow, rest my head in your lap?
Otherwise, homelessness is what my fate decrees.

Everything is on the move in this earthly grove,
Be it colour or scent of rose, be it morning breeze.

This rain of radiance, this blossoming forth of speech,
A floral shower, a floral stroll, and life flaunting floral sheet.

You defy my comprehension, O, life of love !
Now a heaven, now a hell, how you vex and tease !

The thing which my eager lips love and long to kiss,
Is your silent eloquence, surpassing all speech.

Are these the waves of ruddy wine, or the veins of your mouth,
Are these lips, or a lightning flame, with purple wine replete !

He has kept awake at night, the severance-singed Firaq,
Enter slowly, without a stir, he's just gone to sleep.

Ai jazb-e-nihaan aur koi hai ke wohi hai,
Khilwat-kada-e-dil mein awaaz hui hai.

Kah de tau zara sar tire daaman mein chhipa loon,
Aur yoon tau muqaddar mein mire be-watni hai.

Woh rang ho ya boo ho ke baad-e-sahri ho,
Ai bagh-e-jahan jo bhi yahan hai safri hai.

Yeh baarish-e-anwaar, yeh rangeeni-e-guftaar,
Gul baari-o-gulsairi-o-gul parahani hai.

Ai zindagi-e-ishq mein samjha nahin tujhko,
Jannat bhi jahannam bhi, yeh kya boolajbi hai.

Hai nutq jise choomne ke waaste betaab,
Sau buat ki ik baat tiri be sakhuni hai.

Maujen hain mai-e-surkh ki ya khatt-e-dahan hain,
Lab hain ke koi shola-e-barq-e-ambi hai.

Jaage hain Firaq aaj ghum-e-hijar mein ta subah,
Aahista se aa jaao, abhi aankh lagi hai

Josh Malihabadi
(1898-1982)

JOSH MALIHABADI (1898-1982)

Josh Malihabadi was a poet, a patriot and a public figure whose poetry enthused the hearts of millions of people in the pre-Independence days. A friend of the poor and the dispossessed, Josh exploited to the full the resources of his poetic genius for spreading the message of political and social revolution. He has written *ghazals, rubaies* and *nazms*, all in abundance, but he is essentially a poet of the *nazm* and a specialist of the *rubai*. He may not be a profound thinker, but he is a firebrand poet capable of mesmerising his audience with his verbal fusillades and poetic eloquence.

Josh was born at Lucknow. He inherited his poetic taste from his forebears, for his father, grandfather and great grandfaher all were poets of acknowledged merit. He received his education at Lucknow, Agra, and Aligarh, and studied upto the senior Cambridge. He was greatly influenced by Rabindranath Tagore whom he had met during his sojourn in Calcutta in 1921. Josh spent the best part of his life in Delhi, where he stayed from 1934 till after Independence, with a short stint at Poona and Bombay, where he wrote songs and lyrics for the cinema. He was appointed editor of the Urdu journal, *Aajkal*, and was honoured with Padma Vibushan by the Government of India. Some of his famous publications include : *Shola-o-Shabnam, Harf-o-Hikait, Janoon-o-Hikmat, Ayaat-o-Naghmaat, Sumbal-o-Salaasal,* and *Yaadon Ki Baraat.* In the evening of his life Josh migrated to Pakistan, where he felt alone and alienated. He died in 1982.

جوشؔ ملیح آبادی

پیٹ بڑا بدکار ہے بابا

پیٹ بڑا بدکار

ناداں بیٹھے کشتی پر اور دانا غوطے کھائے

کتّا سوئے گدّے پر اور تھلے چوکیدار

پیٹ بڑا بدکار ہے بابا

پیٹ بڑا بدکار

کوّوں کو اور راگ سنائے کویل بن کے بیچ

منعم کی اور سیج بسائے مفلس کا دلدار

پیٹ بڑا بدکار ہے بابا

پیٹ بڑا بدکار

آدم کا بانکا بیٹا اور بھڑوے پن کا روپ

حوّا کی سندر بیٹی اور رنڈی کا بیوہار

پیٹ بڑا بدکار ہے بابا

پیٹ بڑا بدکار

Josh Malihabadi
The Belly is a Wicked Thing (Pet Bara Badkar)

The belly is a wicked thing.
A vicious thing, O man !

The fool rides ashore in boat, the wise fights the flood,
The watch makes his rounds at night, the dog sleeps in bed.

The belly is a wicked thing,
A vicious thing, O man !

The koel sings to please the crows in the forest glades,
The poor man's love plays the slave and sets the rich man's stage,

The belly is a wicked thing,
A vicious thing, O man !

Adam's son, smart and winsome, plays a villain on the sly,
Eve's daughter, sweet and simple, fleshly trade plies.

The belly is a wicked thing,
A vicious thing, O man !

Pet bara badkaar hai baba,
Pet bara badkaar.

Nadaan baithe kashti par aur danaa gote khaae,
Kutta soe gadde par aur tahle chokidaar.

Pet bara badkaar hai baba,
Pet bara badkaar.

Kawwon ko aur raag sunaae koel ban ke beech,
Mun-im ki aur sej sajaae muflis ka dildaar.

Pet bara hadkaar hai baba,
Pet bara badkaar.

Aadam ka baanka beta aur bharooey pan ka roop,
Hawwa ki sundar beti aur randi ka beohaar.

Pet bara badkaar hai baba,
Pet bara badkaar.

جوشؔ ملیح آبادی

غرورِ ادب

میرے جلسے سے اٹھ آنے پر خفا ہے ہم نشیں

شاعروں کی فطرتِ عالی سے تو واقف نہیں

جوہرِ ذاتی کا جب افسردہ ہوتا ہو وقار

کفر سے بد تر ہے اس موقع پر وضعِ انکسار

ناشناسانِ ادب بھولے ہوئے ہوں جب شعور

ان مواقع پر عبادت کے برابر ہے غرور

دل ہمارا جذبۂ غیرت کو کھو سکتا نہیں

ہم کسی کے سامنے جھک جائیں ہو سکتا نہیں

راہِ خود داری سے مر کر بھی بھٹک سکتے نہیں

ٹوٹ تو سکتے ہیں ہم لیکن لچک سکتے نہیں

حشر میں بھی خسروانہ شان سے جائیں گے ہم

اور اگر پرسش نہ ہوگی تو پلٹ آئیں گے ہم

اہلِ دنیا کیا ہیں اور ان کا اثر کیا چیز ہے

ہم خدا سے ناز کرتے ہیں بشر کیا چیز ہے

28

Josh Malihabadi
Artist's Pride (Gharoor-e-Adab)

You have taken ill, my love, that I quit the poetic meet,
We poets, you do not know, are a highly sensitive breed.

If our personal dignity someone denigrates,
It's worse than sacrilege to meekly tolerate.

When men, unconcerned with art, shame and sense defy,
It's an act of religious faith to show our native pride.

On the sensitive point of honour never can we compromise,
Never can we bend our head before a man of pelf and pride.

We can die for self-respect, but never from our path deflect,
We can break but never bend, howsoever stern the threat.

Even on the Judgment Day we'll walk with regal grace,
And if slighted, we'll return straight to our native place.

What care we for the world and its hollow might,
When we feel free with God, how can man cause us fright?

Mere jalse se uth aane par khafa hai hamnasheen,
Shaairon ki fitrat-e-aali se tu waaqif nahin.

Jauhar-e-zaati ka jab afsurda hota hai waqaar,
Kufr se badtar hai is mauqa pe waza-e-inkasaar.

Na-shanaasaan-e-adab bhoole hue hon jab shaoor,
In nuwaaqa par ibaadat ke baraabar hai gharoor.

Dil hamara jazba-e-ghairat ko kho sakta nahin,
Hum kisi ke saamne jhuk jaaen ho sakta nahin.

Raah-e khud-duuri se mar kar bhi bhatak sakte nahin.
Toot tau sakte hai hum, lekin lachak sakte nahin.

Hashar mein bhi khusarwana shaan se jaaenge hum,
Aur agar pursish na hogi tau palat aaenge hum.

Ahl-e-duniya kya hain aur unka asar kya cheez hai,
Hum khuda se naaz karte hain, bashar kya cheez hai?

جوشؔ ملیح آبادی

بھٹکی ہوئی نیکی

ہر شے کو مسلسل جنبش ہے راحت کا جہاں میں نام نہیں
اس عالمِ سعی و کاوش میں دم بھر بھی ہمیں آرام نہیں
چھائی ہے فضا پر تشنہ لبی مفقود یہاں سیرابی ہے
ہر جسم میں اک بے چینی ہے ہر روح میں اک بیتابی ہے
اس بزمِ خلش کا ہر ذرہ بے چینیوں کے انبوہ میں ہے
اک رعشہ پیہم کاہ میں ہے اک لرزشِ پنہاں کوہ میں ہے
لیلائے سماعت مضطر ہے عشرت کے ترانے سننے کو
ہر نقص کا دامن پھیلا ہے تکمیل کی کلیاں چننے کو
ہیجان ہے چشمِ پستی میں رفعت کا نوشتہ پڑھنے کا
اک دھن ہے ترقی کرنے کی اک جوش ہے آگے بڑھنے کا
ہر موم کو دھن ہے شمع بنے مضطر ہے پگھل جانے کے لیے
ہر سنگ کا سینہ جلتا ہے آتش میں بدل جانے کے لیے
ہر قطرۂ دریا غلطاں ہے موتی پہ تسلط پانے کو
ہر ذرّۂ خاکی اڑتا ہے خورشید سے ٹکّر کھانے کو

Josh Malihabadi
Strayed Virtue (Bhatki Hui Neki)

Everything is on the move, stability is a thing unknown,
In this world of strife and stir, peace and calm are hard to own.

Perpetual thirst grips the earth, fertility is a hollow dream,
Restless lies every man, every soul is restless seen.

The bristling world in every grain is by restlessness besieged,
From humble straw to mighty mount everything is tremour-teased.

The auditory sense is all intent to hear the merry music roll,
Every fault desires at heart to reach the virtue's noble goal.

The lowly eye, deep at heart, loves to scale the mountain tall,
To move ahead, to rise and shine, is the urge inspiring all.

The wax wishes to be a candle, yearns to burn away entire,
Every stone feels the itch to turn into a ball of fire.

Every river-drop is envious of the pearl's glint and grace,
Every grain of eddying dust vies with the sun in space.

Har shai ko musalsal jumbish hai, raahat ka jahaan mein naam nahin,
Is alam-e-saie-o-kaawish mein dam bhar bhi hamen aaraam nahin.

Chhai hai faza par tishna labi, mafqood yahan sairaabi hai,
Har jism mein ik be-chaini hai, har rooh mein ik be-taabi hai.

Is bazm-e-khalish ka har zarra be-chainion ke amboh mei hai.
Ik raasha-e-paiham kaah mein hai, ik larzish-e-pinhaan koh mein hai.

Lailaa-e-smaat muztir hai ishrat ke taraane sun-ne ko,
Har nuqs ka daaman phaila hai takmeel ki kaliaan chun-ne ko

Hejaan hui chashm-e-pasti mein rif-at ka nawishta parhne ka,
Ik dhun hai taraqqi karne ki, ik josh hai aage barhne ka.

Har mom ko dhun hai shama bane, muztir hai pighal jaane ke lieye,
Har sang ka seena jalta hai aatish mein badal jaane ke lieye.

Har qatra-e-darya ghaltaan hai moti pe tasallut paane ko,
Har zarra-e-khaki urta hai khursheed se takkar khaane ko.

31

جوشؔ ملیح آبادی

ہر دل میں غرض اک کاہش ہے امّید کا ساغر بھرنے کی
ہر شے کی تڑپتی فطرت میں خواہش ہے ترقی کرنے کی

وہ چور جو شب کے پردے میں سرقے کی غرض سے آتا ہے
جو نیند کی ماتی بستی پر ظلمت کی طرح چھا جاتا ہے

اک ایسی ہی خواہش اس کو بھی چوری کے لیے اکساتی ہے
جس طرح کی خواہش نورانی دیوتاؤں میں پائی جاتی ہے

سارق بھی فرشتوں ہی کی طرح تسکین و طرب کا جویا ہے
ہر چند کہ اسنے قسمت سے تسکین کا رستہ کھویا ہے

رہبر ہو کہ رہزن دونوں میں تسکین کی خواہش یکساں ہے
ہر چند کہ وہ سیدھی راہ پہ ہے یہ راہ بھٹک کر حیراں ہے

عارف نے یہ سمجھا آسائش اشکوں کو گرا کے ملتی ہے
قاتل نے یہ سمجھا انساں کا وہ خون بہا کر ملتی ہے

صوفی نے یہ سمجھا وہ دل کے پیمانے میں مل جائے گی
میکش کی سمجھ میں یہ آیا مے خانے میں مل جائے گی

المختصر ان تشریحوں سے ہم پر یہ حقیقت کھلتی ہے
کہتے ہیں جسے دنیا میں بدی بھٹکی ہوئی وہ اک نیکی ہے

32

Josh Malihabadi

Every heart would in short fill his bowl with cherished hopes,
It's the universal wish to pursue an ever-rising goal.

The thief that in the cover of dark into a house steals,
And casts a menacing shade on the folks that sleep,

Is also motivated by the same devout desire,
Which in the saints divine ignites the holy fire.

The thief too, like the saints, craves for inner bliss,
Though he has by sheer chance the path of virtue missed.,

Both the sinner and the saint are fired by the wish for peace,
One of them has lost the way, the other treads the pathway steep.

The hermit feels that peace of mind flows from deep penance,
The assassin feels that shedding blood paves the way to calm.

The sophist looks for inner peace in the spiritual ale,
The drinker feels the tavern alone such a thing retails.

All these examples are intended to display;
What we term as vice is virtue gone astray.

Har dil mein gharaz ik kaahish hai umeed ka saaghar bharne ki,
Har shai ki tarapti fitrat mein khwahish hai taraqqi karne ki.

Woh chor jo shab ke parde mein sarqe ki gharz se aata hai,
Jo neend ki maati basti par zulmat ki tarah chha jaata hai,

Ik aisi hi khwahish usko bhi chori ke lieye uksaati hai,
Jis tarah ki khwahish nooraani devtaaon mein paai jaati hai,

Saaraq bhi farishton hi ki tarah taskeen-o-tarab ka joya hai,
Har chand ke us ne qismat se taskeen ka rasta khoya hai.

Rahbar ho ke rahzan donon mein taskeen ki khwahish yaksaan hai,
Har chand woh seedhi raah pe hai, woh raah bhatak kar hairaan hai.

Aarif ne yeh samjha aasaaish ashkon ko gira kar milti hai,
Qaatil ne yeh samjha insaan ka woh khoon baha kar milti hai.

Soofi ne yeh samjha woh dil ke paimaane mein mil jaaegi,
Maikash ki samajh mein yeh aaya maikhaane mein mil jaaegi.

Almukhtesar in tashreehon se hum par yeh haqeeqat khulti hai,
Kahte hain jise duniya mein badi, bhakti hui woh ik neki hai.

Hari Chand Akhtar
(1901-1958)

HARI CHAND AKHTAR (1901-1958)

Pandit Hari Chand Akhtar was born in Hoshiapur district (Punjab) in April 1901. After obtaining an M.A. degree in English Hari Chand worked as a journalist for a few years, and then took up employment in the office of the Punjab Legislative Assembly. During World War II he got an assignment in the Ministry of Information and Broadcasting, and was associated with the task of war propaganda. After the partition, Hari Chand Akhtar migrated to Delhi, where he lived till his death on January 1, 1958.

Besides holding a Master's degree in English, Akhtar was well-grounded in Persian and Urdu literature. He had passed his Munshi Fazil examination after matriculation. Imbued with a deep love of poetry, he had started participating in *"mushairas"* at a young age. He had a large circle of friends and admirers, both Hindus and Muslims, who were specially impressed by his wit and humour, and by his capacity for parody and satire. His mastery of the ghazal is amply reflected in the selection presented in this anthology. As a practitioner of the ghazal, Akhtar respects the classical convention of *"radif"* and *"qafia"* and uses a language which is musical, meaningful and limpid, free from unnecessary ornament or conceit. One of his couplets has become a popular quotation :

ہمیں بھی آپڑا ہے دوستوں سے کام کچھ یعنی
ہمارے دوستوں کے بے وفا ہونے کا وقت آیا

Now I need to seek a favour from my trusted friends,
Time has come for my friends to betray their faith.

ہری چند اختر

☆

غرورِ ضبط سے آہ و فغاں تک بات آ پہنچی

ہوس نے کیا کیا دل سے زباں تک بات آ پہنچی

سکونِ دل سے ناقوس و اذاں تک بات آ پہنچی

خدا والوں کی ہمّت سے کہاں تک بات آ پہنچی

خلافت سے جبین و آستاں تک بات آ پہنچی

خدا اور ابنِ آدم میں یہاں تک بات آ پہنچی

ملی آنکھ اور آہ و فغاں تک بات آ پہنچی

ذرا سی بات تھی لیکن یہاں تک بات آ پہنچی

ہماری داستاں میں ذکرِ قیس و کوہ کن آیا

وہاں سے پھر ہماری داستاں تک بات آ پہنچی

جہانِ دوستی اک جنّتِ ایثار ہوتا ہے

وہاں بھی کاہشِ سودو زیاں تک بات آ پہنچی

36

Hari Chand Akhtar

Self-control has entailed wailing uncontrolled,
Desire-pressed, we have perforce our secret heart exposed.

Starting from the peace of mind, they have come to gong and prayer,
Zealous godly men have wandered far from their original goal.

Betwixt God and Adam's race things have changed a lot,
Beginning with a bold defiance, we have come to bend and bow.

Just a meeting of the eyes, and you see us heaving sighs,
Mark, how a trivial thing assumes a serious role.

Our tale contained a reference to Farhaad and Qais,
This has brought us back again to our tale untold.

The world of friendship ought to be a paradise of sacrifice,
But concern for loss and gain has here too encroached.

Ghroor-e-zabat se aah-o-fughaan tak baat aa pahunchi,
Hawas ne kya kiya dil se zabaan tak baat aa pahunchi.

Sakoon-e-dil se naaqoos-o-azaan tak baat aa pahunchi,
Khuda waalon ki himmat se kahan tak baat aa pahunchi.

Khilafat se jabeen-o-aastaan tak baat aa pahunchi,
Khuda aur ibn-e-Aadam mein yahan tak baat aa pahunchi.

Mili thi aankh aur aah-o-fughaan tak baat aa pahunchi,
Zara si baat thi lekin yahaan tak baat aa pahunchi.

Hamari daastan mein zikar-e-qais-o-kohkan aaya,
Wahan se phir hamari daastaan tak baat aa pahunchi.

Jahaan-e-dosti ik jannat-e-eesaar hota hai,
Wahaan bhi kaahish-e-sood-o-zayaan tak baat aa pahunchi.

شباب آیا کسی بت پر فدا ہونے کا وقت آیا
مری دنیا میں بندے کے خدا ہونے کا وقت آیا

اُنھیں دیکھا تو زاہد نے کہا ایمان کی یہ ہے
کہ اب انسان کو سجدہ روا ہونے کا وقت آیا

تکلّم کی خموشی کہہ رہی ہے حرفِ مطلب سے
اشک آمیز نظروں سے ادا ہونے کا وقت آیا

خدا جانے یہ ہے اوجِ یقیں یا پستیِ ہمت
خدا سے کہہ رہا ہوں نا خدا ہونے کا وقت آیا

ہمیں بھی آپڑا ہے دوستوں سے کام کچھ یعنی
ہمارے دوستوں کے بے وفا ہونے کا وقت آیا

نویدِ سر بلندی دی مُنجّم نے تو میں سمجھا
سگانِ دہر کے آگے دوتا ہونے کا وقت آیا

Hari Chand Akhtar

As the fire of youth awakens, the time of love arrives,
The time to deify a mortal, raise him to the skies.

When on him he cast a glance, the priest exclaimed : "By God !
Worshipping a human idol can now be justified."

The helpless tongue thus exhorts the purport seeking vent :
"Let this task be now assigned to your streaming eyes."

Now I need to seek a favour from my trusted friends,
Time has come when my friends will their trust belie.

God knows what it is, perfect faith or failing strength ?
Lo, I pray to God the Great to save my boat of life !

When the astrologers gave me tidings of scaling higher heights,
I had thought time had come my self-respect to sacrifice.

Shabab aaya kisi but par fida hone ka waqt aaya,
Miri duniya mein bande ke khuda hone ka waqt aaya.

Unhen dekha tau zaahid ne kaha imaan ki yeh hai,
Ke ab insaan ko sijda rawa hone ka waqt aaya.

Takallum ki khamoshi kah rahi hai harf-e-matlib se,
Ke ashk-aamez nazron se ada hone ka waqt aaya.

Hamen bhi aa para he doston se kaam kuchh yaani,
Hamare doston ke be-wafa hone ka waqt aaya.

Khuda jaane yeh hai auj-e-yaqeen ya pasti-e-himmat.
Khuda se kah raha hoon na khuda hone ka waqt aaya.

Naveed-e-sar bulandi di munajjam ne tau main samjha,
Sagaan-e-dahar ke aage doo taa hone ka waqt aaya.

هری چند اختر ☆

شیخ و پنڈت دھرم اور اسلام کی باتیں کریں
کچھ خدا کے قہر کچھ انعام کی باتیں کریں

یہ سنائیں پاک کلمے اوّلیں الہام کے
وہ خدا کے آخری پیغام کی باتیں کریں

ہم کھڑے سنتے رہیں اور دل میں یہ کہتے رہیں
اب یہ رخصت ہوں تو ہم کچھ کام کی باتیں کریں

یاس و حرمان و غم و آلام کی باتیں کریں
آ دلِ ایذا طلب کچھ کام کی باتیں کریں

دوست سے کہہ دیں دلِ بے مدّعا کی داستاں
آج ساقی سے شکست جام کی باتیں کریں

جس کی دنیا آپ سے تھی جس کی دنیا آپ تھے
آؤ اس بد بخت کے انجام کی باتیں کریں

عمر بھر کا عہدِ الفت اِک خیالِ خام تھا
آؤ لیکن اس خیالِ خام کی باتیں کریں

زندگی بے شک ترا انعام ہے یا رب مگر
سن سکے تو کچھ ترے انعام کی باتیں کریں

40

Hari Chand Akhtar

Sheikh and Pandit blow the trumpet of their religious faiths,
Some talk of rich rewards, some of Heaven's rage :

This one talks of revelation, the first to dawn on earth,
That one of the last message that our Lord conveyed.

Impatient we hear them talk and wait for them to end,
So that we may also our own issues debate :

Talk of grief and suffering, of despair and aches,
Come, O, pain-preferring heart, let's discuss your case.

Let's reveal to our friend the state of our desireless heart,
Let the saqi know about the flunking flame of ale.

He whose world was bound with you, who owed to you his life,
Let's now talk about the end of that unfortunate.

The pledge of ever-lasting faith was but an idle thought,
But that idle, wishful thought, let's recapitulate.

Life, O Lord, is no-doubt a rich and rare boon,
But let's talk about the boon granted by your grace.

Sheikh-o-pandit dharam aur islaam ki baaten karen,
Kuchh khuda ke qahr, kuchh inaam ki baaten karen.

Yeh sunaaen pak naghme awaleen ilhaam ke,
Woh khuda ke aakhri paigaam ki baaten karen.

Ham khare sunte rahen aur dil mein yah kahte rahen,
Ab yeh rukhsat hon tau hum kuchh kaam ki baaten karen.

Yaas-o-hirmaan-o-ghum-o-aalaam ki baaten karen,
Aa dil-eeza-talab, kuchh kaam ki baaten karen.

Dost se kah den dil-e-be-mudaa ki daastaan,
Aaj saqi se shikast e-jaam ki baaten karen.

Jis ki duniya aap se thi, jis ki duniya aap the,
Aao us bad-bakht ke anjaam ki baaten karen.

Umr bhar ka ahd-e-ulfat ik khayaal-e-khaam tha,
Aao lekin is khayaal-e-khaam ki baaten karen.

Zindgi be shak tira inaam hai yaarab, magar,
Sun sake tau kuchh tire inaam ki baaten karen.

41

Anand Narain Mulla
(b. 1901)

ANAND NARAIN MULLA (b. 1901)

Anand Narain Mulla was born in Lucknow on October 24, 1901. His father, Jagat Narain Mulla, was a famous advocate of Lucknow. After taking his M.A. degree in English literature, Anand Narain studied Law and started practising as a lawyer. He was appointed the judge of Allahabad High Court in 1954, from which post he retired in 1961.

Despite his professional pre-occupations, Mulla has been pursuing his literary interests with an unflagging zeal. He has by now produced five collections of poetry, and has won several literary awards including the Sahitya Akademy Award, U.P. Ghalib Award, and Iqbal Samaan. He was the chairman of *Anjuman-e-Taraqqi-e-Urdu* for ten years.

Mulla's poetry reflects the social and cultural concerns of his milieu. He was influenced, above all, by Ghalib and Iqbal. A broad-minded Kashmiri Brahmin, Mulla is out and out a nationalist and a secularist. He believes that man needs no other religion than the religion of universal love and brotherhood. Mulla started his career with the *nazm*, thought he is equally competent as a poet of the *ghazal*, to which form he has lent a sense of purpose, and a spirit of humanism.

He has little faith in the aesthetic creed of "art for art's sake". Poetry, for him, is the handmaid to life. He is also a crusader for the cause of Urdu. ""*Urdu*" he once remarked, "is my mother tongue. I can change my religion, but not my mother-tongue."

43

آنند نرائن ملّا

رِشوت

آیا جو ہوا کا اک جھونکا

پربت کی اونچی چوٹی سے

ننّھے منّے سے کچھ کنکر

چٹان بنے جو بیٹھے تھے

وادی میں لڑھک کر آ کے گرے

جس خاک سے اڑ کر پہنچے تھے اس خاک پہ پھر واپس آئے

کچھ کھسیائے کچھ جھنجھلائے

اور اپنی جھیپ مٹانے کو

کچھ چیخے اور کچھ چلّائے

جب کچھ نہ چلی

تب یہ کہہ کر

اک دوسرے کو سمجھانے لگے

اک ادنیٰ اور کم ظرف بشر

چوٹی پہ پہنچ تو سکتا ہے

لیکن اس کا

چوٹی پہ ٹھہرنا مشکل ہے

پھر کان میں چپکے سے بولے

جب تک نہ ہوا کو رِشوت دے

44

Anand Narain Mulla
The Bribe (Rishwat)

By a gust of wind unhinged,
Some tiny bits of rock and stone
Who thought they were themselves the rock,
Hurtling fell from mountain top
Into the vale below,
Were razed to the dust again from where they were upraised.
Some felt embarrassed, some felt enraged,
And to hide their sense of shame,
Some began to shout and rail,
But when nothing did avail,
Thus through mutual counselling
On each other prevailed :
A petty, chicken-hearted being,
May scramble to the top,
But cannot on the top stay
"Unless", someone said in whispers,
"He can bribe the wind and waves."

Aaya jo hawa ka ik jhonka
Parbat ki oonchi choti se
Nanhe munhe se kuchh kanker
Chataan bane jo baithe the
Waadi mein lurhak kar aake gire
Jis khaak se ur kar pahunche the us khaak pe phir waapis aae,
Kuchh khisiaae, kuchh jhunjalaae
Aur apni jhep mitaane ko
Kuchh cheekhe aur kuchh chillae,
Jab kuchh na chali
Tab yeh kah kar
Ik doosre ko samjhaane lage
Ik adna aur kam zarf bashar
Choti pe pahunch tau sakta hai
Lekin uska
Choti pa thahrana mushkil hai,
Phir kaan mein chupke se bole,
Jab tak na hawa ko rishwat de.

آنند نرائن ملّا

دنیا ہے یہ کتنی بڑی چھوٹا ہے کتنا یہ جہاں

اتنے بڑے سنسار میں

میرا فقط اک دیس ہے

اور اس بڑے سے دیس میں

میرے لیے بس اک نگر

اور اس بڑی نگری میں بھی

میرا ہے خالی ایک گھر

اور گھر کے اندر ہے مرا

چھوٹا سا اک کمرہ فقط

جس کے بس اک کونے میں ہے

بستر کسی کا اور مرا

اور مری دنیا ہے یہی

آنسو مرے خوشیاں مری

آہیں مرے نغمے مرے

دو بستروں کی داستاں

سارے کے سارے ہیں یہیں

اور مرے چہرے کی نقاب

آکر اترتی ہے یہیں

دنیا ہے یہ کتنی بڑی چھوٹا ہے یہ کتنا جہاں

46

Anand Narain Mulla
How Small is My World in a World so Wide

I have only one country
In this world so wide,
A single town on the earth
Where I live and bide.
In this big, bewildering town
A small house my needs provides,
In this house one small room
Is my sole preserve and pride;
Where in one corner a bedstead doth lie,
For me and someone else beside.
This forms my whole world,
The place where I laugh and cry,
Where I pour my songs and sighs
And spin my blended yarn of life.
It's here that I discard
The mask which my face doth hide.
How small is my world
In a world so wide !

Itne bare sansaar mein
Mera faqt ik des hai,
Aur is bare se des mein
Mere lieye bas ik nagar,
Aur is bari nagri mein bhi
Mera hai khaali ek ghar,
Aur ghar ke ander hai mira
Chhota sa ik kamra faqt
Jis ke bas ik kone mein hai
Bistar kisi ka aur mira
Aur miri duniya hai yehi
Aansoo mire khushiaan miri.
Aahen miri naghme mire,
Do bistaron ki daastaan.
Saare ke saare hain yahin,
Aur mere chehre ki niqaab
Aakar utarti hai yahin,
Duniya hai yeh kitni bari, chhota hai kitna yeh jahaan !

Akhtar Sheerani
(1905-1948)

AKHTAR SHEERANI (1905-1948)

Mohammed Dawood Khan Akhtar Sheerani was born on May 4th, 1905 in Tonk state (Rajpootana, now Rajasthan). His father, Mehmood Khan Sheerani, was a professor at Oriental College, Lahore. Akhtar too joined his father's college, but beyond passing his Munshi Fazil and Adib Fazil examinations, he showed no special interest in academic achievements. He spent his time in cultivating his poetic taste, and studying English and Urdu literatures on his own. By virtue of his literary and linguistic abilities, Akhtar could secure editorial assignments in several literary journals like *Hamayun* and *Shahkar*. He also tried to run his own journals, *Baharastaan*, *Khayalastaan* and *Rooman*, but such attempts proved abortive as Akhtar lacked the steadiness of purpose so essential to carry such tasks to success. Excessive drinking told on his health and he died on September 9, 1948, at the comparatively young age of 43. His poetical works include: *Naghma-e-Haram*, *Shairistaan*, *Subah-e-Bahaar*, and *Tayyur-e-Aawara*.

Akhtar is quintessentially a romantic poet, a singer, like John Keats, of love and beauty. He builds his poetry round the endearing figures of Salma, Azra, Reehana or Cleopatra. Of all these females whose names—real or fictitious—find a repeated mention in his lyrics, Salma, a beautiful belle of Lahore, exercised the most powerful influence on his life and inspired his best lyrical poetry. Akhtar is a master of the musical line and an adept in portraying the beauties of nature. He has written several memorable poems on *Barsaat* and *Basant*, the two seasons specially dear to a romantic temperament.

49

اختر شیرانی
اعتراف

کسی سے بھی دل لگایا نہ تھا

محبت کا صدمہ اٹھایا نہ تھا

حسینوں کے رونے پہ ہنستے تھے ہم

کبھی ایک آنسو بہایا نہ تھا

کوئی حور ہو یا پری، اپنا سر

کسی آستاں پر جھکایا نہ تھا

سیہ گیسووں کو تمنّا رہی

مگر دل کو ہم نے پھنسایا نہ تھا

زمانے میں وہ کون تھا زہرہ وش

کہ سینے سے جس نے لگایا نہ تھا

بسر کی سدا عیش و عشرت میں عمر

کبھی رنج ہم نے اٹھایا نہ تھا

مگر اک جھلک نے ہمیں کھو دیا

یہ صدمہ تو ہم نے اٹھایا نہ تھا

کیا عشق کے درد میں مبتلا

"فلک تونے اتنا ہنسایا نہ تھا

کہ جس کے عوض یوں رلانے لگا"

Akhtar Sheerani
Confession (Aitraaf)

I hadn't to anyone ever given my heart,
Nor suffered the pangs caused by Cupid's darts :

Never had I shed a tear for the beauties' sake,
When I found them crying, I did simply laugh,

Never before anyone had I bent my head,
Be it a limber elf or a fairy doll.

None was there on this earth even were she starry sweet,
Who hadn't with eager arms hugged me to her heart.

Though they tried long and hard, it was all in vain,
I couldn't be ensnared in their coiling locks.

I had lived all my life in a carefree style,
Alien to the stings of sorrow, immune to the inner smarts.

But a single glimpse and glance, and I was left undone,
Never before had I suffered such a shattering shock.

I am now a prey to love, and rue my hapless lot,
"Did I have surfeit of joy, heavens, in the past,
Why have you made me suffer, what was my fault ?"

Kisi se kabhi dil lagaya na tha,
Mahabbat ka sadma uthaya na tha.

Haseenon ke rone pe hanste the hum,
Kabhi ek aansoo bahaya na tha.

Koi hoor ho ya pari apna sar,
Kisi aastaan par jhukaya na tha.

Seaah gaisuon ko tamanna rahi,
Magar dil ko hum ne phansaya na tha.

Zamaane mein woh kaun tha zuhra wash,
Ke seene se jis ne lagaya na tha.

Basar ki sada aish-o-ishrat mein umr,
Kabhi ranj hum ne uthaya na tha.

Magar ik jhalak ne hamen kho diya,
Yeh sadma tau hum ne uthaya na tha.

Kiya ishq ke dard mein mubtila,
"Falak tu ne itna hansaya na tha.
Ke jis ke iwaz yun rulane laga."

51

اخترؔ شیرانی

عزمِ رنگیں

میں خواب بن کے ترے شبستاں میں آؤں گا

چپکے سے خواب گاہ کے پردے اٹھاؤں گا

دستِ صبا کی طرح تجھے گدگداؤں گا

اور ترے پائے ناز پہ سجدے لٹاؤں گا

میں خواب بن کے تیرے شبستاں میں آؤں گا

ہر چند کہ راہ روکیں گے دیوار و در ترے

آنے نہ دیں گے باغ میں نخل و شجر ترے

چوموں گا دستِ نازنیں آکر مگر ترے

دزدِ حنا کی طرح تجھے گدگداؤں گا

میں خواب بن کے تیرے شبستاں میں آؤں گا

تو میرے پاس آنے سے معذور ہی سہی

میرا فراق بھی تجھے منظور ہی سہی

یہ بھی سہی کہ مجھ سے بہت دور ہی سہی

ان دوریوں کو وصل کا عالم بناؤں گا

میں خواب بن کے تیرے شبستاں میں آؤں گا

52

Akhtar Sheerani
Romantic Intent (Azm-e-Rangeen)

I'll visit your bedroom changed to a dream !
And will quietly lift your boudoir's soft screen,
Gently will I tickle you like the morning breeze,
And will shower kisses on your limber feet,
I'll visit your chamber changed to a dream.

Your doors and walls, I know, will obstruct my way,
The garden trees and plants will hold me at bay,
All the same I'll reach you and kiss your tender palm,
And tickle it in secret like the henna balm.
I'll visit your chamber changed to a dream.

You cannot come to me, I do concede,
This state of severance is the fate's decree,
You are obliged by circumstance to stay away from me,
But I'll change this severance into a happy meet,
I'll visit your chamber changed to a dream !

Main khwab bun ke tere shabastaan mein aaoonga,
Chupke se khwabgah ke parde uthaoonga,
Dast-e-saba ki tarah tujhe gudgadaaonga,
Aur tere pa-e-naz pe sijde lutaaoonga,
Main khwab bun ke tere shabastaan mein aaoonga !

Har chand rah rokenge deewar-o-dar tire,
Aane na denge bagh mein nakhl-o-shajar tire,
Choomoonga dast-e-naz main aa kar magar tire,
Duzd-e-hinna ki tarah tujhe gudgudaaoonga,
Main khwab bun ke tere shabastaan mein aaoonga !

Tu mere paas aane se maazoor hi sahi,
Mera firaq bhi tujhe manzoor hi sahi,
Yeh bhi sahi ke mujh se bahut door hi sahi,
In doorion ko wasal ka aalam banaaoonga,
Main khwab bun ke tere shabastaan mein aaoonga !

اخترؔ شیرانی

تو محوِ خواب ہوگی شبستانِ ناز میں

آسودہ،اپنی خلوتِ رنگیں طراز میں

منہ کو چھپائے سایہ زلفِ دراز میں

سایہ سا بن کے میں بھی نظر میں سماؤنگا

میں خواب بن کے تیرے شبستاں میں آؤں گا

تسلیم ہے بہت سے خلل ہوں گے راہ میں

بے شک تباہیوں کے محل ہوں گے راہ میں

دریا و کوہ و دشت و جبل ہوں گے راہ میں

دریا و کوہ و دشت کو نیچا دکھاؤں گا

میں خواب بن کے تیرے شبستاں میں آؤں گا

بے خواب ہوگی گر تو شبِ مشک بار میں

کھوئی ہوئی ترانہِ ابرِ بہار میں

میں آبسوں گا دیدہِ افسانہ کار میں

اور اِک فسانہ تجھ کو سنا کر سلاؤں گا

میں خواب بن کے تیرے شبستاں میں آؤں گا

54

Akhtar Sheerani

When you in your chamber would lie lost in dreams
Contented in seclusion, nursing fitful gleams,
With your face hid behind your long tresses' shade,
I, too, like a shadow, will spring upon the scene,
I'll visit your chamber changed to a dream !

Many hurdles, I admit, will block my way,
Many a menacing danger will lie for me in wait,
Rivers, hills and forests will my pace delay,
But I'll humble down the forests, hills, rivers and lakes,
I'll visit your chamber changed to a dream !

If you lie sleepless in the fragrant night,
Entranced by the patter of the rain outside,
I'll come and settle in your tell-tale eyes
And soothe you to sleep with a lullaby.
I'll visit your chamber changed to a dream !

Tu mahw-e-khwab hogi shabasttan-e-naz mein,
Aasooda apni khilwat-e-rangeen-taraaz mein,
Munh ko chupaae saya-e-zulf-e-daraaz mein,
Saya sa ban ke main bhi nazar mein samaaoonga,
Main khwab ban ke tere shabastaan mein aaoonga !

Tasleem hai bahut se khalal honge rah mein,
Be-shak tabaahion ke mahal honge rah mein,
Darya-o-koh-o-dasht-o-jabal honge rah mein,
Darya-o-koh-o-dasht ko neecha dikhaaoonga,
Main khwab ban ke tere shabastaan mein aaoonga !

Be-khwab hogi gar tu shab-e-mushkbaar mein,
Khoi hui tarana-e-abr-e-bahaar mein,
Mein aa basoonga deeda-e-afsana kar mein,
Aur ik fasana tujh ko suna kar sulaaoonga,
Main khwab ban ke tere shabastaan mein aaoonga !

اخترؔ شیرانی

قرباں کروں گا تجھ پہ گلِ نوبہار میں

لعل و گہر منگاؤں گا، بہرِ نثار میں

پہناؤں گا گلے میں، ستاروں کے ہار میں

بستر پہ تیرے خلد کی کلیاں بچھاؤں گا

میں خواب بن کے تیرے شبستاں میں آؤں گا

دیکھے گی خواب میں تو نظارے بہار کے

نظروں میں جگمگائیں گے تارے بہار کے

رقصاں لبوں پہ ہوں گے شرارے بہار کے

اور میں ترے لبوں سے شرارے چراؤں گا

میں خواب بن کے تیرے شبستاں میں آؤں گا

56

Akhtar Sheerani

I'll offer vernal flowers at your lotus feet,
I'll order pearls and rubies to decorate you, sweet,
I'll stitch a row of stars to garland your head,
With the buds of paradise, I'll deck your bed.
I'll visit your chamber changed to a dream.

You will be dreaming dreams of vernal sights,
Your eyes will reflect the lovely starry night,
On your lips will leap and frisk joyous sparkling smiles,
I'll steal these sparks from your lips agleam,
I'll visit your chamber changed to a dream !

Qurban karoonga tujh pe gul-e-nau bahaar main,
Lal-o-guhar mangaaoonga bahr-e-nisaar main,
Pahnaaoonga gale mein sitaaron ke haar main,
Bistar pe tere khuld ki kalian bichhaaoonga,
Main khwab ban ke tere shabastaan mein aaoonga.

Dekhegi khwab mein tu nazzare bahaar ke,
Nazron mein jagmagaaenge taare bahaar ke,
Raqsaan labon pe honge sharare bahaar ke,
Aur main tere labon se sharare churaaoonga,
Main khwab ban ke tere shabastaan mein aaoonga !

مگر ہم تہِ خاک پنہاں رہیں گے

چمن زار شاداب و خنداں رہیں گے

درختوں پہ طائر غزل خواں رہیں گے

فضاؤں میں بادل پر افشاں رہیں گے

مگر ہم تہِ خاک پنہاں رہیں گے

گھٹائیں گلستاں پہ چھایا کریں گی

فضائیں یونہی لہلہایا کریں گی

درختوں کے دامن گل افشاں رہیں گے

مگر ہم تہِ خاک پنہاں رہیں گے

چمن کی فضائیں مہکتی رہیں گی

صبا کے اثر سے لہکتی رہیں گی

گل و غنچہ و برگ رقصاں رہیں گے

مگر ہم تہِ خاک پنہاں رہیں گے

یہ شہر اور دیہات بستے رہیں گے

صداؤں سے معمور رستے رہیں گے

بپا زندگانی کے طوفاں رہیں گے

مگر ہم تہِ خاک پنہاں رہیں گے

Akhtar Sheerani
But we Below the Earth Shall Lie

Forever will the gardens bloom,
Birds will sing their merry tunes,
The clouds in sky will sail and fly,
But we below the earth shall lie !

The clouds will hover round the groves,
Refreshing breezes wave and blow,
The trees will always blossom forth,
But we blow the earth shall lie !

The garden air shall fragrance breathe,
Luscious green will be the trees,
Buds and blooms will dance in glee,
But we below the earth shall lie,

Towns and villages will bustle with life,
The paths resound with passersby,
Storms will shake the shores of life,
But we below the earth shall lie.

Chamanzaar shadaab-o-khandaan rahenge,
Darakhton pe taair ghazal khwaan rahenge,
Fazaaon mein badal parafshaan rahenge,
Magar hum tah-e-khak pinhaan rahenge.

Ghataaen gulistaan pe chhaaya karengi,
Fazaaen yunhi lahlahaya karengi,
Darakhton ke daaman gulafshaan rahenge,
Magar hum tah-e-khak pinhaan rahenge.

Chaman ki fazaaen mahakti rahengi,
Saba ke asar se lahakti rahengi,
Gul-o-guncha-o-barg raqsaun rahenge,
Magar hum tah-e-khak pinhaan rahenge.

Yeh shahr aur dehaat baste rahenge,
Sadaaon se maamoor raste rahenge,
Bapa zindgaani ke toofaan rahenge,
Magar hum tah-o-khak pinhaan rahenge.

اخترؔ شیرانی

عروسِ سحر روز آیا کرے گی

فضا نور سے جگمگایا کرے گی

مناظر سحر خیز خنداں رہیں گے

مگر ہم تہِ خاک پنہاں رہیں گے

یہ راتیں یونہی جھلملایا کریں گی

ستاروں کی شمعیں جلایا کریں گی

سرِ چرخ روشن چراغاں رہیں گے

مگر ہم تہِ خاک پنہاں رہیں گے

کہستاں سے چشمے ابلتے رہیں گے

سرِ راہ موتی مچلتے رہیں گے

یہ سیلابِ سیمیں خراماں رہیں گے

مگر ہم تہِ خاک پنہاں رہیں گے

غرض یہ یہ خدائی کے رنگیں نظارے

یہ شام و سحر کے بہاریں نظارے

خراماں ورخشاں و رقصاں رہیں گے

مگر ہم تہِ خاک پنہاں رہیں گے

60

Akhtar Sheerani

Daily will the dawn arrive,
Fill the air with welcome light,
The world will wake to pleasant sights,
But we below the earth shall lie.

The nights will glimmer as heretofore,
The lamps of stars will burn and glow,
The sky a feast of lamps will hold,
But we below the earth shall lie.

Founts on hills will rise and roar,
Sparkling gems will downward roll,
The silver streams will wash the shores,
But we below the earth shall lie.

In short the world's beauteous sights,
The shifting shades of day and night,
Will always strut and shine in pride,
But we below the earth shall lie.

Aroos-e-sahr roz aaya karegi,
Faza noor se jagmagaaya karegi,
Manaazir sehar khez-o-khandaan rahenge,
Magar hum tah-e-khaak pinhaan rahenge.

Yeh raaten yunhi jhilmalaaya karengi,
Sitaron ke shammein jalaaya karengi,
Sar-e-charkh raushan chiragaan rahenge,
Magar hum tah-e-khak pinhaan rahenge.

Kuhastaan se chashme ubalte rahenge,
Sar-e-raah moti pighalte rahenge,
Yeh sailaab-e-seemin khiraaman rahenge,
Magar hum tah-e-khak pinhaan rahenge.

Garz yeh khudaai ke rangeen nazzare,
Yeh sham-o-sahr ke bahaareen nazzare,
Khiramaan-o-rakhshaan-o-raqsaan rahenge,
Magar hum tah-e-khak pinhaan rahenge.

61

Gopal Mittal
(1906-1993)

GOPAL MITTAL (1906-1993)

Gopal Mittal was born in Malerkotla, a place in East Punjab, known for its liberal, secular traditions. He had his schooling at Malerkotla, and college education at Lahore. He had given evidence of his poetic interests even in his school-days, and had started participating in local "mushairas" at a very young age.

After doing his B.A. from Lahore, he set up his own literary journal, *Subah-e-Umeed* at Ludhiana, which, however, didn't survive beyond one issue. It was Maulana Tajwar Najeebadi of Lahore who came to his rescue and offered him an editorial assignment in his journal, *Shahkaar,* at a monthly salary of Rs. 30/-. To supplement his income, he also took up a similar assignment with a film magazine, *Jagat Laxmi,* run by the film actor, Karan Dewan.

His circle of friends in Lahore included literary personalities such as Hafeez Jullundhry, Kanhaiya Lal Kapoor, Abdul Majid Adam, and, of course, Maulana Tajwar.

Mittal lived in Lahore till the communal frenzy of the post-partition period after August 1947, made it impossible for him to hold on to his favourite place. He migrated to India and settled in Delhi, where he spent a greater part of his life. He worked for sometime on the editorial board of the Urdu dailies, *Milap* and *Tej,* and later started his own paper, *Tehrik,* in 1953. Mittal was a broad-minded Hindu poet who had many Muslim friends and admirers.

His complete works, published in 1994, contain a rich fare of *ghazals, nazms* and *qatas,* besides didactic and religious verse.

گوپال متّل

ہیرو

حقیر و ناتواں تنکا

ہوا کے دوش پر پرّاں

سمجھتا تھا کہ بحر و بر پہ میری حکمرانی ہے

مگر جھونکا ہوا کا ایک البیلا

تلون کیش

بے پروا

جب اس کے جی میں آئے رخ پلٹ جائے

ہوا لا آخر ہوا ہے کب کسی کا ساتھ دیتی ہے

ہوا تو بے وفا ہے کب کسی کا ساتھ دیتی ہے

ہوا پلٹی

بلندی کا فسوں ٹوٹا

حقیر و ناتواں تنکا

پڑا ہے خاکِ پستی پر

خدا جانے کوئی رہگیر جب اس کو مسلتا ہے

تو اپنا خوابِ عظمت یاد کرکے اس کے دل پر کیا گزرتی ہے

64

Gopal Mittal
Hero

A flimsy and trivial straw,
On the wings of wind afloat,
Vainly thinks he is the lord of all that lies below.
A gust of wind, mischievous, bold,
Freakish,
Unconcerned,
Forces it to change at will, both its speed and course.
Wind is after all the wind, where it listeth blows,
Who can bank upon its support, never doth it steadfast hold.
The wind suddenly grew hostile,
The poor, broken-winged straw,
Swirling on the earth did fall.
When some careless traveller treads it down his toes,
How it yearns for vanished glory, how nostalgic grows !

Haqeer-o-natwaan tinka,
Hawa ke dosh par parran,
Samajhta tha ke bahr-o-bar pe meri hukamraani hai,
Magar jhonka hawa ka ek albela,
Talawwun kesh,
Be parwah,
Jab us ke ji mein aae, rukh palat jaae,
Hawa aakhir hawa hai, kab kisi ka saath deti hai.
Hawa palti
Bulandi ka fasoon toota,
Haqeer-o-natwaan tinka,
Para hai khaak-e-pasti par,
Khuda jaane koi rahgeer jab isko-masalta hai,
Tau apna khwab-e-azmat yaad karke is ke dil par kya guzarti hai.

گوپال متّل

مسافر

اٹھا رختِ سفر اپنا کہ وقتِ نازک آ پہنچا
مسافر، اب نہیں ہے میزبانی کا ہمیں یارا

یہی لازم ہے تجھ کو کوچ کی کر جلد تیاری
کہ اب برداشت کی حد سے فزوں ہے اپنی ناداری

نہ ایسا ہو کہ تجھ کو بھاگنا دشوار ہو جائے
ہماری مفلسی تیرے لیے آزار ہو جائے

مسافر مفلسی کے سائے میں پلتی ہے خونخواری
جلو میں اس کے دامن تھام کر چلتی ہے خونخواری

بنا دیتی یہ کمبخت رہزن میزبانوں کو
چبا جاتے ہیں بھوکے غیر کیا اکثر یگانوں کو

مسافر مصلحت سے کام لے اب چھوڑ یہ بستی
خدا جانے ہماری مفلسی کیا رنگ لائے گی

سکوں کا دور اب اس سر زمیں سے جانے والا ہے
ہوائیں کہہ رہی ہیں کوئی طوفاں آنے والا ہے

66

Gopal Mittal
Traveller (Musaafir)

Traveller, go, pack your goods, hard times arrive,
No more can we play the host, no more oblige.

High time that you quit, heed my advice,
The state of our poverty now all limits defies.

Make good your escape, 'fore it is too late,
Lest you are also stung by our poor plight.

Hunger and rapacity go side by side,
Thirst for blood and poverty are intimate allies.

Pressed by this wretched foe, the hosts turn hostile,
Human beings, want-compelled, turn fratricides.

Traveller, better leave the town, take care, be wise,
Who knows our indigence springs what surprise !

Peaceful times will reign no more in this luckless land,
A mighty storm is brewing, the winds prophesy !

Utha rakht-e-safar apna ke waqt-e-naazuk aa pahuncha,
Musaafir ! ab nahin hai mezbaani ka hamen yaara,

Yehi laazim hai tujhko, kooch ki kar jald tayyaari,
Ke ab bardaasht ki had se fazoon hai apni naadaari,

Na aisa ho ke tujhko bhagna dushwaar ho jaae,
Hamaari muflisi tere lieye aazaar ho jaae.

Musaafir muflisi ke saae mein palti hai khoonkhwaari,
Jilau mein is ke daaman thaam kar chalti hai khoonkhwaari.

Bana leti hai yeh kambakht rahzan mezbaanon ko,
Chaba jaate hain bhooke ghair kya, aksar yagaanon ko.

Musaafir, maslahit se kaam le, ab chhor yeh basti,
Khuda jaane hamaari muflisi kya rang laaegi,

Sakoon ka daur ab is sar zameen se jaanewala hai,
Hawaaen kah rahi hain koi toofaan aane waala hai.

Makhdoom Mahiuddin
(1908-1969)

MAKHDOOM MAHIUDDIN (1908-1969)

Abu Sayyed Mohammed Makhdoom Mahiuddin was born on February 4, 1908, at Indol, district Medak, in Hyderabad (Deccan). He belonged to a family known for its religious zeal and scriptural scholarship — a family of teachers, preachers and mullas. But Makhdoom was more interested in poetry and politics than in religion. He was specially attracted by the socialistic ideology which was the favourite creed of the *Avant Garde* poets and intellectuals of the early twentieth century. His commitment to the socialist ideals was sincere and steadfast. His love of the proletariat, and his anti-imperialism stand reflected in some of his poems, including "Andhera" and "Mashriq" (East). "Andhera", in particular, recalls, in its mood and imagery, the anti-war poems of W.H. Auden. However, it must be said to Makhdoom's credit that he didn't permit his political zeal to stifle the poet in him. He was the leading light of the Progressive Writers' Movement. As a mark of respect for their comrade, the Communist Party of India has raised a building called "Makhdoom Bhawan" in Hyderabad.

Though Makhdoom is primarily a poet of the *nazm*, he has also proved his ability as a writer of the *ghazal*. In addition, he has displayed his worth in the field of prose. His prose writings comprise the following books: *Hosh ke Nakhun*, (1934), *Tagore aur Uski Shairi* (1935), and a translation of the *History of Bolshevak Party in Russia*. His poetical works include *Surkh Savera, Gul-e-Tar*, and *Busaat-e-Raqs* (Complete works). Makhdoom died in Delhi on 25 August, 1969.

مخدومؔ محی الدین

اندھیرا

رات کے ہاتھ میں اک کاسہِ دریوزہ گری

یہ چمکتے ہوئے تارے، یہ دمکتا ہوا چاند

بھیک کے نور میں، مانگے کے اجالے میں مگن

یہی ملبوسِ عروسی ہے یہی ان کا کفن

اس اندھیرے میں وہ مرتے ہوئے جسموں کی کراہ

وہ عزازیل کے کتّوں کی کمیں گاہ

وہ تہذیب کے زخم

خندقیں،

باڑھ کے تار،

باڑھ کے تاروں میں الجھے ہوئے انسانوں کے جسم

اور انسانوں کے جسموں پہ وہ بیٹھے ہوئے گِدھ

وہ تڑختے ہوئے سر

میتّیں ہاتھ کٹی، پاؤں کٹی

لاش کے ڈھانچے کے اس پار سے اس پار تلک

سرد ہوا

Makhdoom Mahiuddin
Darkness (Andhera)

This night that holds a begging bowl,
These glimmering stars, this glittering moon,
All in borrowed light enclothed,
Which serves them both as bridal wear and as burial cloak;
The cries of dying men in dark,
The dogs of hell on the prowl,
Civilisation maimed and gored,
Trenches,
Walls of barbed wire,
Human bodies fence-enmeshed,
Vultures feasting on the flesh,
Broken skulls,
Truncated corpses,
Beyond the piles of bodies dead,
The wind blowing deathly cold;

Raat ke haath mein ik kaasa-e-daryooza gari,
Yeh chamakte hue taare, yeh damakta hua chaand,
Bheek ke noor mein, maange ke ujaale mein magan,
Yehi malboos-e-aroosi hai yahi inka kafan,
Is andhere mein woh marte hue jismon ke karaah,
Woh azazeel ke kutton ke kameen gaah,
Woh tahzeeb ke zakhm
Khandqein,
Baarh ke taar,
Baarh ke taaron mein uljhe hue insaanon ke jism,
Aur insaanon ke jismon pe woh baithe hue gidh,
Woh tarakhte hue sar,
Mayyaten haath kati, paaon kati,
Laash ke dhaanche ke is paar se us paar talak,
Sard hawa,

71

مخدوم محی الدین

نوحہ و نالہ و فریاد کناں

شب کے سنّاٹے میں رونے کی صدا

کبھی پتّوں کی، کبھی ماؤں کی

چاند کے تاروں کے ماتم کی صدا

رات کے ماتھے پہ آزردہ ستاروں کا ہجوم

صرف خورشیدِ درخشاں کے نکلنے تک ہے

رات کے پاس اندھیرے کے سوا کچھ بھی نہیں

رات کے پاس اندھیرے کے سوا کچھ بھی نہیں

Makhdoom Mahiuddin

Weeping, wailing, lamentation,
Piercing through the silent night,
Cries of children and their mothers,
The moon and stars sorrow-soaked,
The night crowned with weeping stars
All await the radiant sun to vanish and dissolve.

The night has nothing to show but dark,
The night has nothing to show but dark !

Noha-o-naala-o-faryaad kunaan,
Shab ke sannaate mein rone ki sada,
Kabhi bachchon ki kabhi maaon ki,
Chaand ke, taaron ki maatam ki sada,
Raat ke maathe pe aazurda sitaaron ka hajoom,
Sirf khursheed-e-darakhshaan ke nikalne tak hai.

Raat ke pass andhere ke siwa kuchh bhi nahin,
Raat ke pass andhere ke siwa kuchh bhi nahin !

مخدوم محی الدین

مشرق

جہل فاقہ بھوک بیماری نجاست کا مکاں

زندگانی تازگی عقل و فراست کا سماں

وہم زائیدہ خداؤں کا روایت کا غلام

پرورش پاتا رہا ہے جس میں صدیوں کا جذام

جھڑ چکے ہیں دست و بازو جس کے اس مشرق کو دیکھ

کھیلتی ہے سانس سینے میں مریضِ دق کو دیکھ

ایک ننگی نعش بے گور و کفن ٹھٹھری ہوئی

مغربی چیلوں کا لقمہ خون میں لتھڑی ہوئی

ایک قبرستان جس میں نوحہ خواں کوئی نہیں

اِک بھٹکتی روح ہے جس کا مکاں کوئی نہیں

پیکرِ ماضی کا اِک بے رنگ اور بے روح خول

ایک مرگِ بے قیامت ایک بے آواز ڈھول

اِک مسلسل رات جس کی صبح ہوتی ہی نہیں

خوابِ اصحابِ کہف کو پالنے والی زمیں

اس زمینِ موت پر وردہ کو ڈھایا جائے گا

اِک نئی دنیا نیا آدم بنایا جائے گا

74

Makhdoom Mahiuddin
East (Mashriq)

A place of hunger, penury, sickness, of darkness unrelieved,
Where life lies of light and freshness, of strength and sense
    bereaved.

Worshipping superstitious gods, a prey to rituals false,
A place where disease and suffering make a hearty feast.

That which has lost its limbs, behold thou that helpless East,
See how this consumptive patient is struggling for release.

A naked corpse, unwept, unburied, rotting in the cold,
A morsel fit for Western vultures, torn apiece and gored!

A graveyard wild and lonesome, with none to mourn or cry,
A restless soul, strayed from home, without a place to bide.

A hollow mask of vanished past, bereft of life and soul,
A death without resurrection, a drum, dumb and cold.

A long endless night, repelling morning rays,
A land fit for idle dreamers, in a cave encaged.

This land by death husbanded will soon be razed to dust,
A new world, a new man would replace this vale accursed.

Juhl faaqa bhook beemaari najaasat ka makaan,
Zindagaani taazgi aql-o-faraasat ka samaan.

Wahm zaaida khudaaon ka, rawaait ka ghulaam,
Parwarish paata raha hai jis mein sadion ka juzaam.

Jhar chuke hain dast-o-baazoo jis ke us mashrik ko dekh,
Khelti hai saans seene mein mareez-e-diq ko dekh.

Ek nangi naash, be gor-o-kafan, thithri hui,
Maghribi cheelon ka luqma, khoon mein lithri hui;

Ek qabaristaan jis mein noha khwaan koi nahin,
Ik bhatakti rooh hai jiska makaan koi nahin.

Paikar-e-maazi ka ik be rang aur be rooh khaul,
Ek marg-e-be-qayaamat, ek be aawaaz dhol.

Ik musalsal raat jiski subah hoti hi nahin,
Khwaab-e-ishaab-e-kahaf ko paalne waali zameen;

Is zameen-e-maut-parwurda ko dhaaya jaaega,
Ik nai duniya, naya aadam banaaya jaaega.

انتظار

رات بھر دیدۂ نمناک میں لہراتے رہے

سانس کی طرح سے آپ آتے رہے جاتے رہے

خوش تھے ہم اپنی تمنّاؤں کا خواب آئے گا

اپنا ارمان بر افگندہ نقاب آئے گا

نظریں نیچی کیے شرمائے ہوئے آئے گا

کاکلیں چہرے پہ بکھرائے ہوئے آئے گا

آ گئی تھی دلِ مضطر میں شکیبائی سی

بج رہی تھی مرے غم خانے میں شہنائی سی

شب کے جاگے ہوئے تاروں کو بھی نیند آنے لگی

آپ کے آنے کی اِک آس تھی اب جانے لگی

صبح نے سیج سے اٹھتے ہوئے لی انگڑائی

او صبا تو بھی جو آئی تو اکیلی آئی

میرے محبوب مری نیند اڑانے والے

میرے مسجود مری روح پہ چھانے والے

ابھی جا تاکہ مرے سجدوں کا ارماں نکلے

ابھی جا تاکہ ترے قدموں پہ مری جاں نکلے

76

Makhdoom Mahiuddin
Waiting (Intezaar)

All night you kept afloat before my dripping eyes,
Coming and going unperceived like the breath of life.

I was glad that my dreams were about to materialise,
My darling love, face-unveiled, would at my door arrive.

With coiling locks lying encurled on her shining face,
She would come coyness-clad, bending down her lovely eyes.

My restless heart, so it seemed, was feeling somewhat pacified,
Bridal bugles could be heard breaking through the dark inside.

Now the stars are falling asleep having kept awake at night,
My cherished hope of union sweet is dying before my very eyes.

The morning, rising from her bed, spreads her wings and yawns,
O thou softly wafting breeze, why have ye come alone?

O my darling thief, my love, the stealer of my sleep,
Controller of my inner self, O thou goddess sweet!

Come sharp, delay not fulfil my yearnings deep,
Let me fall at your feet, and fade away in perfect ease!

Raat bhar deeda-e-ghumnaak mein lahraate rahe,
Saans ki tarah se aap aate rahe, jaate rahe.

Khush the hum apni tamannaon ka khwab aaega,
Apna armaan bar-afganda niqaab aaega.

Nazren neechi kieye sharmaae hue aaega,
Kaakulen chehre pe bikhraae hue aaega;

Aa gai thi dil-e-muztir mein shakebaai si,
Baj rahi thi mire ghum khaane mein shahnaai si.

Shab ke jaage hue taaron ko bhi neend aane lagi,
Aap ke aane ki ik aas thi ab jaane lagi.

Subah ne sej se ulhte hue li angraai,
O saba tu bhi jo aai tau akele aai.

Mere mahboob, miri neend uraane waale,
Mere masjood miri rooh pe chhaane waale,

Aa bhi jaa ta ke mire sijdon ka armaan nikle,
Aa bhi ja ta ke tire qadmon pe miri jaan nikle.

77

N.M. Rashhid
(1910-1975)

NAZAR MOHAMMED RASHID (1910-1975)

Nazar Mohammed Rashid, popularly known as "Noon-Meem Rashid", was born at Akalgarh in Gujranwala district (now in Pakistan). He received his early education at his home town, and college education at Government College, Lahore. His father, Raja Fazal Ilahi Chishti, was a man of literary taste. He introduced him to the poetry of Hafiz, Saadi, Ghalib and Iqbal.

While at Government College, Lahore, Rashid was selected to edit the Urdu section of the college magazine, *Ravi*. Later, he edited for sometime Tajwar Najeebabadi's journal, *Shahkaar*. He also served for sometime in the Commissioner's office at Multan. At about this time he wrote his first poem in free-verse, *Jurrat-e-Parwaaz*, which is included in his famous collection : *Maawara*.

In 1939, Rashid joined All India Radio as a news editor, and became, after sometime, the Director of Programmes. He also served in the army on a short service commission. After the partition of India he worked as a regional director in Pakistan Radio. An assignment in the UN gave him an opportunity to go abroad and stay at New York. He retired in 1973 and settled down at Chelten (England). He died in a London hospital on October 9, 1975.

Rashid is a practitioner and pioneer of the free-verse poetry in Urdu. His handling of the new form had a startling effect on the readers who were thrilled as much by the newness of his technique, as by the daring thought and imagery of his poems. His works include: *Maawara, Iran Mein Ajnabi, Laa-Insaan,* and *Gumaan ka Mumkin.*

ن۔ م۔ راشد
دریچے کے قریب

جاگ اے شمعِ شبستانِ وصال

مخمل خواب کے اس فرشِ طرب ناک سے جاگ

لذتِ شب سے ترا جسم ابھی چور سہی

آ مری جان مرے پاس دریچے کے قریب

دیکھ کس پیار سے انوارِ سحر چومتے ہیں

مسجدِ شہر کے میناروں کو

جن کی رفعت سے مجھے

اپنی برسوں کی تمنّاؤں کا خیال آتا ہے

سیمگوں ہاتھوں سے اے جان ذرا

کھول لے رنگِ جنوں خیز آنکھیں

اسی مینار کو دیکھ

صبح کے نور سے شاداب سہی

اِسی مینار کے سائے تلے کچھ یاد بھی ہے؟

اپنے بے کار خدا کے مانند

اونگھتا ہے کسی تاریک نہاں خانے میں

Nazar Mohammed Rashid
Near The Window (Dareeche Ke Qareeb)

Wake, ye light of the night of love,
Leave the velvet bed of dreams;
Your limbs, though, haven't recovered from the drunkenness of
    sleep,
Come to the window, O my sweet !
Mark how the morning rays
Kiss the minarets of the mosque,
Whose shooting spire recalls
My long-cherished, deep desire.

Open with your argent hands
Your maddening eyes, wine-red,
Come, watch the minaret tall,
Bathed in the light of morn;
Beneath this minaret's shade (recall ?)
Lies a poor decrepit priest,
In his dungeon half-asleep,

Jaag ai shama-e-shabastaan-e-wisaal
Makhmal-e-khwaab ke is farsh-e-tarabnaak se jaag
Lazzat-e-shab se tira jism abhi choor sahi
Aa miri jaan mire paas dareeche ke qareeb
Dekh kis pyaar se anwaar-e-sahar choomte hain
Masjid-e-shahr ke meenaaron ko
Jin ki rif-at se mujhe
Apni barson ki tamanna ka khyaal aata hai.

Seemgoon haathon se ai jaan zara
Khol mai rang janoon khez aankhen
Isi meenaar ko dekh
Subah ke noor se shadaab sahi,
Isi meenaar ke saaye tale kuchh yaad bhi hai
Apne bekaar khuda ke maanind
Oonghta hai kisi taareek nihaan khaane mein

81

ن ۔ م ۔ راشد

ایک افلاس کا مارا ہوا املا ئے حزیں

ایک عفریت ۔۔۔۔اداس

تین سو سال کی ذلت کا نشاں

ایسی ذلت کہ نہیں جس کا مداوا کوئی

دیکھ بازار میں لوگوں کا ہجوم

بے پناہ سیل کے مانند رواں

جیسے جنّات بیابانوں میں

مشعلیں لے کے سرِ شام نکل آتے ہیں

ان میں ہر شخص کے سینے کے کسی گوشے میں

ایک دلہن سی بنی بیٹھی ہے

ٹمٹماتی ہوئی ننّھی سی خودی کی قندیل

لیکن اتنی بھی توانائی نہیں

بڑھ کے ان میں سے کوئی شعلہ جو آلہ بنے

ان میں مفلس بھی ہیں بیمار بھی ہیں

زیرِ افلاک مگر ظلم سہے جاتے ہیں

Nazar Mohammed Rashid

Idle like his idle God —
An apparition, sick and sad;
A humiliation, centuries long,
Irremediable, unredeemed !

Watch the jostling crowds of men,
Overflooding the thoroughfare,
Like the ghosts in wilderness wielding burning brands,
That suddenly spring to sight as the shades descend.
In the heart of every man
Glimmers the flame of self-respect,
Tremulous like a timorous bride,
That lacks the courage to change
The fading spark to a mighty blaze,
Some among the crowd are poor, some of them are sick,
Yet they suffer uncomplaining beneath the heavens high.

Ek iflaas ka maara hua mulla-e-hazeen,
Ek ifreeat-udaas
Teen sau saal ki zillat ka nishaan,
Aisi zillat ke nahin jis ka madaawa koi.

Dekh bazaar mein logon ka hajoom
Be panah sail ke maanind rawaan,
Jaise jinnaat bayaabaanon mein
Mashalen le ke sar-e-shaam nikal aate hain.
Un mein har shakhs ke seene ke kisi goshe mein
Ek dulhan si bani baithi hai
Timtamaati hui nanhi si khudi ki qandeel
Lekin itni bhi tawanaai nahin
Barh ke in mein se koi shola-e-jawwala bane
In mein muflis bhi hain beemaar bhi hain
Zer-e-iflaak magar zulam sahe jaate hain.

ن ۔ م ۔ راشدؔ

ایک بوڑھا سا تھکا ماندہ سا رہوار ہوں میں

بھوک کا شاہسوار

سخت گیر اور تنومند بھی ہے

میں بھی اس شہر کے لوگوں کی طرح

ہر شبِ عیش گزر جانے پر

بہرِ جمعِ خس و خاشاک نکل جاتا ہوں

چرخ گرداں ہے جہاں

شام کو پھر اسی کاشانہ میں لوٹ آتا ہوں

بے بسی میری ذرا دیکھ کہ میں

مسجدِ شہر کے میناروں کو

اس دریچے میں سے پھر جھانکتا ہوں

جب انھیں عالمِ رخصت میں شفق چومتی ہے

Nazar Mohammed Rashid

I'm an old, jaded horse,
And hunger, my rider,
Is ruthless and strong.
Like the rest of city folks,
As the night of revelry ends
I too set out for fuel and fodder;
At sundown I return to my den again
Utterly helpless, once again I watch,
From near my window,
The crimson eve fondly kiss
The minarets of the mosque.

Ek boorha sa thaka maanda sa rahwaar hoon main
Bhook ka shahsawaar
Sakhtgeer aur tanumand bhi hai,
Main bhi is shahr ke logon ki tarah
Har shab-e-aish guzar jaane par
Bahr-e-jama-e-khas-o-khaashaak nikal jaata hoon,
Charkh gardaan hai jahaan
Shaam ko phir usi kaashaane mein laut aata hoon
Be basi meri zara dekh ke main
Masjid-e-shahr ke meenaaron ko
Is dareeche mein se phir jhaankta hoon
Jab inhen aalam-e-rukhsat mein shafaq choomti hai.

سبا ویراں

سلیماں سر بہ زانو اور سبا ویراں

سبا ویراں، سبا آسیب کا مسکن

سبا آلام کا انبارِ بے پایاں

گیاہ و سبزہ و گل سے جہاں خالی

ہوائیں تشنہِ باراں

طیور اس دشت کے منقار زیرِ پر

تو سر مہ در گلو انساں

سلیماں سر بہ زانو اور سبا ویراں

سلیماں سر بہ زانو، ترش رو، غمگیں، پریشاں مو

جہانگیری، جہاں بانی فقط طرۂ آہو

محبت شعلہ پرّاں، ہوس بوئے گلِ بے بو

زرازِ دہر کمتر گو

سبا ویراں کہ اب تک اس سر زمیں پر ہیں

کسی عیّار کے غارت گروں کے نقشِ پا باقی

سبا باقی، نہ مہر وئے سبا باقی

سلیماں سر بہ زانو،

اب کہاں سے قاصدِ فرخندہ پے آئے

کہاں سے کس سبو سے کاسہِ پیری میں مے آئے

Nazar Mohammed Rashid
Saba in Ruins (Saba Weeraan)

Sulemaan is crestfallen, Saba lies in ruins;
Saba, a ruin—a haunt of ghosts,
A flood of sorrows uncontrolled,

No trace of bud or leaf or grass,
Dry, thirsty wind blows;
Birds have hid their beaks in feathers,
Men are sitting dumb and choked,
Sulemaan is down-hearted, Saba, a wild and barren wold.

Sulemaan—depressed, dejected, dishevelled,
Kingship—a flighty, fleeting stag,
Lust, a rose without the scent, love a flame eluding grasp.

Keep the secert guarded close,
Saba—a sheer stretch of ruin
Tramped beneath the marauders' feet, ravaged by the reign of fraud,
Saba and her moon-like beauties are now a thing of past.

Sulemaan sits crestfallen,
Who'll bring the welcome news, who'll rap the door ?
Where's the wine, where the flask to fill the empty, aged bowl ?

Sulemaan sar ba-zanoo aur Saba weeraan
Saba weeraan, Saba aaseb ka maskin,
Saba aalaam ka ambaar-e-be paayaan

Gayaah-o-sabza-o-gul se jahaan khaali,
Hawaaen tishna-e-baaraan
Tayyoor is dasht ke minqaar zer-e-par
Tau surma dar galu insaan
Sulemaan sar ba-zaanoo aur saba weeraan.

Sulemaan sar ba-zanoo, tursh roo, ghamgeen, pareeshan-moo
Jahangeeri, jahanbaani faqt tarrara-e-aahoo,
Mahabbat shola-e-parraan, hawas boo-e-gul-e-be-boo.

Za raaz-e-dahar kamlu go
Saba weeran ke ab tak is zameen par hain
Kisi ayyaar ke gharatgaron ke naqsh-e-pa baqi,
Saba baqi na mahroo-e-Saba baqi.

Sulemaan sar ba-zanoo,
Ab kahan se qaasid-e-farkhunda pai aae
Kahan se, kis saboo se kaasa-e-peeri mein mai aae ?

Asrar-ul-Haq Majaz
(1911-1955)

ASRAR-UL-HAQ MAJAZ (1911-1955)

Majaz was born at Radauli near Lucknow on October 19, 1911. He received his schooling at Lucknow, and college education at Agra and Aligarh. He had shown his poetic talent even during his schooldays at Lucknow where, under the influence of his friend and counsellor, Moin Ehsan Jazbi, he had started writing poetry. At Aligarh he was influenced, among others, by Fani Badayuni. Majaz also studied at St. John College, Agra, where in the company of his easy-going friends, he got addicted to drinking which ruined his physical and mental health, and made him a prey to nervous breakdown.

Leaving his M.A. (Urdu) studies halfway, he took up employment with All India Radio where he also edited the radio journal, *Aawaz*. But he gave up this job after a year due to differences with his boss, Ahmed Shah Bukhari ('Pitras'). On the morning of December 5, 1955, he was found lying unconscious on the terrace of a tavern in Lucknow. The end came the same day in a hospital in Lucknow.

Romance and revolt are the two important strands of Majaz's poetry. His famous poem, 'Aawaara', is the cry of an anguished heart, struggling in vain, to break the bonds of cant and convention. "Khwab-e-Sehar", on the other hand, records the poet's feeling of hope and relief at the long-awaited dawn of a new socialist order, which alone, he feels, can deliver man from centuries of slavery to superstition and exploitation.

In his style, Majaz adheres to the conventional kind of rhymed verse, and is not enamoured of the new forms of blank verse and free-verse poetry.

Majaz's collected works are available under the title, *Aahang*.

89

اسرارالحق مجاز
مہمان

آج کی رات اور باقی ہے

کل تو جانا ہی ہے سفر پہ مجھے

زندگی منتظر ہے منہ پھاڑے

زندگی، خاک و خون میں لتھڑی

آنکھ میں شعلہ ہائے تند لیے

دو گھڑی خود کو شاداماں کر لیں

آج کی رات اور باقی ہے

چلنے ہی کو ہے اک سموم ابھی

رقص فرما ہے روحِ بربادی

بربریت کے کاروانوں سے

زلزلے میں ہے سینہ گیتی

ذوقِ پنہاں کو کامراں کر لیں

آج کی رات اور باقی ہے

ایک پیمانہ مے سرجوش

لطفِ گفتار، گرمیِ آغوش

بوسے ۔۔۔۔ اس درجہ آتشیں بوسے

پھونک ڈالیں جو میری کشتِ ہوش

Majaz
Visitor (Mehmaan)

I have only one more night,

To-morrow I shall pack and go,
Life with its jaws agape,
Mud-splashed, bloody-faced,
With eyes aflame, lies in wait.
Let's enjoy a little while,
I have only one more night.

A scorching gale is about to blow,
Ruin sits artride the globe,
The earth is all ashudder with fright,
Mauled by the savage hordes,
Let our hearts be satisfied,
I have only one more night.

A glass of wine with foaming beads,
Warm embraces, whisperings sweet,
Kisses—flaming hot and wild,
Sense-dissolving in their heat !

Aaj ki raat aur baaqi hai

Kal tau jaana hi hai safar pe mujhe,
Zindagi muntezir hai munh phaare,
Zindagi, khaak-o-khoon mein lithri,
Aankh mein shola haae tund lieye
Do ghari khud ko shaadmaan kar lein,
Aaj ki raat aur baaqi hai.

Chalne hi ko hai ik samoom abhi,
Raqs farma hai rooh-e-barbaadi
Barbareeat ke kaarwaanon se
Zalzale mein hai seena-e-geeti.
Zauq-e-pinhaan ko kaamraan kar lein,
Aaj ki raat aur baaqi hai.

Ek paimaana-e-mai-e-sar josh,
Lutaf-e-guftaar, garmi-e-aaghosh,
Bose—is darja aatisheen bose,
Phoonk daalen jo meri kisht-e-hosh !

91

مجاز

روح نغ بستہ ہے تپاں کر لیں
آج کی رات اور باقی ہے
ایک دو اور ساغرِ سرشار
پھر تو ہونا ہی ہے مجھے ہشیار
چھیڑنا ہی ہے سازِ زیست مجھے
آگ برسائیں گے لبِ گفتار
کچھ طبیعت تو ہم رواں کر لیں
آج کی رات اور باقی ہے
پھر کہاں یہ حسیں سہانی رات
یہ فراغت، یہ کیف کے لمحات
کچھ تو آسودگیِ ذوقِ نہاں
کچھ تو تسکینِ شورشِ جذبات
آج کی رات اور باقی ہے
آج کی رات اور باقی ہے

92

Majaz

Let the frigid soul revive,
I have only one more night.

Give me more of ale, I pray,
To-morrow I shall work and wake.
I cannot turn away from life,
From harsh reproach and hectic haste.
Let my drooping spirits revive,
I have only one more night.

Rarely comes such lovely night,
Such leisure, such deep delight,
Passions crave fulfilment,
Hunger must be satisfied.
Let it be eternalised, —
I have only one more night.

Rooh-e-yakh basta ko tapaan kar lein,
Aaj ki raat aur baaqi hai.

Ek do aur saaghar-e-sarshaar,
Phir tau hona hi hai mujhe hoshiaar,
Chherna hi hai saaz-e-zeest mujhe,
Aag barsaaenge lab-e-guftaar;
Kuchh tabeeat tau hum rawaan kar lein,
Aaj ki raat aur baaqi hai.

Phir kahaan yeh haseen suhaani raat,
Yeh faraaghat, yeh kaif ke lamhaat,
Kuchh tau aasoodgi-e-zauq-e-nihaan,
Kuchh tau taskeen-e-shorish-e-jazbaat.
Aaj ki raat jaawedaan kar lein,
Aaj ki raat aur baaqi hai.

خوابِ سحر

مہر صدیوں سے چمکتا ہی رہا افلاک پر
رات ہی طاری رہی انسان کے ادراک پر
عقل کے میدان میں ظلمت کا ڈیرا ہی رہا
دل میں تاریکی، دماغوں میں اندھیرا ہی رہا
اک نہ اک مذہب کی سعیِ خام بھی ہوتی رہی
اہلِ دل پر بارشِ الہام بھی ہوتی رہی
آسمانوں سے فرشتے بھی اترتے ہی رہے
نیک بندے بھی خدا کا کام کرتے ہی رہے
ابنِ مریم بھی اٹھے، موسیٰ و عمران بھی اٹھے
رام و گوتم بھی اٹھے، فرعون و ہاماں بھی اٹھے
اہلِ سیف اٹھتے رہے، اہلِ کتاب آتے رہے
ایں جناب آتے رہے اور آں جناب آتے رہے
حکمراں دل پر رہے صدیوں تلک اصنام بھی
ابرِ رحمت بن کے چھایا دہر پر اسلام بھی
مسجدوں میں مولوی خطبے سناتے ہی رہے
مندروں میں برہمن اشلوک گاتے ہی رہے

94

Majaz
Dream of Dawn (Khwab-e-Sehar)

For ages has the radiant sun been shining in the skies,
But human mind has always struggled in the shade of night.

Darkness has held its sway since the world began,
Not a ray was allowed to light the head or heart of man.

Religion too from time to time has made her vain forays,
The rain of revelation too has purified this place.

Angels too from time to time have descended on this earth,
Noble souls have also been displaying their precious worth.

Moses, Umraan, Mary's Jesus—all showed their spiritual might,
Ram, Gautam, Faroun, Haaman, all have their hands tried.

Wielders of the pen and sword have also walked this globe,
The world has been graced by unnumbered reverend folk.

For centuries has the human heart to idols been a prey,
Islam too, like vernal cloud, has fertilised this clay.

Mullahs have been sermonising in the holy mosques,
Brahamins have been chanting hymns in their synogogues.

Mehar sadion se chamakta hi raha iflaak par,
Raat hi taari rahi insaan ke idraak par.

Aql ke maidaan mein zulmat ka dera hi raha,
Dil mein taariki, dimaaghon mein andhera hi raha.

Ik na ik mazhab ki sai-e-khaam bhi hoti rahi,
Ahl-e-dil par baarish-e-ilhaam bhi hoti rahi.

Aasmaanon se farishte bhi utarte hi rahe,
Nek bande bhi khuda ka kaam karte hi rahe.

Ibn-e-Mariam bhi uthe, Moosa-o-Umraan bhi uthe,
Ram-o-Gautam bhi uthe, Faroun-o-Haaman bhi uthe;

Ahle-e-saif uthte rahe, ahl-e-kitab aate rahe,
Een janb aate rahe, aur aanjanab aate rahe.

Hukamraan dil par rahe sadion talak isnaam bhi,
Abr-e-rahmat ban ke chhaya dahr par islaam bhi.

Masjidon mein maulvi khutbe sunaate hi rahe,
Mandiron mein brahamin ashlok gaate hi rahe.

مجازؔ

آدمی منّت کشِ اربابِ عرفاں ہی رہا
دردِ انسانی مگر محرومِ درماں ہی رہا

اک نہ اک در پر جبینِ شوق گھستی ہی رہی
آدمیت ظلم کی چکّی میں پستی ہی رہی

رہبری جاری رہی پیغمبری جاری رہی
دین کے پردے میں جنگِ زر گری جاری رہی

اہلِ باطن علم کے سینوں کو گرماتے رہے
جہل کے تاریک سائے ہاتھ پھیلاتے رہے

یہ مسلسل آفتیں، یہ یورشیں، یہ قتلِ عام
آدمی کب تک رہے اوہامِ باطل کا غلام

ذہنِ انسانی نے اب اوہام کے ظلمات میں
زندگی کی سخت طوفانی اندھیری رات میں

کچھ نہیں تو کم سے کم خوابِ سحر دیکھا تو ہے
جس طرف دیکھا نہ تھا اب تک ادھر دیکھا تو ہے

96

Majaz

Man has been supplicating saints and sages wise,
Human misery, all the same, has all recipes defied.

Human brow has always bent at this or that threshold,
Humanity has always suffered inequities untold.

There has been no dearth of leaders, or of prophets wise,
Greed for gold has plied its trade wearing religious guise.

Feeling hearts have tried to leaven knowledge with the light of
love,
The clouds of darkness, nevertheless, have always hung over this
earth,

Such struggle, such suffering, such heinous carnage !
How long has man been to superstition a slave !

Human mind has at last awakened from its heavy sleep,
In the stormy night of life, in the superstitious deep,

Has at least dreamt a dream of the golden dawn,
Looked at last towards the East, where none before had glanced.

Aadmi mannat kash-e-arbaab-e-irfaan hi raha,
Dard-e-insaani magar mehroom-e-darmaan hi raha.

Ik na ik dar par jabeen-e-shauq ghisti hi rahi,
Aadmeeat zulam ki chakki mein pisti hi rahi.

Rahbari jaari rahi paighambari jaari rahi,
Deen ke parde mein jang-e-zargari jaari rahi.

Ahl-e-baatin ilm ke seenon ko garmaate rahe,
Juhal ke taarik saae haath phailaate rahe.

Yeh musalsal aafaten, yeh yorishen, yeh qatal-e-aam,
Aadmi kab tak rahe ohaam-e-baatil ka ghulaam !

Zehn-e-insaani ne ab ohaam ke zulmaat mein,
Zindagi ki sakht toofaani andheri raat mein,

Kuchh nahin tau kam se kam khwab-e-sahar dekha tau hai,
Jis taraf dekha na tha ab tak udhar dekha tau hai.

Faiz Ahmed Faiz
(1911-1984)

FAIZ AHMED FAIZ (1911-1984)

Faiz Ahmed Faiz was born in Sialkot and educated at Lahore. He began his career as a lecturer in English at Amritsar. During World War II, he joined the Welfare Department of the Army, and became Lt. Colonel. However, with his strong sense of independence, and a commitment to the socialist ideology, he could not for long brook the shackles of military discipline. He turned to journalism and distinguished himself as editor of *The Pakistan Times*. He was charged with complicity in the Rawalpindi conspiracy case, and was sentenced to four years' imprisonment in 1951. Two of his poetical collections, *Dast-e-Saba* and *Zindaan Nama*, are the products of this period of imprisonment.

As a poet Faiz began with the conventional themes of love and beauty, but soon these conventional themes get submerged in the larger social and political issues of the day. The romance of love gets fused with the travails of the afflicted humanity, and Faiz uses his poetry to champion the cause of socialistic humanism. This turning away from romance to realism is clearly suggested in his poem : *Mujh se Pehli si Mahabbat Miri Mehboob na Maang* (Ask me not my love, for the love of former days).

In his style and diction, Faiz may be called an inheritor of the tradition of Ghalib. His admiration of Ghalib is also reflected in the title of his first published work, *Naqsh-e-Faryaadi,* which comes straight from the opening line of *Dewan-e-Ghalib,* An admirer of Karl Marx and a poet of the proletariat, Faiz was honoured by Soviet Russia with the prestigious Lenin award for peace. His complete works have been published under the title, *Nuskhahaai Wafa.* Because of the sincerity and intensity of his thought and sentiment, and because of this consummate art, his poetry is read and admired on both sides of the Indian subcontinent.

فیض احمد فیضؔ

نثار میں تیری گلیوں کے اے وطن کہ جہاں

چلی ہے رسم کہ کوئی نہ سر اٹھا کے چلے

جو کوئی چاہنے والا طواف کو نکلے

نظر چرا کے چلے، جسم و جاں بچا کے چلے

ہے اہلِ دل کے لیے اب یہ نظمِ بست و کشاد

کہ سنگ و خِشت مقیّد ہیں اور سگ آزاد

بہت ہے ظلم کے دستِ بہانہ جُو کے لیے

جو چند اہلِ جنوں تیرے نام لیوا ہیں

بنے ہیں اہلِ ہوس، مدّعی بھی، منصف بھی

کسے وکیل کریں، کس سے منصفی چاہیں

مگر گزارنے والوں کے دن گزرتے ہیں

ترے فراق میں یوں صبح و شام کرتے ہیں

بجھا جو روزنِ زنداں تو دل یہ سمجھا ہے

کہ تیری مانگ ستاروں سے بھر گئی ہوگی

چمک اٹھے ہیں سلاسل تو ہم نے جانا ہے

کہ اب سحر ترے رخ پر بکھر گئی ہوگی

100

Faiz Ahmed Faiz
"Hail to Thee, My Native Land"

Hail to thee, my native land, hail to thy ways !
Where none is allowed to walk with his head upraised;
If ever someone ventures out on a pilgrimage,
Warily, warily should he walk, lest he be waylaid.

There now exists for bolder hearts a novel, penal code,
Dogs are free to bark and bite, stones are kept encaged.

Enough for the tyrants seeking an excuse,
A few audacious lovers, with your love crazed;
The sensual men masquerade both as plaintiff and as judge,
Whom to ask for justice, whom to supplicate ?

Yet your lovers, somehow, manage to survive,
In your separation creep from day to night.

As the vent in the wall vanishes in the dark,
We conjecture that your hair is getting spangled with the stars;
When our chains emit a glow in the dungeon gloom,
Your lovely face, we imagine, blushes in the morning bloom.

Nisar main teri galion ke, ai watan ke jahan,
Chali hai rasm ke koi na sar utha ke chale,
Jo koi chaahne wala tawaaf ko nikle,
Nazar chura ke chale, jism-o-jaan bacha ke chale.

Hai ahl-e-dil ke lieye ab yeh nazm-e-bast-o-kushaad,
Ke sang-o-khisht muqaid hain aur sag azaad.

Bahut hai zulam ke dast-e-bahana-joo ke lieye,
Jo chand ahl-e-janoon tere naam-lewa hain,
Bane hain ahl-e-hawas, muddai bhi, munsif bhi,
Kise wakil karen, kis se munsifi chaahen.

Magar guzaarne waalon ke din guzarte hain,
Tire firaq main yoon subah-o-shaam karte hain.

Bujha jo rozan-e-zindaan, tau dil yeh sumjha hai,
Ke teri maang sitaaron se bhar gai hogi,
Chamak uthe hain salaasal tau hum ne jaana hai,
Ke ab sehar tire rukh par bikhar gai hogi.

فیض احمد فیضؔ

غرض تصوّرِ شام و سحر میں جیتے ہیں
گرفتِ سایۂ دیوار و در میں جیتے ہیں

یونہی ہمیشہ اُلجھتی رہی ہے ظلم سے خلق
نہ ان کی رسم نئی ہے، نہ اپنی ریت نئی

یونہی ہمیشہ کھلائے ہیں ہم نے آگ میں پھول
نہ ان کی ہار نئی ہے نہ اپنی جیت نئی

اِسی سبب سے فلک کا گِلا نہیں کرتے
ترے فراق میں ہم دل برا نہیں کرتے

گر آج تجھ سے جدا ہیں تو کل بہم ہوں گے
یہ رات بھر کی جدائی تو کوئی بات نہیں

گر آج اَوجِ پہ ہے طالعِ رقیب تو کیا
یہ چار دن کی خدائی تو کوئی بات نہیں

جو تجھ سے عہدِ وفا استوار رکھتے ہیں
علاجِ گردشِ لیل و نہار رکھتے ہیں

102

Faiz Ahmed Faiz

This is how we spend our time, imagining dawns and eves,
Confined within the stony walls, this is how we live and breathe !

Men have fought with tyranny ever since the world began,
Our suffering and their torture have always gone hand in hand.

We have always sown flowers amidst the flames,
Their defeat and our triumph are neither new nor strange.

That's why we grumble not against the tyrannous fate,
Despite separation, we do not feel dismayed.

If to-day we sit apart, to-morrow we unite,
This parting for just one night doesn't give us fright;

If to-day the rival's star scales the upper skies,
We shouldn't feel unnerved by his transient might.

Those who are committed to you firmly in their mind,
Have the strength to face and fight the challenges of time.

Gharz tasawwur-e-shaam-o-sehar mein jeete hain;
Garift-e-saya-e-deewar-o-dar mein jeete hain.

Yoonhi hamesha ulajhti rahi zulam se khalaq;
Na un ki rasm nai hai na apni reet nai,

Yoonhi hamesha khilaae hain hum ne aag mein phool;
Na un ki haar nai hai; na apni jeet nai,

Isi sabab se falak ka gila nahin karte,
Tire fiarq mein hum dil bura nahin karte.

Gar aaj tujh se juda hain tau kal baham honge,
Yeh raat bhar ki judaai tau koi baat nahin,

Gar aaj auj par hai taala-e-raqib tau kya ?
Yeh chaar din ki khudaai tau koi baat nahin.

Jo tujh se ahd-e-wafa istawaar rakhte hain,
Ilaaj-e-gardish-e-lail-o-nihaar rakhte hain.

☆

یادِ غزالِ چشماں، ذکرِ سمن عذاراں

جب چاہا کرلیا ہے گنجِ قفس بہاراں

آنکھوں میں درد مندی، ہونٹوں پہ عذر خواہی

جانانہ وار آئی شامِ فراقِ یاراں

ناموسِ جان و دل کی بازی لگی تھی ورنہ

آساں نہ تھی کچھ ایسی راہِ وفا شعاراں

مجرم ہو خواہ کوئی، رہتا ہے ناصحوں کا

روئے سخن ہمیشہ سوئے جگر فگاراں

شاید قریب پہنچی صبحِ وصال ہمدم

موجِ صبا لیے ہے خوشبوئے خوش کناراں

ہے اپنی کشتِ ویراں، سرسبز اس یقیں سے

آئیں گے اس طرف بھی اک روز ابر و باراں

آئے گی فیضؔ اک دن بادِ بہار لے کر

تسلیمے فروشاں، پیغامِ مے گساراں

104

Faiz Ahmed Faiz

Remembering the doe-like eyes, conjuring up the jasmine-face,
We create, when we want, a blooming garden in the cage.

Compassion brewing in the eyes, apology flowing from the lips,
Thus came the parting eve, like a beauteous belle on stage.

Life and death hung in balance, our very honour was at stake,
Otherwise, it wasn't easy to traverse the path of faith.

Whosoever be at fault, we the poor wounded hearts
Always have to bear the brunt of the censors' rage.

Perhaps the union morn arrives, I can smell, my friend,
The softly-blowing morning breeze, rich with soft incense.

What sustains my withering crop is my firm belief,
That rainy clouds will surely bless this land one day.

Surely will the vernal breeze one day bring, O Faiz,
Greetings from the tavern-keeper, tidings from the tavern mates.

Yaad-e-ghazaal-chashmaan, zikar-e-saman-azaaraan,
Jab chaha kar liya hai kunj-e-qafas baharaan.

Aankhon mein dardmandi, honton pe uzar khwahi,
Janaana-waar aai shaam-e-firaq-e-yaaraan.

Naamoos-e-jaan-o-dil ki baazi lagi thi, warna,
Aasaan na thi kuchh aisi rah-e-wafa-shiaaraan.

Mujrim ho khwah koi, rahta hai naasihon ka,
Roo-e-sakhum hamesha soo-e-jigar figaraan.

Shaaid qarib pahunchi subah-e-wisaal, humdum,
Mauj-e-saba lieye hai khushboo-e-khush kinaraan.

Hai apni kisht-e-weeran sar sabz is yaqeen se,
Aaenge is taraf bhi ik roz abr-o-baraan.

Aaegi Faiz ikdin baad-e-bahaar le kar,
Tasleem-e-mai firoshaan, paighaam-e-mai gusaraan.

فیض احمد فیضؔ

چند روز اور مری جان

چند روز اور مری جان فقط چند ہی روز

ظلم کی چھاؤں میں دم لینے پہ مجبور ہیں ہم

اور کچھ دیر ستم سہہ لیں، تڑپ لیں، رو لیں

اپنے اجداد کی میراث ہے معذور ہیں ہم

جسم پر قید ہے، جذبات پہ زنجیریں ہیں

فکر محبوس ہے، گفتار پہ تعزیریں ہیں

اپنی ہمّت ہے کہ پھر بھی جیے جاتے ہیں

زندگی کیا کسی مفلس کی قبا ہے جس میں

ہر گھڑی درد کے پیوند لگے جاتے ہیں

لیکن اب ظلم کی میعاد کے دن تھوڑے ہیں

اِک ذرا صبر، کہ فریاد کے دن تھوڑے ہیں

عرصۂ دہر کی جھلسی ہوئی ویرانی میں

ہم کو رہنا ہے پہ یونہی تو نہیں رہنا ہے

اجنبی ہاتھوں کا بے نام گرانبار ستم

آج سہنا ہے، ہمیشہ تو نہیں سہنا ہے

چند روز اور، مری جان فقط چند ہی روز

106

Faiz Ahmed Faiz
A Few Days More, My Love

A few days more, my love, just a few days,
We are obliged to live beneath the tyranny's sway.
Suffer a little longer, grovel and bewail,
Sufferance is our legacy, how can we escape ?

Our body is in bondage, our feeling are enchained,
Censor sits on our speech, thought lies restrained.
If we continue to live credit goes to our will.
Life, it seems, is a poorman's cloak
Where every minute a painful patch is stitched on to mend the
 holes.

But, hold thy cheer, the tyranny's reign is in its last stride,
A little patience, and you'll see better days arrive ?

In this world's blasted wilds,
We are to stay but not like this,
The blatant wrongs at alien hands,
Which we bear to day, we will not bear for aye;

A few days more, my love, just a few days !

Chand roz aur miri jaan ! faqt cand hi roz
Zulm ki chhaaon mein dam lene pe majboor hain hum,
Aur kuchh der sitam sah lein, tarap len, ro lein,
Apne ijdaad ki meeraas hai, maazoor hain hum;

Jism par qaid hai, jazbaat pe zanjeeren hain,
Filkar mahboos hai, guftaar pe taazeren hain,
Apni himmat hai ke hum phir bhi jieye jaate hein !
Zindagi kya kisi muflis ki qaba hai jismen
Har ghari dard ke paiwand lage jaate hain ?

Lekin ab zulm ki mayyaad ke din thore hain,
Ik zara sabar, ke faryuud ke din thore hain.

Arsa-e-dahar ki jhulsi hui weeraani mein
Hum ko rahna hai pe yunhi tau nahin rahna hai,
Ajnabi haathon ka be naam, giraanbaar sitam,
Aaj sahna hai, hamesha tau nahin sahna hai.........

Chand roz aur, miri jaan ! faqt chand hi roz.

Meeraji
(1912-1949)

SANA ALLAH SANI DAAR MEERAJI
(1912-1949)

Meeraji was born in Lahore on May 25, 1912, and died in Bombay on November 4, 1949. Though he lived for only thirty-seven years, his poetic output is astonishing. His complete works, published from London in 1988, contain a rich variety of poetry, representing *geets, ghazals,* and *nazms,* both of the rhyming and the free-verse type. In addition, he has made translations from foreign languages including English, French, Russian, Japanese, Chinese, Persian, Sanskrit, etc. His favourite topics are love, beauty and death, his special contribution lies in giving a new direction to Urdu poetry and poetics. Along with Nazar Mohammed Rashid, he is a leading poet of the Progressive Movement in Urdu.

Meeraji was born and brought up in an affluent and affectionate family. His father, Munshi Mohammed Mahtab-ul-Din was an engineer in Indian Railways. But Meeraji left his home and family for certain inexplicable reasons, and spent his life as a homeless wanderer making his living by writing songs, and by doing editorial work for several Urdu journals, such as *Adbi Duniya* (Lahore), *Saqi* (Delhi), and *Khayaal* (Bombay). Seemingly an unwordly ascetic, Meeraji was a sensitive and intelligent man, a jilted lover, sad at heart and sick in body, always perplexed, always questing, and turning to poetry for release.

Akhtar-ul-Iman, the poet's friend, with whom he spent the last days of his life in Poona and Bombay, describes how lonely and miserable was his existence in the end. Drinking and smoking had told upon his health and he had to receive psychiatric therapy for his ailment. He died in King Edward Memorial Hospital, Bombay.

109

میرا جی

کلرک کا نغمۂ محبّت

سب رات مری سپنوں میں گزر جاتی ہے اور میں سوتا ہوں

پھر صبح کی دیوی آتی ہے،

اپنے بستر سے اٹھتا ہوں، منہ دھوتا ہوں،

لایا تھا کل جو ڈبل روٹی

اس میں سے آدھی کھائی تھی

باقی جو بچی وہ میرا آج کا ناشتہ ہے

دنیا کے رنگ انوکھے ہیں

جو میرے سامنے رہتا ہے اس کے گھر میں گھر والی ہے،

اور دائیں پہلو میں اک منزل کا ہے مکاں، وہ خالی ہے

اور بائیں جانب اِک عیّاش ہے جس کے یہاں اک اُڈاشتہ ہے

اور ان سب میں اِک بھی ہوں لیکن بس تو ہی نہیں

فارغ ہوتا ہوں ناشتے سے اور اپنے گھر سے نکلتا ہوں

دفتر کی راہ پہ چلتا ہوں،

رستے میں شہر کی رونق ہے، اک تانگہ ہے، دو کاریں ہیں

تانگوں پر برقِ تبسّم ہے،

باتوں کا میٹھا ترنّم ہے،

110

Meeraji
Love Song of A Clerk

The night slips away in dreams, and I go to sleep,
Then comes the goddess Morn;
I arise and wash my face.
The loaf of bread that I had bought,
Was half consumed by me at night,
The rest will serve as breakfast for the morrow morn.
Strange are the ways of life !
He who lives opposite has a married wife;
The single-storeyed house on right is not occupied.
On my left lives a rake with a mistress by his side;
I too live in this part, but without you, alas !
Except the fragrance of your locks, I've every joy of life.
I finish my breakfast and set out from home
On the road to office.
The road is all abustle, a tonga and two cars,
The tonga flashes bright smiles,
The riders chatter music-like.

Sab raat miri sapnon mein guzar jaati hai aur main sota hoon,
Phir subah ki devi aati hai,
Apne bistar se uthta hoon, munh dhota hoon,
Laaya tha kal jo double roti
Us mein se aadhi khaai thi
Baqi jo bachi woh mira aaj ka naashta hai.
Duniya ke rang anokhe hain,
Jo mere saamne rahta hai, uske ghar mein ghar wali hai,
Aur daaen pehloo main ik manzil ka hai makaan, woh khali hai,
Aur baaen jaanib ik ayyaash hai jis ke yahan ik dasshta hai,
Aur in sab mein ik main bhi hoon, lekin bas tu hi nahin.
Farigh hota hoon naashte se aur apne ghar se nikalta hoon,
Daftar ki raah pe chalta hoon,
Raste mein shahr ki raunaq hai, ik tonga hai, do kaaren hain,
Tangon par barq-e-tabassum hai,
Baaton ka meetha tarunnam hai,

میراجی

اک ساتا ہے دھیان یہ رہ رہ کر، قدرت کے دل میں ترحم ہے
ہر چیز تو ہے موجود یہاں اک تُو ہی نہیں، اک تو ہی نہیں
اور میری آنکھوں میں رونے کی ہمّت ہی نہیں، آنسو ہی نہیں
جوں توں رستہ کٹ جاتا ہے اور بندی خانہ آتا ہے
چل کام میں اپنے دل کو لگا یوں کوئی مجھے سمجھاتا ہے
میں دھیرے دھیرے دفتر میں اپنے دل کو لے جاتا ہوں
نادان ہے دل، مورکھ بچّہ ۔۔۔اک اور طرح دے جاتا ہوں
پھر کام کا دریا بہتا ہے اور ہوش مجھے کب رہتا ہے
جب آدھا دن ڈھل جاتا ہے تو گھر سے افسر آتا ہے
اور اپنے کمرے میں مجھ کو چپراسی سے بلواتا ہے
یوں کہتا ہے، ووں کہتا ہے لیکن بیکار ہی رہتا ہے
میں اسکی ایسی باتوں سے تھک جاتا ہوں تھک جاتا ہوں
اور دل میں آگ سلگتی ہے : میں بھی جو کوئی افسر ہوتا
اس شہر کی دھول اور گلیوں سے کچھ دور مرا پھر گھر ہوتا
اور تُو ہوتی
لیکن میں تو اک منشی ہوں تُو اونچے گھر کی رانی ہے
یہ میری پریم کہانی ہے اور دھرتی سے بھی پرانی ہے
112

Meeraji

I'm with this thought obsessed: doth God mercy possess ?
Everything is here in plenty, but for you, but for you !
And I have no strength to cry, nor a tear in my eyes.

Somehow the way doth end, and I reach the office cage;
"Get absorbed in your work," someone gives the counsel sage.
My silly heart, a senseless child, takes me to a different side.
But when the flood of work flows, I'm carried by its tide.

When half the day is almost done, lo, my boss arrives;
Sends a peon, calls me by;
Asks me to do this or that, but himself simply sits and chats.
I feel bored, utterly fagged,
Sit smouldering deep inside: If I were the boss,
Away from these dusty lanes I would then reside,
With you, my dear, as my consort !
But I'm a petty clerk, and you a queen, exalted, high.
This is my tale of love, a tale as old as life.

Uksaata hai dhayaan yeh rah rah kar : qudrat ke dil mein tarahum hai ?
Har cheez tau hai maujood yahan, ik tu hi nahin, ik tu hi nahin,
Aur meri aankhon mein rone ki himmat hi nahin, aansu hi nahin.

Joon toon rasta kat-ta hai, aur bandi khana aata hai,
"Chal kaam mein apne dil ko laga" yoon koi mujhe samjhata hai,
Phir kaam ka darya bahta hai aur hosh mujhe kab rahta hai,
Nadaan hai dil, moorakh bachcha, ik aur taraf le jaata hai,

Jab aadha din dhal jaata hai, tau ghar se afsar aata hai,
Aur apne kamre mein mujhko chapraasi se bulwaata hai,
Yoon kahta hai, woon kahta hai, lekin bekaar hi rahta hai,
Main uski aisi baaton se thak jaata hoon, thak jaata hoon.
Aur dil mein aag sulagti hai : main bhi jo koi afsar hota,
Is shahr ki dhool aur galion se kuchh door mira phir ghar hota
Aur tu hoti.
Lekin main tau ik munshi hoon, tu oonche ghar ki rani hai,
Yeh meri prem kahani hai, aur dharti se bhi purani hai.

میرا جی

سندباد کی واپسی

مانا سلامتی ہے کنارے پہ بحر کے

دلچسپ حادثوں کی خبر اب میں لاؤں گا

جو دل بجھے ہوئے ہیں، فسردہ ہیں ان کو آج

میں جلوہ ہائے موج و گہر سے برجھاؤں گا

چھا جائے سب کی روح پہ اک دامِ جستجو

وہ سحر زا طلسم کا نغمہ سناؤں گا

یہ زندگی بھی ایک تگ و دو ہے مستقل

ہمدم سفر کا عمر کو سب کی بناؤں گا

گوشے میں عافیت کے نہ بیٹھے کبھی کوئی

مسلک مرا یہی ہے ہر اک کو بتاؤں گا

سو تجربے ہیں راہِ سفر میں چھپے ہوئے

میں ان کو اپنی عمر کا حاصل بناؤں گا

طاری ہے اک جمود سا روحِ حیات پر

ہر نقشہ جمود کو یکسر مٹاؤں گا

لیکن عطا ہوں سحر کی خاصیتیں مجھے

مل جائیں لفظ لفظ میں کیفیتیں مجھے

Meeraji
Return of Sindbaad (Sindbaad Ki Waapsi)

The shore is a safe resort, this much I concede,
But I'll bring exciting news of happenings on the sea.

I'll bring for the hearts deep-depressed with grief,
Glimpses of the wave and pearl gathered from the surging deep.

I'll sing enchanting songs full of magic sweet,
Which will stir the listeners' soul, fill them with the questing zeal.

Life is a ceaseless quest, a struggle unrelieved,
I'll teach every man to shun the life of ease.

"Never should you rest content with a life of ease."
This is my principle, this is what I preach.

Experiences lying ambushed along the unknown paths,
Will provide the guerdon of my daring feats.

The spirit of dull inertia has swamped the zest of life,
I'll see that this spirit is rooted out from land and lea.

May God grant me the gift of perfect speech !
May I get the right word to articulate my zeal !

Maana salaqmti hai kinaare pe bahr ke,
Dilchasp haadison ki khabar ab main laaoonga.

Jo dil bujhe hue hain, fasurda hain unko aaj,
Main jalwa haaey mauj-o-guhar se rijhaaoonga

Chha jaae sab ki rooh pe ik daam-e-justjoo,
Woh sehar za talism ka naghma sunaaoonga.

Yeh zindagi bhi ek tag-o-daw hai musteqil,
Hamdam safar ka umr ko sabki banaoonga.

Goshe ke aafeat ke na baithe kabhi koi,
Maslik mera yahi hai, har ik ko bataonga.

Sau tajurbe hain raah-e-safr mein chhipe hue,
Main unko apni umr ka haasil banaoonga.

Taari hai ik jamood sa rooh-e-hayaat par,
Har naqsha-e-jamood ko yaksar mitaaoonga.

Lekin ita hon seher ki khaaseeaten mujhe,
Mil jaaen lafz lafz mein kaifeeaten mujhe !

115

اغوا

چاند خموش ہے فضا خاموش

راہ خموش ہے ہوا خاموش

سارے عالم پہ چھائی خاموشی

نیند کی پر سکوں بے ہوشی

دھیرے دھیرے قدم اٹھائیں ہم

اور بستی کو چھوڑ جائیں ہم

دیکھو، محدود زندگی کیوں ہو

غیر کے بس میں سرخوشی کیوں ؟

آؤ بھولو سماج کی باتیں

اپنی ہیں اب سے چاندنی راتیں

آؤ پابندیوں کو بھولو تم

آؤ آزادیوں کو چھولو تم

دل کی افسردگی کو دور کرو

دل سے پژمردگی کو دور کرو

آج کی رات ہے مسرّت کی

آج ہر بات ہے مسرّت کی

Meeraji
Elopement

The moon is silent, calm the breeze,
The earth is quiet, the pathway sleeps.

Stillness reigns over the world,
People lie sleep-enfurled.

Let's move with steps subdued,
And quietly bid this place adieu.

Why should life be lived in chains ?
Why should joy be others' domain ?

Come, forget the social cant,
Let's enjoy the moonlit sands.

Come, reject the moral code,
Live in freedom, be thou bold.

Dispel the grief and gloom of heart,
Let dejection hence depart.

To-night is the night of joy,
Nothing should this mood destroy.

Chaand khamosh hai, faza khaamosh,
Raah khamosh hai, hawa khaamosh.

Saare aalam pe chhaai khaamoshi,
Neend ki pursakoon be hoshi,

Dhire dhire qadam uthaaen hum,
Aur basti ko chhor jaaen hum.

Dekho, mahdood zindagi kyon ho,
Ghair ke bas mein sar khushi kyon ho ?

Aao, bhoolo samaaj ki baaten,
Apni hain ab se chaandni raaten.

Aao, paabandion ko bhoolo tum,
Aao, aazaadion ko chhoo lo tum,

Dil ki afsurdagi ko door karo,
Dil se pazhmurdagi ko door karo.

Aaj ki raat hai musarrat ki,
Aaj har baat hai musarrat ki.

میراجی

کشتئ غم چھوڑ دو۔۔۔ آزاد

اپنی ہستی کو اب کرو۔۔۔ آزاد

ہاتھ میں ہاتھ تھام لو میرا

اب سے بس اک نام لو میرا

زندگی چار دن ہے چار ہی دن

دل میں چاہت ہے چار دن ساکن

رات ایسی نہ آئے گی پھر سے

وقت ایسا نہ لائے گی پھر سے

چاند خاموش ہے فضا خاموش

سارا عالم ہے نیند میں بے ہوش

چپکے چپکے قدم اٹھائیں ہم

آؤ آؤ یہاں سے جائیں ہم

Meeraji

Leave the boat of life—free,
Let all restraints disperse and flee.

Hold my hand in thy grasp,
Enshrine my name in your heart.

Life is but a passing show,
Transient is the passion's flow.

Never again this night will come.
Time and tide wait for none.

The earth and moon are silence-steeped,
The world lies drugged with sleep.

With cautious tread and stealthy feet,
Let's quit this crippling street

Kashti-e-umr chhor do—aazad,
Apni hasti ko ab karo—aazad !

Haath mein haath thaam lo mera,
Ab se bas ik naam lo mera.

Zindagi chaar din hai, chaar hi din,
Dil mein chaahat hai chaar din saakin.

Raat aisi na aaegi phir se,
Waqt aisa na laaegi phir se.

Chaand kaamosh hai, faza khaamosh,
Saara aalam hai neend mein be hosh.

Chupke chupke qadam uthaaen hum,
Aao, aao, yahan se jaaen hum.

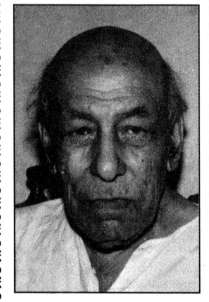

Moin Ahsan Jazbi
(b. 1912)

MOIN AHSAN JAZBI (b. 1912)

Jazbi was born on August 21, 1912, at Mubarakpur, district Azam Garh (U.P.). Poetic temperament came to him in legacy. His grandfather, Abdul Ghafoor, was an accomplished poet who wrote under the pen name *Mateer*. Also, the general atmosphere in Jazbi's family was conducive to the gowth of the poetic spirit. No wonder he had started writing poetry at an early age and had written his first *ghazal* at the age of 16. Notwithstanding his taste and talent, and his academic qualifications—he was M.A., Ph.D. in Urdu from Aligarh—his genius remained unrecognised in the beginning, but when his first poem was published in the montly journal of Lahore, *Humayun*, it was widely acclaimed by the readers.

Jazbi was an active member of the Progressive Writers' Movement. He was also a pioneer of the new *ghazal*. He was for long associated with Aligarh University from where he retired as a Reader. Jazbi's publications include *Firozaan* (a poetic collection), *Hali Ka Siaasi Shaoor* (a research dissertation), *Sakhun-e-Mukhtesar* (a poetic collection), and *Gudaaz-e-Shab* (complete works).

Among the awards bestowed on him may be mentioned *Modi Ghalib Award, Mir Akademy Award, Uttar Pradesh Akademy Award,* and *Iqbal Sammaan.*

معین احسن جذبیؔ

☆

مرنے کی دعائیں کیوں مانگوں جینے کی تمنا کون کرے

یہ دنیا ہو یا وہ دنیا اب خواہشِ دنیا کون کرے

جب کشتی ثابت و سالم تھی ساحل کی تمنا کس کو تھی

اب ایسی شکستہ کشتی پر ساحل کی تمنا کون کرے

وعدے کی وفا تم سے نہ ہوئی گو جان پہ میرے بن ہی گئی

گر جھوٹا ہوں جھوٹا ہی سہی اب تم کو جھوٹا کون کرے

ہاں وادیِ ایمن بھی ہے وہی ہاں برق کا مسکن بھی ہے وہی

اور ہوش کا خرمن بھی ہے وہی پر ان سے تقاضا کون کرے

جو آگ لگائی تم نے تھی اس کو تو بجھایا اشکوں نے

جو اشکوں نے بھڑکائی ہے اس آگ کو ٹھنڈا کون کرے

دنیا نے ہمیں چھوڑا جذبیؔ ہم چھوڑ نہ دیں کیوں دنیا کو

دنیا کو سمجھ کر بیٹھے ہیں اب دنیا دنیا کون کرے

122

Moin Ahsan Jazbi

Why should I pray for death, why seek a longer life ?
Be it this world or the next, both I now despise.

When the boat was fit and fine, who was keen to reach the shore?
Now with these tattered sails, who'll on the shore arrive ?

You didn't fulfil your word, though I nearly lost my life,
I'm a liar, I concede, but what are you ? Who'll decide ?

Mount Sinai is the same, the seat of lightning is unchanged,
Reason's store is rich and ripe, but none to clamour for the sight.

The fire once by you inflamed, was quelled by my tears,
But the fire fuelled by tears, who is going to pacify ?

When the world has spurned us off, why shouldn't we spurn it
     back,
We know what the world is worth, who for it will yearn and sigh
     ?

Marne ki duaaen kyon maangoon, jeene ki tamanna kaun kare,
Yeh duniya ho, ya woh duniya, ab khwahish-e-duniya kaun kare ?

Jab kashti saabat-o-saalam thi, saahil ki tamanna kisko thi,
Ab aisi shikasta kashti par saahil ki tamanna kaun kare ?

Waade ki wafa tum se na hui, go jaan pe mere ban hi gai,
Gar jhoota hoon jhoota hi sahi, ab tum ko jhoota kaun kare ?

Haan waadi-e-aiman bhi hai wuhi, barq ka maskin bhi hai wuhi,
Aur hosh ka khirman bhi hai wuhi, par un se taqaaza kaun kare ?

Jo aag lagaai thi tum ne, us ko tau bujhaaya ashkon ne,
Jo ashkon ne bharkaai hai, us aag ko thanda kaun kare ?

Duniya ne hamen chhora Jazbi, hum chhor na den kyon duniya ko,
Duniya ko samjh kar baithe hain, ab duniya duniya kaun kare ?

جذبیؔ

موت

اپنی سوئی ہوئی دنیا کو جگالوں تو چلوں
اپنے غم خانے میں دھوم مچالوں تو چلوں
اور اِک جامِ مئے تلخ چڑھا لوں تو چلوں
ابھی چلتا ہوں ذرا خود کو سنبھا لوں تو چلوں
جانے کب پی تھی کہ ابھی تک ہے مئے غم کا خمار
دھندلا دھندلا نظر آتا ہے جہانِ بیدار
آندھیاں چلتی ہیں دنیا ہوئی جاتی ہے غبار
آنکھ تو مل لوں ذرا ہوش میں آلوں تو چلوں
وہ مرا سحر وہ اعجاز کہاں ہے لانا
میری کھوئی ہوئی آواز کہاں ہے لانا
میرا ٹوٹا ہوا وہ ساز کہاں ہے لانا
اک ذرا گیت بھی اس ساز پہ گالوں تو چلوں

124

Jazbi
Death

Let me rouse my slumbering world, then I shall proceed,
Let me stir this house of dark, then I shall proceed;
Let me quaff another goblet of this bitter ale,
Allow me to recoup a little, then I shall proceed.

I know not when I drained the cup, still I feel the heat,
The workday world appears to me in mist and smoke concealed,
A fierce gale seems to blow, dust flies in wreaths,
Let me wake and shake a little, then I shall proceed.

Whither is gone my magic might, bring it back please,
Where have I lost my voice, give my tongue its speech,
Bring my broken lyre again, stir its strings from sleep,
Let me play a tune or two, then I shall proceed.

Apni soi hui duniya ko jaga loon tau chaloon,
Apne ghum khaane mein ik dhoom macha loon tau chaloon,

Aur ik jaam-e-mai-e-talkh charha loon tau chaloon,
Abhi chalta hoon, zara khud ko sambhaaloon tau chaloon.

Jaane kab pi thi abhi tak hai mai-e-ghum ka khumaar,
Dhundla dhundla sa nazar aata hai jahaan-e-bedaar,

Aandhiaan chalti hain, duniya hui jaati hai ghubaar,
Aankh tau mal loon, zara hosh mein aa loon tau chaloon.

Woh mira sehar, woh aijaaz kahan hai, laana,
Meri khoi hui aawaaz kahaan hai, laana,

Mera toota hua woh saaz kahaan hai, laana,
Ik zara geet bhi is saaz pe ga loon tau chaloon.

جذبی

میں تھکا ہارا تھا اتنے میں جو آئے بادل
کسی متوالے نے چپکے سے بڑھادی بوتل
اُف وہ رنگین پر اسرار خیالوں کے محل
ایسے دو چار محل اور بنالوں تو چلوں
میری آنکھوں میں ابھی تک ہے محبّت کا غرور
میرے ہونٹوں کو ابھی تک ہے صداقت کا غرور
میرے ماتھے پہ ابھی تک ہے شرافت کا غرور
ایسے وہموں سے بھی اب خود کو نکالوں تو چلوں

Jazbi

I was feeling lost and weary, when the clouds assailed the sky,
A fellow drinker passed to me a ruddy bottle on the sly,
Which made me build pleasing castles, rising tall and high,
Let me build some more of these, then I shall proceed.

Pride of love lights up my eyes,
Still my lips in truth delight,
In gentlemanliness I pride,
Let these superstitions die, then I shall proceed.

Main thaka haara tha, itne mein jo aae badal,
Kisi matwaale ne chupke se barha di botal,
Uf woh rangeen, purasraar khayaalon ke mahal,
Aise do chaar mahal aur banaloon tau chaloon.

Meri aankhon mein abhi tak hai mahabbat ka gharoor,
Mere honton ko abhi tak hai sadaaqat ka gharoor,
Mere maathe pe abhi tak hai, sharaafat ka gharoor,
Aise wahmon se bhi ab khud ko nikaaloon tau chaloon.

Aal Ahmed Saroor
(b. 1912)

AAL AHMED SAROOR (b. 1912)

Born in a middle-class family of Badayun (U.P.), Saroor had his schooling at Victoria High School, Ghazipur, and his college eduction in Agra and Aligarh. After taking his B.Sc degree in science, he switched over to English literature, did his Master's degree from Aligarh, and started working as a lecturer in English. Later, in pursuance of his special interest in Urdu, he did another M.A. in Urdu, and moved to the department of Urdu as a lecturer, first in Aligarh, then in Lucknow. By dint of his abilities, he soon acquired a signal reputation as a poet, critic, and scholar.

Like many other Urdu poets, Saroor was influenced by the poetry of Mir, Ghalib, Iqbal, Fani and Hasrat. In addition, he had imbibed the influence of English Romantic poetry and English literary criticism, which influence stands reflected in his critical writings.

Among the various national movements Saroor was impressed, in particular, by Mahatma Gandhi's struggle for Independence, though not by his creed of non-violence, by the socialist idology of Soviet Russia, and by the Progressive Movement in Urdu poetry. However, he adhered in poetry to the traditional form of rhymed verse. He found a special fascination in the sights and sound of Nature, and enjoyed, like Wordsworth, his ramblings amid rivers, rocks and meadows. Not an upholder of "art for art's sake" he considers poetry as a serious art form, charged with aesthetic, social, and ethical responsibilities.

His poetical works include *Salsabeel* (1935) and *Zauq-e-Janoon* (1955).

129

آلِ احمد سرورؔ
سعیِ وفا

مجھے ہر ناصحِ مشفق یہی تلقین کرتا ہے

کہ بزمِ ہند میں سعیِ وفا کرنے سے کیا حاصل

مریضِ ناتواں کا حال اب ناگفتنی سمجھو

دوا کرنے سے کیا حاصل دعا کرنے سے کیا حاصل

حرم کے کارنامے دیر میں مقبول کیا ہوں گے

بتوں کے سامنے ذکرِ خدا کرنے سے کیا حاصل

یہاں ہر موج کے حلقے میں سَو گرداب پنہاں ہیں

سفینہ نظر طوفانِ بلا کرنے سے کیا حاصل

جہاں نفرت کی آندھی ہو، تعصّب کی ہوائیں ہوں

اک ایسے دشت میں خیمہ بپا کرنے سے کیا حاصل

حریفوں کی سیاست سے اندھیرا ہی سہی گھر میں

نگاہِ لطفِ شمعِ انجمن کچھ اور کہتی ہے

غبارِ کارواں میں چھپ گئی منزل تو کیا غم ہے

افق سے پھوٹتی ننھّی کرن کچھ اور کہتی ہے

Aal Ahmed Saroor
Love's Labour (Saieye Wafa)

Every kind counsellor gives me this advice,
Love's labour on Indian soil is an act futile.

The poor debilitated patient cannot now survive,
Be it prayer or regimen, nothing can restore his life.

How can the acts of mosques find favour with the shrines?
To talk of God in front of idols is an idle exercise.

A hundred whirlpools lie ambushed in every ringlet of the wave,
Why push your precious boat into the jaws of sea-sprites?

Where bigotry reigns unchecked, winds of malice blow,
Why make your habitat in such a barren wild?

Though the scheming over-lords have plunged our house in total dark,
The assembly lamp, still aglow, tells a different tale.

What matters if the destination lies hid in whirling dust,
The ray springing from the East will surely light our way.

Mujhe har naasih mushfiq yehi talqeen karta hai,
Ke bazm-e-Hind mein saieye wafa karne se kya haasil,

Mareeze-e-natawaan ka haal ab na guftani samjho
Dawa karne se kya haasil, dua karne se kya haasil,

Haram ke kaarnaame der mein maqbool kya honge,
Buton ke saamne zikar-e-khuda karne se kya haasil.

Yahaan har mauj ke halqe mein sau girdaab pinhaan hain,
Safina nazr-e-toofaan-e-bala karne se kya haasil.

Jahan nafrat ki aandhiho, taassab ki hawain hon,
Ik aise dasht mein khaima bapa karne se kya haasil.

Hareefon ki sayaasat se andhera hi sahi ghar mein,
Nigah-e-lutaf-e-shama-e-anjuman kuchh aur kahti hai,

Ghubar-e-karwaan mein chhup gai manzil tuu kyu ghum hai,
Ufaq se phoot-ti nanhi kiran kuchh aur kahti hai.

آلِ احمد سرورؔ

بڑی پُر شور ہے زاغ و زغن کی نغمہ آرائی
مگر جمہور کی طرزِ سخن کچھ اور کہتی ہے

کہاں تک پستیٔ اہلِ وطن پر نوحہ خوانی ہو
حدیثِ عظمتِ اہلِ وطن کچھ اور کہتی ہے

وہی مئے آج بھی ہے تاجؔ کے جامِ بلّوریں میں
اودھ کی شام کے وہ مے کدے آباد ہیں اب بھی

قفس کیا، حلقہ ہائے دام کیا، رنجِ اسیری کیا
یقیں کی روشنی جاگے تو دل آزاد ہیں اب بھی

یہ صدیوں کی حنا بندی کبھی تو رنگ لائے گی
بہاروں میں مری سعیِ وفا بھی جگمگائے گی

132

Aal Ahmed Saroor

The crows and kites have no-doubt filled the air with maddening
    roar,
But the saner voice of demos transcends their noisy lays.

No more should we moan and groan about our fallen state,
The great tradition of our past will not let us suffer dismay.

The crystal goblet of the Taj is still agleam with ancient wine,
The evening taverns of Audh are all abuzz with glad encores.

Who fears the cage and chain, who grieves for being interned ?
Given the strength of inner faith, the heart can cast away the
yoke.

The centuries of careful tending will surely come to fruit,
Love's labour will burst in bloom, let the spring breezes blow !

Bari purshor hai zaagh-o-zagan ki naghma aaraai,
Magar jamhoor ki tarz-e-sakhum kuchh aur kathi hai,

Kahan tak pasti-e-ahl-e-watan par noha khwaani ho,
Hadees-e-azmat-e-ahl-e-watan kuchh aur kahti hai.

Wohi mai aaj bhi hai Taj ke jaam-e-billaurin mein,
Audh ki shaam ke woh maikade aabaad hein ab bhi;

"Qafas kya, halqa haa-e-daam kya, ranj-e-aseeri kya"
Yaqeen ki roshni jaage tau dil aazaad hain ab bhi.

Yeh sadion ki hina bandi kabhi tau rang laaegi,
Bahaaron mein meri saieye wafa bhi jagmagaaegi.

آلِ احمد سرور

کل اور آج

وہ بھی کیا لوگ تھے آسان تھیں راہیں جن کی

بند آنکھیں کیے اک سمت چلے جاتے تھے

عقل و دل، خواب و حقیقت کی نہ الجھن نہ خلش

مختلف جلوے نگاہوں کو نہ بہلاتے تھے

عشق سادہ بھی تھا، بے خود بھی، جنوں پیشہ بھی تھا

حسن کو اپنی اداؤں پہ حجاب آتا تھا

پھول کھلتے تھے تو پھولوں میں نشہ ہوتا تھا

رات ڈھلتی تھی تو شیشوں پہ شباب آتا تھا

نرم رو وقت کے دھارے پہ سفینے تھے رواں

ساحل و بحر کے آئیں نہ بدلتے تھے کبھی

ناخداؤں پہ بھروسہ تھا مقدر پہ یقیں

چادرِ آب سے طوفاں نہ ابلتے تھے کبھی

چاندنی کیف اثر، روح فزا ہوتی تھی

ابر آتا تھا تو بدمست بھی ہوجاتے تھے

دن میں شورش بھی ہوا کرتی تھی ہنگامے بھی

رات کی گود میں منہ ڈھانپ کے سو جاتے تھے

134

Aal Ahmed Saroor
Yesterday and Today (Kal Aur Aaj)

What sort of folks they were whose paths were always smoothly
    paved,
Blindfolded did they walk to their goal straight.
No clash of dream and truth for them, no quarrel of head and
heart,
Nor did the shifting scenes their eager eyes engage.

Love was then a passion pure, self-oblivious, frenzic too,
Coy beauty shied away from superfluous, vain dispaly.
Roses always smelled sweet when they came to bloom,
With the ripening of the night, the goblets swelled their sails.

Delightful was the moon-lit night, refreshing to the soul,
Intoxicating were the clouds that filled the skiey bowl.
The day was marked with merry din and enterprise galore,
Folks stretched and slept at ease when the night approached.

Softly sailed the ship of life, gently flowed the waves,
The sea and shore didn't change their normal ways.
people banked upon their pilots, relied upon their fate,
Never did the level rivers burst in sudden spates.

Who bhi kya log the aasaan thein raahen jinki,
Band aankhen kieye ik simat chale jaate the,
Aql-o-dil, khwab-o-haqeeqat ki na uljhan, na khalish,
Mukhtalif jalwe nigaahon ko na bahlaate the.

Ishq saada bhi tha, be khud bhi janoon pesha bhi,
Husn ko apni adaaon pe hijaab aata tha,
Phool khilte the tau phoolon mein nasha hota tha,
Raat dhalti thi tau sheeshon pe shabab aata tha.

Chaandni kaif asar, rooh afzaa hoti thi,
Abr aata tha tau badmast bhi ho jaate the,
Din mein shorish bhi hua karti thi, hangaame bhi,
Raat ki gaud mein munh dhaanp ke so jaate the.

Narm rau waqt ke dhaare pe safeene the rawan,
Saahil-o-bahar ke aaeen na badalte the kabhi,
Naakhudaaon pe bharosa tha, muqaddar pe yaqeen,
Chaadar-e-aab se toofaan na ubalte the kabhi.

135

آلِ احمد سرورؔ

ہم کہ طوفانوں کے پالے بھی ستائے بھی ہیں

برق و باراں میں وہی شمع جلائے کیوں کر

یہ جو آتش کدہ دنیا میں بھڑک اٹھا ہے

آنسوؤں سے اسے ہر بار بجھائے کیوں کر

کردیا برق و بخارات نے محشر برپا

اپنے دفتر میں لطافت کے سوا کچھ بھی نہیں

گھر گئے وقت کی بے رحم کشاکش میں مگر

پاس تہذیب کی دولت کے سوا کچھ بھی نہیں

یہ اندھیرا، یہ طلاطم، یہ ہواؤں کا خروش

اس میں تاروں کی سبک نرم ضیا کیا کرتی

تلخئ زیست سے کڑوا ہوا عاشق کا مزاج

بگمہِ یار کی معصوم ادا کیا کرتی

سفر آساں تھا تو منزل بھی بڑی روشن تھی

آج کس درجہ پر اسرار ہیں راہیں اپنی

کتنی پرچھائیاں آتی ہیں تجلی بن کر

کتنے جلووں سے الجھتی ہیں نگاہیں اپنی

136

Aal Ahmed Saroor

We who are storm-bred, oppressed by circumstance,
Can we burn the lights of yore in the lightning and the gale ?
The world is suddenly overwhelmed with conflagration wild,
Can our overflowing tears quench the flames that rage ?

Rain and lightning have wrought a havoc in our old abode,
We have nothing to fight this flood except our sensitive souls,
The relentless whirling wheel of time has caught us as it rolls,
Except our civilised self we have no shield in store.

Such darkness, such deadly storm, such tempestuous gales,
How can the glimmering stars dissipate the gloom ?
Reality's harsh touch and taste have embittered the lover's mood,
How can an amorous glance roll back the menacing doom ?

When the path was smooth, the goal was clear,
To-day the path is intricate,
Shadows masquerade as light,
Shifting scenes perplex the gaze.

Hum ke toofaanon ke paale bhi, sataae bhi hain,
Barq-o-baaraan mein wohi shamein jalaaen kaise,
Yeh jo aatish kada duniya mein bharak utha hai,
Aansuon se use har baar bujhaaen kaise ?

Kar diya barq-o-bukhaaraat ne mahshar barpa,
Apne daftar mein litaafat ke siwa kuchh bhi nahin,
Ghir gaye waqt ki be raham kashakash mein magar,
Paas tahzeeb ki daulat ke siwa kuchh bhi nahin.

Yeh andhera, yeh talaatum, yeh hawaaon ka kharosh,
Is mein taaron ki subak, narm zaya kya karti,
Talkhi-e-zeest se karwa hua aashiq ka mizaaj,
Nigah-e-yaat ki maassoom ada kya karti ?

Safar aasaan tha tau manzil bhi bari roshan thi,
Aaj kis darja purasraar hain raahen apni,
Kitni parchaaiaan aati hain tajalli ban kar,
Kitne jalwon se ulajhti hain nigaahen apni.

137

Ali Sardar Jafri
(b. 1913)

ALI SARDAR JAFRI (b. 1913)

Sardar Jafri was born on November 26, 1913 at Balrampur, where his forebears had for long established themselves as members of the high class gentry. The poet's family was affluent and educated. It was, besides, a deeply religious family. Yet, the young poet Ali Sardar—though he was fond of good living and good clothes—was not particularly impressed by the pomp and show which, for him, underscored the tragic gap between the rich and the poor. Rejecting his father's proposal for getting traditional education in Ismalic lore, Ali Sardar opted for the Western type of modern education. Even during his schooldays he had shown a keen interest in poetry and politics. He was specially inspired by the socialist ideology of Communist Russia, which ideology he has espoused all his life. Because of his rebellious writings and speeches he had to go to jail a number of times and this caused a disruption in his studies both at Aligarh and Lucknow universities.

Ali Sardar Jafri is an important pillar of the Progressive Writers' Movement in Urdu. He has contributed to the Progressive Writer's cause through the medium, not only of his poetry, but also of his prose writings in various literary journals such as *Naya Adab, Naya Zamana,* and *Gufatgoo.* His poetical works such as *Khoon ki Lakir, Asia Jaag utha, Patthar ki Deewar, Ek Khwab Aur, Lahu Pukaarta Raha,* and *Parwaaz,* are sufficient to give him an assured place in the world of art and thought. He has won several awards including *Nehru Soviet Land Award, Ghalib Award,* and *Iqbal Sammaan.* In recognition of his outstanding contribution to Urdu litrerature he was honoured with the highest literary award of the country, *Jnan Peeth Award (1997).*

علی سردار جعفری

نوالا

ماں ہے ریشم کے کار خانے میں

باپ مصروف سوتی مل میں ہے

کوکھ سے ماں کی جب سے نکلا ہے

بچّہ کھولی کے کالے دِل میں ہے

جب یہاں سے نکل کے جائے گا

کار خانوں کے کام آئے گا

اپنے مجبور پیٹ کی خاطر

بھوک سرمائے کی بڑھائے گا

ہاتھ سونے کے پھول اگلیں گے

جسم چاندی کا دھن لٹائے گا

کھڑکیاں ہوں گی بینک کی روشن

خون اس کا دیے جلائے گا

یہ جو نتّھا ہے بھولا بھالا ہے

خونی سرمائے کا نوالا ہے

پوچھتی ہے یہ اس کی خاموشی

کوئی مجھ کو بچانے والا ہے؟

Ali Sardar Jafri
Morsel (Niwala)

In textile works the father works,
The mother sweats in silken mills;
Since he saw the light of day,
The boy groans in dingy bills.
When he leaves his dungeon dark,
In workshop will he sweat and starve,
Feed the greed of mighty rich,
To quell his chronic hunger itch.
His hands will dig out golden fruit,
His sweat will silver bars produce;
His blood will serve as oil for lamps
To light the windows of the banks.
The little, feeble, innocent child,
Is a morsel fit for Mammonites.
His eloquent silence supplicates :
"Will someone come to change my fate ?"

Maan hai resham ke kaarkhaane mein,
Baap masroof sooti mill mein hai,
Kokh se maan ki jab se nikla hai,
Bachcha kholi ke kaale dil mein hai;
Jab yahaan se nikal ke jaaega,
Kaarkhaanon ke kaam aaega;
Apne majboor pet ki khatir,
Bhook sarmaae ki barhaaega;
Haath sone ke phool uglenge,
Jism chaandi ka dhan lutaaega.
Khirkiyaan hongi bank ki roshan,
Khoon is ka diye jalaaega;
Yeh jo nanha hai, bhola bhala hai,
Khooni sarmaae ka niwala hai.
Poochhti hai yeh is ki khaamoshi,
Koi mujh ko bachaane wala hai ?

علی سردار جعفری

میرا سفر

پھر اک دن ایسا آئے گا

آنکھوں کے دیے بجھ جائیں گے

ہاتھوں کے کنول کمھلائیں گے

اور برگِ زباں سے نطق و صدا

کی ہر تتلی اڑ جائے گی

اک کالے سمندر کی تہہ میں

کلیوں کی طرح سے کھلتی ہوئی

پھولوں کی طرح سے ہنستی ہوئی

ساری شکلیں کھو جائیں گی

خون کی گردش، دل کی دھڑکن

سب راگنیاں سو جائیں گی

اور نیلی فضا کی مخمل پر

ہنستی ہوئی ہیرے کی یہ کنی

یہ میری جنّت، میری زمیں

اِس کی صبحیں اِس کی شامیں

بے جانے ہوئے، بے سمجھے ہوئے

اک مشتِ غبارِ انساں پر

شبنم کی طرح رو جائیں گی

142

Ali Sardar Jafri
My Journey (Mera Safar)

The day will come when my eyes,
Will forever lose their light,
The lotuses of my hands will wither,
And the butterflies of speech,
Will leave my tongue and roam the skies.
The gleaming lips and blooming cheeks,
Like buds and blossoms scattering smiles,
Will sink into the shadowy seas,
To leave a void, dark and wide.
Blood will freeze, heart will stop,
And silent lie the lyre of life.
This my darling, beauteous earth,
In azure velvet robed and decked,
My paradise, my heaven blest,
The star-studded golden crest,
Without knowing the tragic fact,
Will come and drench my humble dust,
With tears of dew at dawn and dusk.

Phir ik din aisa aaega,
Aankhon ke diye bujh jaaenge,
Haathon ke kanwal kumhlaaenge,
Aur barg-e-zaban se nutaq-o-sada
Ki har titil ur jaaegi;
Ik kaale samunder ki tah mein,
Kalion ki tarah se khilti hui,
Phoolon ki tarah se hansti hui
Saari shaklen kho jaaengi;
Khoon ki gardish, dil ki dharkan
Sab raagniaan so jaaengi,
Aur neeli faza ki makhmal par,
Hansti hui heere ki yeh kani,
Yeh meri jannat, meri zamin,
Is ki subhen, iski shaamen,
Be jaane hue, be samjhe hue,
Ik musht-e-ghubar-e-insaan par,
Shabnam ki tarah ro jaaengi;

143

علی سردار جعفری

ہر چیز بھلا دی جائے گی

یادوں کے حسیں بت خانے سے

ہر چیز اٹھا دی جائے گی

پھر کوئی نہیں یہ پوچھے گا

سردار کہاں ہے محفل میں

لیکن میں یہاں پھر آؤں گا

پتّوں کے ذہن سے بولوں گا

چڑیوں کی زباں سے گاؤں گا

جب بیج ہنسیں گے

اور کونپلیں اپنی انگلی سے

مٹی کی تہوں کو چھیڑیں گی

میں پتّی پتّی کلی کلی

اپنی آنکھیں پھر کھولوں گا

سر سبز ہتھیلی پر لے کر

شبنم کے قطرے تولوں گا

میں رنگِ حنا، آہنگِ غزل،

اندازِ سخن بن جاؤں گا

144

Ali Sardar Jafri

Everything will be forgot,
Every relic of the past,
Will be shoved aside at last;
None will ever care to ask :
Where's the master of the house, where's Ali Sardar ?
But I shall visit the earth again,
Shall speak in children's lisping tongue,
And sing in sparrow's twittering vein.
When seeds begin to wake and smile,
And tender saplings upward rise,
And push the veil of earth aside,
To every leaf and every bud,
I'll lend my sparkling eyes;
And on my palms, green and fresh,
Dewy gems will roll and rest,
Transformed to henna's tint,
To silver speech, the Muse's lilt,

Har cheez bhula di jaaegi,
Yaadon ke haseen but-khane se,
Har cheez utha di jaaegi,
Phir koi nahin yeh poochhega :
Sardar kahan hai mehfil mein ?

Lekin main yahan phir aaoonga,
Bachchon ke dahan se boloonga,
Chirion ki zaban se gaaoonga,
Jab beej hansenge dharti mein,
Aur kaunplen apni ungali se,
Mitti ki tahon ko chherengi,
Main patti, patti, kali, kali,
Apni aankhen phir kholoonga,
Sarsabz hatheli par le kar
Shabnam ke qatre toloonga,
Main rang-e-henna, aahang-e-ghazal,
Andaaz-e-sakhun ban jaaoonga,

145

علی سردار جعفری

رخسارِ عروسِ نو کی طرح

ہر آنچل سے چھن جاؤں گا

جاڑوں کی ہوائیں دامن میں

جب فصلِ خزاں کو لائیں گی

رہرو کے جواں قدموں کے تلے

سوکھے ہوئے پتّوں سے میرے

ہنسنے کی صدائیں آئیں گی

میں ایک گریزاں لمحہ ہوں

ایّام کے افسوں خانے میں

میں ایک تڑپتا قطرہ ہوں

مصروفِ سفر جو رہتا ہے

ماضی کی صراحی کے دل سے

مستقبل کے پیمانے میں

میں سوتا ہوں اور جاگتا ہوں

اور جاگ کے پھر سو جاتا ہوں

صدیوں کا پرانا کھیل ہوں میں

میں مر کے امر ہو جاتا ہوں

Ali Sardar Jafri

Like the bride's lovely face,
I shall shine through every veil.
When winter comes and blows the gale,
Bringing autumn in its trail,
From beneath the traveller's feet,
In withered grass and faded leaves,
You will hear me laugh and speak.
I'm the moment flowing fast,
In the Time's elfin grasp;
A little, restless, tremulous drop,
Ever on the travel path.
Flowing from the flask of past,
I slip into the future's glass,
Where I sleep and wake by turns,
And fall again in slumber fast.
For centuries has this game been rife
I die to earn immortal life.

Rukhsaar-e-aroos-e-nau ki tarah,
Haraanchal se chhin jaaoonga,
Jaaron ki hawaaen daman mein
Jab fasl-e-khizan ko laaengi,
Rahrau ke jawan qadmon ke tale,
Sookhe hue patton se mere,
Hansne ke sadaaen aaengi.

Main ek gurezaan lamha hoon,
Ayyaam ke afsoon khane mein,
Main ek tarpta qatra hoon,
Masroof-e-safar jo rahta hai,
Maazi ki suraahi ke dil se
Mustaqbil ke paimaane mein,
Main sota hoon aur jaagta hoon,
Aur juug ke phir so jaata hoon,
Sadion ka purana khel hoon main,
Main mar ke amar ho jaata hoon.

علی سردار جعفری

تین شرابی

ذکر نہیں یہ فرزانوں کا
قصہ ہے اِک دیوانوں کا
ماسکو، پیرس اور لندن میں
دیکھے میں نے تین شرابی
سرخ تھیں آنکھیں روح گلابی
نشہِ مے کا تاج جبیں پر
فکرِ فلک پر پاؤں زمیں پر
بے خبر اپنی لغزشِ پا سے
باخبر اپنے عہدِ وفا سے
دخترِ رز کے در کے بھکاری
اپنے قلب و نظر کے شکاری
قدم قدم پر بہک رہے تھے
مہک رہے تھے چہک رہے تھے
ایک نے شاید وہسکی پی تھی
دوسرے نے شمپین کی بوتل
تیسرے نے وہ پگھلی چاندی
ووڈکا کی سیال حسینہ
وہ شے جس کی تابشِ رخ سے
شیشے کو آجائے پسینہ

148

Ali Sardar Jafri
Three Drunks (Teen Sharabi)

This is not the wise-men's tale,
But of three demented males.

In London, Paris and Moscow,
I saw three drunken guys—
Rosy-spirited, ruddy-eyed.

Booze had made them feel like kings,
With feet on earth, and thought on wings,
Forgetful of their staggering gait,
Committed to the cup and ale.

Beggars at the door of wine,
Captives of their sensual minds,
Rocking, rolling all the while,
Singing, swinging, scattering smiles.

One perhaps had drunken whisky,
The other had drained champagne,
The third on silver juice was tipsy,
"Vodka" was his darling's name—
That beauteous dame which with its heat,
Puts the very glass to shame.

Zikar nahin yeh farzaanon ka,
Qissa hai ik deewaanon ka.

Moscow, Paris aur London mein
Dekhe main ne teen sharabi,
Surkh thi aankhen, rooh gulabi !

Tishna-e-mai ka taj jabeen par,
Fikar falak par, paaon zameen par,
Be khabar apni laghzash-e-pa se,
Be khabar apne ahd-e-wafa se.

Dukhtar-e-raz ke dar ke bhikari,
Apne qalab-o-nazar ke shikari,
Qadam qadam par bahak rahe the,
Mahak rahe the, chahk rahe the.

Ek ne shaaid whisky pi thi,
Doosre ne champagne ki botal,
Teesre ne woh pighli chaandi,
Vodka ki sayaal haseena,
Woh shai jis ki taabish-e-rukh se,
Sheeshe ko aa jaae passena.

149

رات نے اپنی کالی زباں سے

خونِ شفق کے دل کو چاٹا

چار طرف خاموشی چھائی

پھیل گیا ہر سو سناٹا

جنتِ پیرس کے پہلو میں

سین کی موجوں کو نیند آئی

ڈسنے لگی مجھ کو تنہائی

میخانے میں جاکر میں نے

آگ سے دل کی پیاس بجھائی

بند بہت تھے لیکن وہ سب

اپنے نشے میں کھوئے ہوئے تھے

جاگ رہی تھیں آنکھیں لیکن

دل تو سب کے سوئے ہوئے تھے

کوئی نہیں تھا ان میں میرا

میں یہ بیٹھا سوچ رہا تھا

کب یہ ظالم رات کٹے گی

کب واپس آئے گا سویرا

Ali Sardar Jafri

The night with its sable tongue,
Licked away the wounded eve,
The whole world was plunged in dark,
Everything was silence-steeped;
In the lap of heavenly Paris,
The Seine dozed off to sleep;
Stung by loneliness complete,
To a tavern did I creep,
And, consuming liquid fire, calmed down my inner heat.

The place contained many a drinker,
They were all drowned in wine,
Though their eyes were all awake,
Fast asleep were their minds.
I was sitting self-withdrawn,
A stranger amid the drunken throng;
Waiting for the end of night,
Wishing for the birth of dawn.

Raat ne apni kaali zabaan se,
Khoon-e-shafaq ke dil ko chaata,
Chaar taraf khaamoshi chhaai,
Phail gaya har soo sannata;
Jannat-e-paris ke pahloo mein,
Seine ki maujon ko neend aai,
Dasne lagi mujh ko tanhaai,
Maikhane mein ja kar main ne,
Aag se dil ki pyaas bujhaai.

Rind bahut the lekin woh sab,
Apne nashe mein khoey hue the,
Jaag rahi theen aankhen lekin
Dil tau sab ke soey hue the,
Koi nahin tha un mein mera,
Main yeh baitha soch rah tha,
Kab yeh zaalim raat kategi,
Kab waapis aaega savera.

علی سردار جعفری

اتنے میں اِک قامتِ رعنا

قدم قدم پر پھول کھلاتا

ہونٹوں سے معصوم تبسّم

آنکھوں سے بجلی برساتا

میخانے میں جھوم کے آیا

جم گئیں ساری نظریں اٹھ کر

رہ گئے سب کے ارماں گھٹ کر

ٹوٹ گئے عزت کے موتی

پُور ہوئے غیرت کے شیشے

چھپ گئے سب منہ جام کے پیچھے

اس نازک لمحے میں مَیں نے

حرص و ہوس کو رقصاں دیکھا

زَد میں نظامِ زَرداری کی

روحِ بشر کو لرزاں دیکھا

مجبوری کو عریاں دیکھا

ذکر نہیں یہ فرزانوں کا

قصہ ہے اِک دیوانوں کا

152

Ali Sardar Jafri

There and then a beauteous shape,
Spreading fragrance round the place,
Tempting with her winsome smiles,
Striking lightning with her eyes,
Dancing, twisting, slipped inside.

The gazers stood petrified,
Everyone was heaving sighs.
Honour shed her virgin gloss,
Sense of shame got dissolved,
Faces vanished behind the glass.

At that crucial point of time,
I saw lust and greed unleashed,
The soul of man all ashudder,
Helplessness fully revealed;
While Capitalism did bounce and leap.

This is not the wise-men's tale,
But of mad, demented males.

Itne mein ik qaamat-e-raana,
Qadam, qadam par phool khilata,
Honton se maasoom tabassum,
Aankhon se bijli barsaata,
Maikhane mein jhoom ke aaya.

Jam gaien saari nazaren uth kar,
Rah gaye sab ke armaan ghut kar,
Toot gaye izzat ke moti,
Choor hue ghairat ke sheeshe,
Chhup gaye sab munh jaam ke peechhe.

Is nazuk lamhe mein main ne,
Hirs-o-hawa ko raqsaan dekha,
Zad mein nizaam-e-zar daari ke,
Rooh-e-bashar ko larzaan dekhta,
Majboori ko uriaan dekha.

Zikar nahin yeh farzaanon ka,
Qissa hai ik deewaanon ka.

ایک خواب اور

خواب اب حسنِ تصوّرِ کے افق سے ہیں پرے

دِل کے اِک جذبہِ معصوم نے دیکھے تھے جو خواب

اور تعبیروں کے تپتے ہوئے صحراؤں میں

تشنگی آبلہ پا، شعلہ بکف موجِ سراب

یہ تو ممکن ہی نہیں بچپن کا کوئی دِن مل جائے

یا پلٹ آئے کوئی ساعتِ نایابِ شباب

پھوٹ نکلے کسی افسردہ تبسّم سے کرن

یا دمک اٹھے کسی دستِ بریدہ میں گلاب

جانے کس موڑ پہ کس راہ میں کیا بیتی ہے

کس سے ممکن ہے تمنّاؤں کے زخموں کا حساب

آستینوں کو پکاریں گے کہاں تک آنسو

اب تو دامن کو پکڑتے ہیں لہو کے گرداب

در بدر ٹھوکریں کھاتے ہوئے پھرتے ہیں سوال

اور مجرم کی طرح ان سے گریزاں ہے جواب

سرکشی، پھر میں تجھے آج صدا دیتا ہوں

میں ترا شاعرِ آوارہ و بیباک و خراب

پھینک پھر جذبہِ بیتاب کی عالم پہ کمند

ایک خواب اور ابھی اے ہمّتِ دشوار پسند !

Ali Sardar Jafri
One Dream More (Ek Khwab Aur)

Gone are those golden dreams, beyond the reach of thought,
Which were woven in the past by my innocent heart.
And the hope of fulfilment, lost in the burning wilds,
Contends with thirst and blistered feet and mirages spurting sparks.
Nothing can bring back the childhood, or the precious wealth of youth,
It's indeed a wishful thought to resurrect the past.
Vain to hope that faded lips will illume with smiles,
Or that the wounded hands a rose sprig will hold aloft.
Who knows what all has happened, at what place or time,
Who can keep a count of wounds suffered by human kind,
How long can we wipe our tears with the sleeves of our shirt,
Our very hem is trailing now in the whirlpool of blood.
Many a question unattended flits about from place to place,
And the answer, like a criminal, tries to hide its ugly face.
Hear me, O Spirit rebellious, again I give the call,
I, a poet of ill-repute, a reckless, roving bard;
Cast again on the world the magic of your stirring thoughts,
Dream another daring dream, O danger-loving resolve !

Khwab ab husn-e-tasawwur ke ufaq se hain pare,
Dil ke ik jazba-e-maasom ne dekhe the jo khwab,
Aur taabiron ke tapte hue sahraaon mein,
Tishnagi aabla pa, shola-ba-kaf mauj-e-saraab;
Yeh tau mumkin nahin bachpan ka koi din mil jaae,
Ya palat aae koi saait-e-nayaab-e-shabab;
Phoot nikle kisi afsurada tabassum se kiran,
Ya damak uthe kisi dast-e-bureeda mein gulab.
Jaane kis more pe, kis raah mein kya beeti hai
Kis se mumkin hui tamannaaon ke zakhmon ka hisaab.
Aasteenon ko pukaarenge kahan tak aansoo,
Ab tau daaman ko pakarte hain lahu ke girdaab.
Dar badar thokren khaate hue phirte hain swaal,
Aur mujrim ki tarah un se gurezaan hai jawaab.
Sar kashi, phir main tujhe aaj sada deta hoon,
Main tira shair-e-aawara-o-bebaak-kharaab,
Phaink phir jazba-e-betaab ki aalam pe kamand,
Ek khwab aur abhi, ai himmat-e-dushwar pasand !

155

Majid Amjad
(1914-1974)

MAJID AMJAD (1914-1974)

Majid Amjad was born in Jhang (Pakistan) on June 29, 1914. His father, Mian Mohammed Ali, had performed second marriage when his first wife, the poet's mother, was still living. Resenting this act of infidelity, Majid's mother had returned to his parents' home along with the boy poet. It was Majid's maternal grandfather who looked after the poet's early education, and initiated him into the elementaries of Urdu and Persian literature. Majid couldn't forget the injustice done to his mother, and the travails of homelessness and poverty that this act had entailed. He was married to his cousin sister—his maternal uncle's daughter—but it wasn't a happy alliance, despite the fact that Majid's wife was an educated lady who also became the headmistress of a high school. Majid had no children, nor any brother or sister, though he had a stepbrother and a stepsister.

After doing his B.A. from Lahore, Majid worked for several years as an editor of a semi-government journal, *Arooj-e-jhang*. A greater part of his life was spent in Sahiwaal (Montgomery), from where he retired as Assistant Food Controller in 1972, two years before his death in 1974. The Government of Pakistan had granted him a stipend of Rs. 500/- per month in recognition of his services to Urdu. His complete poetical works containing about 600 pages of *ghazals* and *nazms* were published posthumously in 1987 under the title *Loh-e-Dil*.

Majid is a poet of wonder and quest, fond of pondering the fundamentals of life and nature. His poetry is a fine blend of art and thought, of deep emotion and observation, couched in a refreshingly meaningful diction, metrically arranged, though not always in the traditional rhyming order. According to Taj Saeed, the editor of the poet's "Kuliaat", "After Iqbal, Majid is a very great Urdu poet."

مجید امجد

آٹوگراف

کھلاڑیوں کے خود نوشت دستخط کے واسطے

کتابچے لیے ہوئے

کھڑی ہیں منتظر حسین لڑکیاں

ڈھلکتے آنچلوں سے بے خبر حسین لڑکیاں

مہیب پھاٹکوں کے ڈولتے کواڑ چیخ اٹھے

ابل پڑے الجھتے بازوؤں، چچختی پسلیوں کے پُر ہراس قافلے

گرے، بڑھے، مُڑے،، بھنور ہجوم کے

کھڑی ہیں یہ بھی راستے پہ اک طرف

بیاضِ آرزو بکف

نظرِ نظر میں نار سا پر ستشوں کی داستاں

لرز رہا ہے دم بدم

کمانِ ابرواں کا خم

کسی عظیم شخصیت کی تمکنت

حنائی انگلیوں میں کانپتے ورق پہ جھک گئی

تو زر نگار پلوؤں سے جھانکتی کلائیوں کی تیز نبض رک گئی

Majid Amjad
Autograph

Waiting for the cricketers' autographs,
Holding booklets in their hands,
Mindless of their slipping veils,
Stand the beauteous, eager dames.
The doors screech,
Out pours the restive crowd, jostling with their arms and chests,
Falling, rising, bending, turning, like a whirpool unleashed.
They too wait on one side,
Their loved booklets on their palms,
Their glance reflects hopeless longing,
The arched eyebrows, bow-like bent,
Flicker as they breathe.
If a condescending gaze,
Filtering through their hennaed fingers settles on the trembling page,
Their pulse, beneath the glimmering veils, suddenly drops and fails.

Khilaarion ke khud-nawisht dastkhat ke waaste
Kitaabche lieye hue
Khari hain muntezir haseen larkiaan
Dhalkate aanchlon se be khabar larkiaan.
Maheeb phaatkon ke dolte kiwar cheekh uthe
Ubal pare ulajhhte baazuon, chatakhti paslion ke pur haraas qaafle,
Gire, barhe, mure, bhanwar hajoom ke.

Hain yeh bhi raaste pe ik taraf
Bayaaz-e-aarzoo ba-kaf,
Nazar nazar mein naarasa parastishon ki daastaan
Larz raha hai dam badam
Kamaan-e-abruaan ka khum,
Kisi azim shakhseeat ki tamkanat
Hinaai ungalion mein kaanpte warq pe jhuk gai,
Tau zarnigaar palluon se jhaankti kalaaion ki tez nabz ruk gai.

159

مجید امجدؔ

کوئی جب ایک نازِ بے نیاز سے
کتابچوں پہ کھینچتا چلا گیا
حروفِ کج تراش کی لکیر سی
تو کھم گئیں لبوں پہ مسکراہٹیں شریر سی
وہ باؤلر، وہ ایک مہوشوں کے جمگھٹوں میں گِھر گیا

وہ صفحۂ بیاض پر
بصد غرور کلِک گوہریں پھری
حسین کھلکھلاہٹوں کے درمیاں، وکٹ گری

میں اجنبی میں بے نشاں
میں پا بہ گِل
نہ رفعتِ مقام ہے، نہ شہرتِ دوام ہے
یہ لوحِ دل، یہ لوحِ دل
نہ اس پہ کوئی نقش ہے، نہ اس پہ کوئی نام ہے

Majid Amjad

When someone in a casual way,
On their booklet scribbles away,
A few crooked lines and signs,
The dames a gleeful smile betray.

The bowler stood amidst the beauties, all around impaled,
His proud, pearl-scattering pen, ran across the page,
The damsels tittered, and the wicket fell.

I, a stranger, unknown, un-named,
Level with the trodden dust,
No place of pride, no settled fame;
The tablet of my heart, alas !
Bears no sign, boasts no name !

Koi jab ek naaz-e-be nayaaz se
Kitaabchon pe kheinchta chala gaya
Haroof-e-kaj taraash ki lakeer si,
Tau tham gaien labon pe muskraahten shareer si.

Woh bowler, woh ek mahwashon ke jamghaton mein ghir gaya
Woh safa-e-bayaaz par
Ba-sad gharoor kilk-e-gohareen phiri
Haseen khilkhilaahton ke darmiaan wicket giri.

Main ajnabi, main be nishaan
Main pa ba gil
Na rifat-e-maqaam hai, na shuhrat-e-dawaam hai,
Yeh loh-e-dil, yeh loh-e-dil
Na is pe koi naqsh hai, na is pe koi naam hai.

مجید امجدؔ

دستک

کس نے دروازہ کھٹکھٹایا ہے

جا کے دیکھوں تو کون آیا ہے

کون آیا ہے مرے دوارے پر

رات آئی کہاں بچارے پر

میرے چھپر سے ٹیک کر کاندھا

کون استادہ ہے تھکا ماندہ

میری کٹیا میں آؤ، سستالو

یہ مرا ساغرِ شکستہ لو

میری چھاگل سے گھونٹ پانی پیو

اک نئے عزم کی جوانی پیو

ٹمٹماتے دیے کی جھلمل میں

جوت سلگالو اک نئی دل میں

یہ میرے آنسوؤں کی شبنم لو

پاؤں کے آبلوں کی مرہم لو

یہ مجھے افتخار دو، بیٹھو

سر سے گٹھڑی اتار دو، بیٹھو

162

Majid Amjad
A Knock at The Door (Dastak)

Who is knocking at my door ?
Let me go and see;
Who at this nightly hour
Doth my shelter seek ?
Who is this tired stranger
Reclined against my thatched eaves ?
Come, relax inside my hut,
Here, share my broken cup;
Slake your thirst from my can
Let your crumpled soul expand.
Let this twinkling earthen lamp,
Revive your spirits, drain your damp;
Let my tears serve as balm
For your blistered feet and arms.
Come, grace my humble seat,
Remove your bundle, stretch your feet.

Kis ne darwaaza khatkhataaya hai ?
Jaa ke dekhun tau kaun aaya hai,
Kaun aaya mere dwaare par,
Raat aai kahaan bechaare par ?
Mere chhappar se tek kar kaandha
Kaun istaada hai, thaka maanda ?
Meri kutia mein aao, susta lo,
Yeh mira saagir-e-shikasta lo,
Meri chhagal se ghoont paani peo,
Ik naye azm ki jawaani peo,
Timtamate dieye ki jhilmil mein,
Jot sulga lo ik nai dil mein;
Yeh mire aansuon ki shabnam lo
Paaon ke aablon ki marham lo,
Yeh mujhe iftekhaar do, baitho,
Sar se gathri utaar do, baitho.

مجید امجدؔ

میرے زانو پہ اپنا سر رکھ کر

طاق پر کاہشِ سفر رکھ کر

نیند کی انجمن میں کھوجاؤ

منزلوں کے سپن میں کھوجاؤ

خواب، وادی و کہسار کے خواب

دشت و دریا و آبشار کے خواب

خواب، اندھیری طویل راہوں کے

کنج صحرا کی خیمہ گاہوں کے

جہاں اِک شمع ابھی فروزاں ہے

جہاں اِک دل تپاں ہے سوزاں ہے

تم لپٹ جاؤ ان خیالوں سے

اور میں کھیلوں تمہارے بالوں سے

تم کہاں ہو؟ کہاں؟ جواب تو دو

او میرے میہماں جواب تو دو

تم نے دروازہ کھٹکھٹایا تھا

کس کی دستک تھی کون آیا تھا

کس نے نیندوں کو میری ٹوکا تھا

کوئی جھونکا تھا؟ کوئی دھوکا تھا

164

Majid Amjad

Rest your head in my lap,
Forget your hard travails, relax.
Lose yourself in slumber sweet,
Dream of golden goals in sleep;
Dreams of meadows, mountains tall,
Of woods, rivers and waterfalls,
Dreams of dark, unending paths,
Of welcome camps in deserts dark,
Where a lamp is still agleam,
A feeling heart spreads its beams;
Enwrap yourself in blissful thoughts,
While I caress your locks.

Where are you, O, where, speak!
O my guest, respond at least.
Was it you who had knocked,
Who was he who came unasked?
Who had disrupted my sleep
Was it wind, or fancy's feat?

Mere zaanoo pa apna sar rakh kar
Taaq par kaahish-e-safar rakh kar
Neend ki anjuman mein kho jaao,
Manzilon ke sapan mein kho jaao!
Khwab, wadi-o-kuhsaar ke khwab,
Dasht-o-darya-o-aabshaar ke khwab,
Khwab, andheri taweel raahon ke,
Kunj-e-sahra ki khaimagaahon ke,
Jahan ik shama abhi firozaan hai,
Jahan ik dil tapaan hai, sozaan hai,
Tum lipat jaao in khayaalon se,
Aur main kheloon tumhaare baalon se,

Tum kahan ho, kahan ? jawaab tau do,
O, mire maihmaan jawaab tau do,
Tum ne darwaaza khatkhataaya tha
Kis ki dastak thi, kaun aaya tha ?

Kis ne neendon ko meri toka tha,
Koi jhonka tha ? koi dhoka tha ?

165

مجید امجدؔ

بس اسٹینڈ پر

"خدایا اب کے یہ کیسی بہار آئی"

خدا سے کیا گلہ بھائی۔۔۔

خدا تو خیر کس نے اس کا عکسِ نقشِ پا دیکھا

نہ دیکھا بھی تو دیکھا اور دیکھا بھی تو کیا دیکھا

مگر توبہ مری توبہ، یہ انساں بھی تو آخر اک تماشا ہے

یہ جس نے پچھلی ٹانگوں پر کھڑا ہونا بڑے جتنوں سے سیکھا ہے

ابھی کل تک جب اس کے ہونٹ محرومِ زخِدا تھے

ابھی کل تک جب اس کے ابروؤں تک موئے پیچاں تھے

ردائے صدِ زماں اوڑھے، لرزتا، کانپتا، بیٹھا

ضمیرِ سنگ سے بس ایک چنگاری کا طالب تھا

"مگر اب تو یہ اونچی میٹوں والے جلو خانے میں بستا ہے"

ہمارے ہی لبوں سے مسکراہٹ چھین کر اب ہم پہ ہنستا ہے

خدا اس کا، خدائی اس کی، ہر شے اس کی۔۔۔ ہم کیا ہیں

"چمکتی موٹروں سے اڑنے والی دھول کا ناچیز ذرّہ ہیں"

166

Majid Amjad
At The Bus-Stand

"What a spring is this, O God!"
"But God, O brother, is not at fault.
And then, who has seen even a trace of His foot-mark?
Though unseen, He yet is seen, and when seen, is not defined.
But, Good gracious ! how strange is man!
Who learnt, after infinite pains, to stand upon his hind legs;
Till the time his lips hung helpless without the supporting chin,
When his shaggy hair hung heavily on his eyebrows,
Beneath the weight of centuries buried did he lay,
Waiting for the heart of stone to yield forth a spark."

"But now in multi-storeyed mansions doth this man reside,
Snatching smiles from our lips mocks us with his cunning smile,
To him belongs everything : God, earth, these sights and scenes,
What are we but flying dust scattered by his limousines!

"Khudayaa ab ke yeh kaisi bahaar aai"
"Khuda se kya gila bhai!..........
Khuda tau khair kis ne us ka naqsh-e-pa dekha,
Na dekha bhi tau dekha aur dekha bhi tau kya dekha
Magar, tauba miri tauba! yeh insaan bhi tau aakhir ik tamashaa hai,
Yeh jis ne pichhli taangon par khara hona bare jatnon se seekha hai,
Abhi kal tak jab us ke hont mahroom-e-zanakhdaan the,
Abhi kal tak jab us ke abruon tak moo-e-pechaan the,
Ridaa-e-sad zamaan aurhe, larzta, kaanpta, baitha,
Zameer-e-sang se bas ek chingaari ka taalib tha"

"Magar ab tau yeh oonchi mamtion wale jilau khane mein basta hai
"Hamaare hi labon se muskraahat chheen kar ab hum pe hansta hai,
Khuda us ka, khudaai uski, har shai uski — hum kya hain?
"Chamakti motoron se urne wali dhool ka na cheez zarra hain?"

مجید امجدؔ

ہماری ہی طرح جو پائمالِ سطوتِ میری و شاہی ہیں

لکھوکھا پا پیادہ، آبدیدہ، دل زدہ، واماندہ راہی ہیں

جنہیں نظروں سے گم ہوتے ہوئے رستوں کی گم پیا لکیروں میں

دکھائی دے رہی ہیں آنے والی منزلوں کی دھندلی تصویریں

"ضرور اک روز بدلے گا نظامِ قسمتِ آدم

سجے گی اک نئی دنیا، بسے گا اک نیا عالم

شبستاں میں نئی شمعیں، گلستاں میں نیا موسم"

"وہ رُت اے ہم نفس، جانے کب آئے گی

وہ فصلِ دیر رس، جانے کب آئے گی

یہ نو نمبر کی بس، جانے کب آئے گی"

168

Majid Amjad

"Those who are, like us, by these overlords oppressed,
The downtrodden millions, tired, tearful, deep-depressed,
They in their receding paths, enveloped in the gloomy past,
Catch a glimpse of their goal, dim-descried, afar !"

"One day will surely change the picture of the fate of man,
A few world, a new order, will replace the present sham,
New lamps will light the hall, a new spring will bless the land."

Who knows when the new spring will bless the garden vines,
Who knows when it will ripen, the long-ripening human mind,
Who knows when it comes, the bus number nine !

*"Hamari hi tarah jo paaimaal-e-satwat-e-meeri-o-shaahi hain,
Lakhokha pa payada, aabdeeda, dil-zada, waamaanda rahi hain,
Jinhen nazaron se gum hote hue raston ki gum-paima lakeeron mein
Dikhaai de rahi hain aane waali manzilon ki dhundali tasweeren."*

*"Zaroor ik roz badlega nizaam-e-qismat-e-aadam,
Sajegi ik nai duniya, basega ik naya aalam,
Shabastaan mein nai shamein, gulistaan mein naya mausim."*

*"Woh rut ai hum nafas ! jaane kab aaegi,
Woh fasl-e-der-ras jaane kab aaegi,
Woh nau number ki bus jaane kab aaegi."*

Jaan Nisaar Akhtar
(1914-1976)

JAAN NISAAR AKHTAR (1914-1976)

Jaan Nisaar Akhtar was born at Gwalior, though Khairabad, a township in U.P. was his ancestral home. He had his schooling in Gwalior and college education at Aligarh University, from where he passed his M.A. examination in Urdu. Poetry came to him in legacy, for his father, Muztir Khairabadi, and his uncle. Bismal Khairabadi, both were accredited poets of their time.

Akhtar began his career as a lecturer in Urdu at Victoria College, Gwalior. In 1943 he got married to Safia, sister of the famous Urdu poet, Majaz. He enjoyed several years of happy wedded life, but then came the tragic shock of Safia's death, which left the poet completely shattered. The poem, *Safia Ke Mazaar Par,* included in this anthology may be called the poet's memorial to his wife.

Akhtar died of heart stroke in Bombay on August 18, 1976. His poetical works include *Salaasal, Taar-e-Garebaan, Nazr-e-Butaan, Jaawedaan, Ghar Aangan, Khaak-e-dil,* and *Pichhle Pahr.* He was given the Soviet Land Nehru Award for his collection, *Khaak-e-dil,* and was also honoured with Sahitya Akademi Award posthumously.

جاں نثار اختر

☆

رنج و غم مانگے ہے، اندوہ و بلا مانگے ہے

دِل وہ مجرم ہے جو خود اپنی سزا مانگے ہے

چپ ہے ہر زخمِ گلو، چپ ہے شہیدوں کا لہو

دستِ قاتل ہے کہ محنت کا صِلہ مانگے ہے

دِل ہر اک حال سے بے گانہ ہوا جاتا ہے

اب توجّہ، نہ تغافل، نہ ادا مانگے ہے

تُو ہے اِک دولتِ نایاب مگر کیا کہیے

زندگی اور بھی کچھ تیرے سوا مانگے ہے

سانس ویسے ہی زمانے کی رکی جاتی ہے

وہ بدن اور بھی کچھ تنگ قبا مانگے ہے

کھوئی کھوئی یہ نگاہیں، یہ خمیدہ پلکیں

ہاتھ اٹھاکے کوئی جس طرح دعا مانگے ہے

لاکھ منکر سہی پر ذوقِ پرستش میرا

آج بھی ایک صنم ایک خدا مانگے ہے

172

Jaan Nisaar Akhtar

It demands more of pain, sorrow, suffering, shocks,
It insists on being punished, this culprit of my heart.

Muted lies the wounded throat, silent too the martyr's blood,
It's the assassin's hand alone that clamours for reward.

The heart is growing unconcerned to every state of bliss or bale,
Attention, indifference, or grace — it remains immune to all.

You are a rare wealth indeed, but we must concede,
That life has other needs too, besides you, O precious heart !

The world is already feeling choked in these difficult times,
Yet my love wants a robe tighter still and taut.

Ah, these looks all confused, eyelashes bent and arched,
Like a man, hands stretched, praying to his god.

Though we may deny the truth, yet my zeal devout,
Even to-day craves an idol, needs a living god.

Ranj-o-ghum maange hai, andoh-o-bala maange hai,
Dil woh mujrim hai jo khud apni saza maange hai.

Chup hai har zakhm-e-gulu, chup hai shaheedon ka lahu,
Dast-e-quatil hai ke mehnat ka sila maange hai.

Dil har ik haal se begaana hua jaata hai,
Ab tawajjuh, na taghaaful, na ada maange hai.

Tu hai ik dault-e-nayaab, magar kya kahieye,
Zindagi aur bhi kuchh tere siwa maange hai.

Saans waise hi zamaane ki ruki jaati hai,
Woh badan aur bhi kuchh tang qaba maange hai.

Khoi khoi yeh nigaahen, yeh khameeda palken,
Haath uthaae koi jistarah dua maange hai.

Laakh munkir sahi, par zauq-e-parastish mera,
Aaj bhi ek sanam, ek khuda maange hai.

خاموش آواز

کتنے دنوں میں آئے ہو ساتھی

میرے سوتے بھاگ جگانے

مجھ سے الگ اس ایک برس میں

کیا کیا بیتی تم پہ نہ جانے

دیکھو کتنے تھک سے گئے ہو

کتنی تھکن آنکھوں میں گُھلی ہے

آؤ تمھارے واسطے ساتھی

اب بھی مری آغوش کُھلی ہے

اتنے دن کے بعد کہیں تم

آئے ہو ساجن میرے دوارے

آج اندھیرے انگنا مورے

ناچ اٹھے ہیں چاند ستارے

دیکھو کیسی رات حسیں ہے

جیسے میرا پیار بھکلا ہو

آج تو ایسی جوت ہے جیسے

چاند زمیں سے آن ملا ہو

174

Jaan Nisaar Akhtar
Silent Voice (At Safia's Tomb)

You have come after long
To wake my sleeping stars,
What all you suffered, all alone,
For full one year, far apart !

See, you look weak and we
Your eyes reflect a weary gaze,
Come, my love, I deeply yearn
To hold you tight in my embrace.

You have come to me to-day
After such a tedious wait,
Lo, my house is suddenly lit
With dancing moon and starry fays.

Mark, how lovely is the night !
As if my love has come to bloom,
Preternatural is the light,
As if the earth has met the moon.

Kitne dinon mein aae ho saathi
Mere sote bhaag jagaane,
Mujh se alag is ek baras mein
Kya kya beeti tum pe ne jaane.

Dekho kitne thak se gaye ho,
Kitni thakan aankhon mein ghuli hai,
Aao tumhaare waaste, saathi,
Ab bhi miri aaghosh khuli hai.

Itne din ke baad kahin tum
Aae ho saajan mire dwaare
Aaj andhere angana more,
Naach uthe hain chaand sitaare.

Dekho kaisi raat haseen hai
Jaise mera pyaar khila ho,
Aaj tau aisi jot hai jaise
Chaand zameen se aan mila ho.

جاں نثار اخترؔ

آؤ میں تم سے روٹھ سی جاؤں

آؤ مجھے تم ہنس کے منالو

مجھ میں سچ مچ جان نہیں ہے

آؤ مجھے ہاتھوں پر اٹھالو

دِل کی دھڑکن ڈوب بھی جائے

دِل کی صدائیں تھک نہ سکیں گی

مِٹ بھی جاؤں پھر بھی تم سے

میری وفائیں تھک نہ سکیں گی

یہ تو پوچھو مجھ سے چھٹ کر

تیرے دل پر کیا کیا گزری

تم بن میری ناؤ تو ساجن

ایسی ڈوبی پھر نہ ابھری

ایک تمہارا پیار بچا ہے

ورنہ سب کچھ لُٹ سا گیا ہے

ایک مسلسل رات کہ جس میں

آج مِرا دم گھُٹ سا گیا ہے

176

Jaan Nisaar Akhtar

I'll affect to be wroth,
Bring me round with your smiles,
I'm really dead and lost,
Lift me up, grant me life !

Though my heart has ceased to throb,
The voice of past doth ring the same,
Even though I'm razed to dust,
My love for you knows no change.

Ask me how from you removed
I spent my days and nights,
Once sunk, this boat of life
Never did to the surface rise.

I have lost all in life,
Except your love which yet survives,
Enfolded in this endless night,
I feel somewhat choked inside.

Aao main tum se rooth si jaaoon,
Aao mujhe tum hans ke manalo,
Mujh mein sach much jaan nahin hai,
Aao mujhe haathon par utha lo.

Dil ki dharkan doob bhi jaae,
Dil ki sadaaen thak na sakengi,
Mit bhi jaaoon phir bhi tum se
Meri wafaaen thak na sakengi.

Yeh tau poochho mujh se chhut kar
Tere dil par kya kya guzri,
Tum bin meri naao tau saajan.
Aisi doobi phir na ubhri.

Ek tumhaara pyaar bacha hai,
Warna sab kuchh lut sa gaya hai,
Ek musalsal raat ke jis mein,
Aaj mira dam ghut sa gaya hai.

Ehsaan Daanish
(1914-1982)

EHSAAN-UL-HAQ EHSAAN DAANISH
(1914-1982)

Ehsaan Daanish was born at Bagpat in Meerut district (U.P.). He derived his surname, "Daanish", from his father, Qazi Daanish Ali. Despite his stock of "daanish"— which literally means wisdom or prudence—Ehsaan's father was cheated by his friends and relations and reduced to poverty. He was forced to migrate from Bagpat to Kandhla in Muzaffar Nagar district, where the boy poet had his upbringing and elementary schooling up to class III. Economic difficulties at home compelled him to leave school and do sundry odd jobs for subsistence. His mother sold her copper utensils to pay for his educational expenses, but the money thus gathered was hardly sufficient for the other pressing needs of the family. Consequently, Ehsaan Daanish was made to fend for himself. He worked as a labourer at a building site, a chowkidar at a printing press, a petition-writer in the municipal corporation, a gardener, and a cook. He had thus a close brush with poverty. But he didn't lose his courage, not did he waver in his commitment to the Muse.

In spite of the heavy odds that he had to face, he succeeded in getting his first poetic collection, *Hadees-e-Adab*, published. Later, he set up his own publishing house called *Maktaba-e-Daanish*. A poet of the labouring classes, Ehsaan hated capitalism. He dedicated his poetry to students, peasants, and the downtrodden masses. He was influenced, among others, by Iqbal and Josh Malihabadi, who too, like him, had espoused the cause of the weak and the dispossessed. Besides being a specialist of the *nazm*, he was a successful prose writer.

He died in Lahore on March 21, 1982. His literary output includes *Hadees-e-Adab, Dard-e-Zindagi, Nawa-e-kaargar, Aatish-e-Khamosh* and *Chiragaan*.

احسان دانشؔ

☆

رعنائیِ کونین سے بیزار ہمیں تھے

ہم تھے ترے جلووں کے طلب گار ہمیں تھے

پتّھر کبھی گلیوں میں برستے تھے ہمیں پر

دیوانہ گرِ کوچہ و بازار ہمیں تھے

ہے فرق طلب گار و پرستار میں اے دوست

دنیا تھی طلب گار، پرستار ہمیں تھے

دیدے کے نگاہوں کو تصوّر کا سہارا

راتوں کو ترے واسطے بیدار ہمیں تھے

پچھتاؤ گے، دیکھو، ہمیں بیگانہ سمجھ کر

مانو گے کسی وقت کہ غم خوار ہمیں تھے

بازارِ ازل یوں تو بہت گرم تھا لیکن

لے دے کے محبّت کے خریدار ہمیں تھے

ہاں آپ کو دیکھا تھا محبت سے ہمیں نے

جی سارے زمانے کے گنہگار ہمیں تھے

احسانؔ ہے بے سود گلہ ان کی جفا کا

چاہا تھا انھیں ہم نے ، خطاوار ہمیں تھے

180

Ehsaan Daanish

We were the ones who found the world wanting in delight,
We were the ones who sought your glimpse, for your grace
applied.

We were the ones subjected to heavy rain of stones,
We were the manic wanderers in streets and lanes descried.

A seeker and a worshipper are two different things,
The world was your seeker, we your acolytes.

We it were who kept awake for your sake at night,
Enlivening with hues of hope, reality, sable-dyed.

You'll regret treating us, mind you, stranger-like,
That we were your friends indeed, you'll sure realise.

The celestial mart lay abuzz with many a crier and buyer,
But the precious stuff of love, we alone did buy.

We were the ones who cast on you a longing, loving glance,
We were the only culprits in the world so wide.

In vain do we complain against his tyrannous ways, Ehsaan,
We were the ones who fell for him, we must be penalised.

Raanaai-e-kauneen se bezaar hameen the,
Hum the tire jalwon ke talabgaar hameen the.

Paththar kabhi galion mein baraste the hameen par,
Deewana gar-e-koocha-o-bazaar hameen the.

Hai farq talabgaar-o-parastaar mein, ai dost,
Duniya thi talabgaar, parastaar hameen the.

De de ke nigaahon ko tasawwur ka saharaa,
Raaton ko tire waaste bedaar hameen the.

Pachhtaaoge, dekho, hamen begaana samajh kar,
Maanoge kisi waqt ke ghumkhwar hameen the.

Bazaar-e-azal yoon tau bahut garm tha lekin,
Le de ke mahabbat ke kharidaar hameen the.

Haan aap ko dekha tha mahabbat se hameen ne,
Ji saare zamaane ke gunahgaar hameen the.

Ehsaan hai be sood gila un ki jafa ka,
Chaha tha unhen hum ne, khatawaar hameen the.

احسان دانشؔ

سادھو کی چِتا

ہمِنشیں کشمیر سے لاہور کو آتے ہوئے

اِک سماں دیکھا جگر پر نیشِ غم کھاتے ہوئے

گِر چکا تھا طاقِ مغرب سے چراغِ آفتاب

بند تھی جزدانِ تاریکی میں فطرت کی کتاب

لخظہ لخظہ تیرہ تر ہوتی فضائے سرمگیں

سنگ پاروں پر اچٹتی بوندیاں گیلی زمیں

ابر کے دامن میں کوندے کی لپک چشموں کا شور

ہلکی ہلکی بوندیوں کا سلسلہ جھرنوں کا زور

مُیل کی اِک دیوار کے نیچے قریبِ رہ گزر

ایک سادھو کی چِتا، تصویرِ انجامِ بشر

بوندیوں میں آگ کا پرتَو چٹانوں پر جھلک

مست بادل کی گرج سے کوہساروں میں دمک

آگ کے خونخوار جبڑوں سے دھواں اٹھتا ہوا

پیچ و خم کھا کر زمیں سے آسماں اٹھتا ہوا

ہر طرف بھیگے ہوئے پیڑوں کے پتّے سوگوار

خوف سے ٹھنڈی ہوا کو ہلکا ہلکا سا بخار

182

Ehsaan Daanish
Hermit's Pyre

Coming down to Lahore from the mountainside,
I saw a chilling scene which shook me deep inside.

The sun had set in the West, everywhere the dark did creep,
Folded lay the book of nature, as if all the world did sleep.

Thicker grew the pall of night, as the minutes flew,
The earth was wet with drops of rain, glistening like the dew.

Lightning flashed, fountains roared, the sky was overcast,
A gentle drizzle filled the air, you could hear the waterfalls.

On the edge of narrow path, below the culvert wall,
Burnt a hermit's funeral pyre—the end awaiting all !

The droplets mirrored the flaming fire, the rocks glimmered and
glowed,
In the lightning flash did shimmer the mountains ranged in
rows.

From the gory jaws of fire rose the billowing smoke,
Spiralling up towards the sky, spreading like a parasol.

Sorrow-soaked stood the trees with their drooping leaves,
Feverish grew the cool-breeze, as if terror-seized.

Humnasheen Kahsmir se Lahore ko aate hue,
Ik samaan dekha jigar par nesh-e-ghum khaate hue.

Gir chuka tha taaq-e-maghrib se chiraag-e-aaftaab,
Band thi juzdaan-e-taareeki mein fitrat ki kitaab.

Lahza lahza teera-tar hoti fazaa-e-surmageen,
Sang paaron par uchat-tin boondian, geeli zameen.

Abr ke daaman mein konde ki lapak, chashmon ka shor,
Halki halki boondion ka silsala, jharnon ka zor.

Pul ki ik deewar ke neeche, qareeb-e-rah-guzar,
Ek saadhu ki chitaa, tasweer-e-anjaam-e-bashar.

Boondion mein aag ka partaw, chitanon par jhalak,
Mast badal ki garaj se kohsaaron mein damak.

Aag ke khoonkhwar jibron se dhuaan uth-ta-hua,
Pech-o-khum kha kar zameen se aasmaan uth-ta hua.

Har taraf bheege hue peron ke patte sogawaar,
Khauf se thandi hawa ko halka halka sa bukhaar.

183

احسانؔ دانش

کھولتا سینہ، سلگتی کھوپڑی، پکتا بدن
بڑبڑاتی آگ جھلاتی لپٹ جلتا کفن
ٹوٹتی نبضیں چٹختی ہڈیاں اڑتے شرار
لوتھڑوں کی سنسناہٹ سرخ شعلوں کی ڈکار
ہر طرف لہرا رہاتھا بے ثباتی کا عَلم
موت کی دیوی کے خونیں قہقہوں کا زیر و بم
میرے قصرِ زندگی میں زلزلہ سا آ گیا
روح کے آئینہ خانے میں دھندلکا چھا گیا
بزمِ عشرت اٹھ گئی طنبورِ غم بجنے لگا
عبرت اٹھی آرزو بیٹھی تمنّا سو گئی
یاس نے انگڑائی لی امّید زخمی ہو گئی
رات بھر میرے دلِ محزوں کی بے تابی رہی
خواب پر غالب پریشانی بے خوابی رہی
اب بھی وہ منظر کبھی جب یاد آتا ہے مجھے
زندگی میں موت کا نقشہ دکھاتا ہے مجھے

184

Ehsaan Daanish

The boiling breast, smouldering skull, the body getting baked.
Sputtering fire, raging flames, and the coffin all ablaze.

Burning veins, crackling bones, cinders whirling past,
Susurrating chunks of flesh, flames belching sparks.

Everywhere fluttered the flag of all-conquering change,
Loud laughs of victor death everywhere did range.

The whole edifice of my life was shaken in its roots,
On the mirror of my heart fell a layer of soot.

The mood of joy died down, sorrow played its drum,
Sadder grew the tuneful lyre, weighed with deep concern.

Hopes and dreams sat subdued, chastening thoughts arose,
Despair shook its languour off, fledgling hopes froze.

Retlessness was my lot all through the night,
Not even in my dreams could I feel respite.

Even now when at times I recall that chilling sight,
Flashing comes before my eyes, that scene of death-in-life !

Khaulta seena, sulagti khopri, pakta badan,
Burburati aag, jhillaati lapat, jalta kafan.

Toot-tin nabzen, chatakhti haddian, urte sharaar,
Lothron ki sansanaahat, surkh sholon ki dakaar.

Har taraf lahra raha tha be sabaati ka alam,
Maut ki devi ke khoonin qahqahon ka zer-o-bum.

Mere qasr-e-zindagi mein zalzala sa aa gaya,
Rooh ke aaeena khane mein dhundalka chha gaya.

Bazm-e-ishrat uth gai, tamboor-e-ghum bajne lage,
Zarbat-e-tashweesh se saaz-e-alam bajne lage.

Ibrat uthi, aarzoo baithi, tamanna so gai,
Yaas ne angraai li, umeed zakhmi ho gai.

Raat bhar mere dil-e-mahzoon ki betaabi rahi,
Khwab par ghalib pareshaani-e-be khwabi rahi.

Ab bhi woh manzir kabhi jab yaad aata hai mujhe.
Zindagi mein maut ka naqsha dikhata hai mujhe.

دیہات کی شام

شام کے اندھیرے میں دن کا اجالا کھو گیا

آگ کے چو گرد دہقانوں کا جمگھٹ ہو گیا

ہالیوں کو مل گیا دن بھر کی محنت سے فراغ

ٹمٹمایا گاؤں کی چوپال میں دھندلا چراغ

مشورے ہونے لگے نشو و نما کے باب میں

سادہ خاطر بہہ چلے تقریر کے سیلاب میں

یہ وہ ہیں جن پر تغافل کارگر ہوتا نہیں

جن کے دل میں کبر و نخوت کا گزر ہوتا نہیں

جن کی گردِ رہگزر ہے غازۂ روئے بہار

جن کا شانہ روز سلجھاتا ہے زلفِ روزگار

بازووں پر جن کے نازاں فطرتِ گلشن طراز

کاوشوں سے جن کی حسنِ انجمن مائل بہ ناز

واہ رے دیہات کے تازہ تمدن کی بہار

سادگی میں بھی ہے کیا کیا تیرا دامن زرنگار

دِل یہ کہتا ہے فراقِ انجمن سہنے لگوں

شہر کی رنگینیاں چھوڑوں یہیں رہنے لگوں

Ehsaan Daanish
Village Evening

The light of day disappeared in the darkening eve,
The farmers sat crouching round the faggots' heat.

The ploughmen had gained at last their hard-earned respite,
An earthen lamp began to glimmer at the meeting site.

Then began confabulation about improving village life,
And the simple village folks were swept along the flowing tide.

These folks are alien to the bane of slothful life,
They are the ones who transcend the taint of selfish pride.

On their shoulder rests the burden of the world's heavyweight,
The dust of their daily rounds serves to deck the spring's face.

On the strength of their arms prides Nature's creative force,
It is their effort that bestows on beauty's face a youthful glow.

Kudos to your simple grace, O village culture undebased,
What a charm lies concealed even in your simple ways.

Now I feel I should renounce the company of my urban mates,
Quit the colourful urban sights, and your charms embrace !

Shaam ke andhere mein din ka ujala kho gaya,
Aag ke chaugird dahqaanon ka jamghat ho gaya.

Haalion ko mil gaya din bhar ki mehnat se faraagh,
Timatamaya gaaon ki chaupaal mein dhundala chiragh

Mashware hone lage nashw-o-numa ke baab mein,
Saada khatir bah chale taqreer ke sailaab mein.

Yeh woh hain jin par taghaaful kaargar hota nahin,
Jin ke dil mein kibr-o-nikhwat ka guzar hota nahin.

Jin ki gard-e-rahguzar hai ghaaza-e-roo-e-bahaar,
Jin ka shaana roz suljhaata hai zulf-e-rozgaar.

Baazoo-on par jin ke naazaan fitrat-e-gulshan taraaz,
Kawishon se jin ki husn-e-anjuman maayal ba naaz.

Waah re dehaat ke saada tamaddun ki bahaar,
Saadgi mein bhi hai kya kya tera daaman zar nigaar.

Dil yeh kahta hai firaq-e-anjuman sahne lagoon,
Shahr ki rangeenian chhoroon, yahin rahne lagoon.

Sikander Ali Wajd
(1914-1983)

SIKANDER ALI WAJD (1914-1983)

Sikander Ali Wajd was born on January 22, 1914, at Veejapur, district Aurangabad, in Maharashtra. He was educated at Osmania University, Hyderabad, from where he obtained his B.A. degree in 1935. In 1937 he passed the Hyderabad civil service examination, and joined the judicial service. In 1956 he was made the Sessions Judge, from which post he sought premature retirement in 1964.

Wajd had given proof of his literary abilities even during his student days. He was chosen to edit the college magazine, *Nau Ras* in 1930, while in 1936 he was given the editorial responsibility of the university journal, *Mujalla Osmania*. In the meantime, he had earned considerable fame as a poet in poetic symposiums and literary circles. His poetical works include *Lahu Tarang* (1944), *Aaftaab-e-Taza* (1952), and *Auraaq-e-Musawwar* (1963). A selection of his poetry was published by *Anjuman-e-Taraqqi-e-Urdu* in 1954. His complete works were published under the title, *Kalaam-e-Wajd*, in 1975. Wajd died in Aurangabad on 16 May, 1983.

The three poems included in this anthology demonstrate the poet's mastery of the different art forms and styles. While the *nazm* on *Ajanta* displays his graphic and descriptive skill, his poem, *Tahseen-e-Na-Shanaas*, gives us an idea of the poet's attitude to poetry, which he regards as a serious mission rather than a pleasurable pastime. The ghazal "Yaad aata hai", bears testiony to his lyrical and musical ability and shows his capacity for expressing emotion without affectation.

Wajd was honoured by the government of India with *Padma Shree*. He was also appointed member of the Rajya Sabha from Maharashtra in 1972.

سکندر علی وجد

☆

خوش جمالوں کی یاد آتی ہے

بے مثالوں کی یاد آتی ہے

جن سے دنیائے دِل مُنوّر تھی

ان اُجالوں کی یاد آتی ہے

جن کی آنکھوں میں تھا سرُورِ غزل

ان غزالوں کی یاد آتی ہے

سادگی لاجواب ہے جن کی

ان سوالوں کی یاد آتی ہے

ذِکر سنتے ہی نوجوانی کا

کچھ خیالوں کی یاد آتی ہے

جانے والے کبھی نہیں آتے

جانے والوں کی یاد آتی ہے

وجد لطفِ سخن مبارک ہو

باکمالوں کی یاد آتی ہے

190

Sikander Ali Wajd

Winsome beauties come to mind,
Those peerless beings, where to find ?

Whither gone those brightening morns,
That once whelmed our heart and mind ?

Entrancing eyes with lyrical grace,
Those doe-like shapes spring to mind !

The questions disarmingly simple,
Again obsess our heart and mind.

Mention of the time of youth,
Stirs up certain thoughts in mind,

Departing mates never return,
But their memories live behind.

Kudos, Wajd, to your art !
You recall the masterminds.

Khush jamaalon ki yaad aati hai,
Be misaalon ki yaad aati hai.

Jin se duniya-e-dil munawwar thi,
Un ujaalon ki yaad aati hai.

Jin ki aankhon mein tha saroor-e-ghazal,
Un ghazaalon ki yaad aati hai.

Saadgi la-jawaab hai jinki,
Un sawaalon ki yaad aati hai.

Zikar sunte hi naujawaani ka,
Kuchh khayaalon ki yaad aati hai.

Jaane wale kabhi nahin aate,
Jaane waalon ki yaad aati hai.

Wajd, lutaf-e-sakhun mubaarik ho,
Ba kamaalon ki yaad aati hai.

سکندر علی وجدؔ

اجنتا

جہاں خونِ جگر پیتے رہے اہلِ ہنر برسوں

جہاں گھلتا رہا رنگوں میں آہوں کا اثر برسوں

جہاں کھنچتا رہا پتھر پہ عکسِ خیر و شر برسوں

جہاں قائم رہے گی جنّتِ قلب و نظر برسوں

جہاں نغمے جنم لیتے ہیں رنگینی برستی ہے

دکن کی گود میں آباد وہ خوابوں کی بستی ہے

جگر کے خون سے کھینچے گئے ہیں نقشِ لاثانی

تصدّق جن کے ہر خط پر تحیّر خانہ مانی

مشکّل ہے شباب و حسن میں تخئیلِ انسانی

تقدّس کے سہارے جی رہا ہے ذوقِ عریانی

حسینانِ اجنتا کا جنوں سرتاج ہے گویا

یہاں جذبات کے اظہار کی معراج ہے گویا

گلستاں سے جو گزرا کارواں فصلِ بہاری کا

بہانہ مل گیا اہلِ جنوں کو حسن کاری کا

چٹانوں پر بنایا نقشِ دل کی بے قراری کا

سکھایا گر اسے جذبات کی آئینہ داری کا

192

Sikander Ali Wajd
Ajanta

Where the talent was for long forced to drink its blood,
Where for years the painters' colours on their sighs were fed,
Where the tale of bliss and bale the solid rocks reflect,
Where the paradise of peace shall for ever rest,
    Where lovely hues fill the earth, melody takes its birth,
    That vale of golden dreams in Deccan's lap doth lurk.

The artists' own blood had fed these images nonpareil,
Before which even Maani's art would fade away and pale,
Imagination here lies in beauteous forms impaled,
Love of beauty, pure and nude, drapes itself on sacred veils;
    Ajanta's beauties here have reached the height of frenzy
    bold,
    Thought and feeling have attained the final, perfect goal.

As the caravan of spring strolls along the garden paths,
Men of art, frenzy-seized, express themselves in graphic arts,
Pour the restlessness of heart on eternal stones and rocks,
Make them interpret emotion blent with serious thought.

Jahan khoon-e-jigar peete rahe ahl-e-hunar barson,
Jahan ghulta raha rangon mein aahon ka asar barson,
Jahan khinchta raha paththar pe aks-e-khair-o-shar barson,
Jahan qaayam rahegi jannat-e-qalab-o-nazar barson;
    Jahan naghme janam lete hain, rangeeni barsti hai,
    Decaan ki god mein aabaad woh khwaabon ki basti hai.

Jigar ke khoon se kheinche gaye hain naqsh-e-lasaani,
Tasaddaq jin ke har khat par tahayyur khana-e-Maani,
Mushakkle hai shabab-o-husn mein takhayyul-e-insaani,
Taqaddas ke sahaare ji raha hai zauq-e-uriaani;
    Haseenaan-e-Ajanta ka janoon sartaaj hai goya,
    Yahan jazbaat ke izhaar ki meraaj hui goya.

Gulistaan se jo guzra karwaan fasal-e-bahaari ka,
Bahaana mil gaya ahl-e-janoon ko husn kaari ka;
Chitaanon par banaaya naqsh dil ki beqaraari ka,
Sikhayaa gur use jazbaat ki aaeena daari ka.

سکندر علی وجدؔ

دلِ کہسار میں محفوظ اپنی داستاں رکھ دی
جگرداروں نے بنیادِ جہانِ جاوداں رکھ دی
کہیں پیدا ہے ساری کیفیت صحنِ گلستاں کی
کہیں رونق نظر آتی ہے بازار و شبستاں کی
کہیں حیرت زبانِ حال ہے،حالِ پریشاں کی
لکیریں ہیں کہ شریانیں دلِ انسان و حیواں کی
کہیں ظلمت کے پیچھے روشنی محسوس ہوتی ہے
کہیں تو موت میں بھی زندگی محسوس ہوتی ہے
ہنر مندوں نے تصویروں میں گویا جان بھر دی ہے
ترازو دِل میں ہو جاتی ہے وہ کافر نظر دی ہے
اداؤں سے عیاں ہے لذتِ دردِ جگر دی ہے
کھلیں گے راز اس ڈر سے دہن پر مہر کر دی ہے
یہ تصویریں بظاہر ساکت و خاموش رہتی ہیں
مگر اہلِ نظر پوچھیں تو دل کی بات کہتی ہیں

194

Sikander Ali Wajd

Thus they store their chosen tales in the breast of mounts and caves,
Leave behind for future times lasting monuments of faith.

Here we see deftly etched garden scenes and sights,
There we turn to gaze upon a town abuzz with life.
Here, sense and speech stand stunned by a deep-distressing sight,
Are these lines or pulsing veins athrob beneath the living hide?
Sometime we can see the light breaking through the veil of night,
Somewhere even death appears instinct with the force of life.

These geniuses, so it seems, have made these pictures come alive,
A sharp, penetrating glance springs from their painted eyes.
In their gestures we can read the feelings of their secret heart,
Sealed are their lips and tongues, so they don't betray their thought.
Still and silent are these images to the careless eye,
But they speak when approached by some wise, discerning guy.

Dil-e-kuhsaar mein mehfooz apni daastaan rakh di,
Jigardaaron ne buniyaad-e-jahaan-e-jaawedaan rakh di.

Kahin paida hai saari kaifeeat sehan-e-gulshan ki,
Kahin raunaq nazar aati hai bazaar-o-shabastaan ki,
Kahin hairat zabaan-e-haal hai, haal-e-pareshaan ki
Lakiren hain ke shariaanen dil-e-insaan-o-haiwaan ki.

Kahin zulmat ke peechhe roshni mahsoos hoti hai,
Kahin tau maut mein bhi zindagi mahsoos hoti hai.

Hunarmandon ne tasweeron mein goya jaan bhar di hai,
Taraazoo dil mein ho jaati hai woh kaafir nazar di hai;
Adaaon se ayaan hai lazzat-e-dard-jigar di hai,
Khulenge raaz is dar se dahan par muhar kar di hai.

Yeh tasweeren bazaahar saakit-o-khaamosh rahti hain,
Magar ahl-e-nazar poochhen tau dil ki baat kahti hain.

تحسینِ ناشناس

ناداں، مجھے درکار نہیں داد کا صدقہ

لیا شعر مرا کاسہِ درویزہ گری ہے؟

ہے شہرتِ ارزاں کی طلب اہلِ ہوس کو

محتاجئِ عالم کا سبب بے ہنری ہے

میں کچھ نہیں، سب کچھ ہے مرا حسنِ تخیّل

اِس حسن کا زیور مری آشفتہ سری ہے

یہ زندہ حقیقت ہے کہ ہر شعرِ دل آویز

معراجِ کمالاتِ خیالِ بشری ہے

ملحوظ رہے فکرِ فلک رس کا تقدّس

یہ رہ گزرِ منزلِ پیغامبری ہے

رنگین بہانہ ہے فقط نظم و غزل کا

مقصود حقیقت کی یہاں پردہ دری ہے

ہے آتشِ دل ساغرِ صہبائے سخن میں

خشکی مرے لب کی مری آنکھوں کی تری ہے

میرے لیے طاعت ہے مری شعلہ نوائی

تیرے لیے اک مشغلہِ خوش بصری ہے

Sikander Ali Wajd
Praise of The Ignorant (Tahseen-e-Na-Shanaas)

Do I need your acclamation, O, thou simple soul ?
Treat not my poetic works as a begging bowl.

Only selfish, sensual men hanker after popular fame,
Dearth of talent is the cause of our self-belittling role.

This is the imagination's marvel, what am I, otherwise ?
Frenzy is the jewel that decks fancy's beauteous brow.

It's an undeniable fact that all heart-delighting verse.
To the sharp, perceptive mind its essential beauty owes.

Imagination shouldn't break the edicts of the moral code,
A poet must prove himself worthy of the prophet's role.

A song or lyric is indeed a pleasing alibi,
To unmask the face of truth is the poet's goal.

The fire of heart lies distilled in the goblet of my Muse,
The dryness of my lips derives from my eyes' flow.

For me it is a sacred mission to put my flaming heart in verse,
To you these stirring strains seem just an entertaining mode.

Nadaan, mujhe darkaar nahin daad ka sadqa,
Kya shair mira kaasa-e-daryooza gari hai ?

Hai shuhrat-e-arzaan ki talab ahl-e-hawas ko,
Muhtaaji-e-aalam ka sabab be-hunari hai.

Main kuchh nahin, sab kuchh hai mira husn-e-takhayyul
Is husn ka zewar miri aashufta sari hai.

Yeh zinda haqeeqat hai ke har shair-e-dilaawez,
Meraaj-e-kamaalaat-e-khayaal-e-bashri hai.

Malhooz rahe fikar-e-falak-ras ka taqaddas,
Yeh rah guzr-e-manzil-e-paighambri hai.

Rangeen bahana hai faqt nazm-o-ghazal ka,
Maqsood haqeeqat ki yahaan parda dari hai.

Hai aatish-e-dil saghir-e-sahbaa-e-sakhun mein,
Khushki mire lab ki miri aankhon ki tari hai,

Mere lieye taayat hai miri shola nawaai,
Tere lieye ik mashghala-e-khush basri hai.

197

Akhtar-ul-Imaan
(1915-1996)

AKHTAR-UL-IMAAN (1915-1996)

Akhtar-ul-Imaan was born on November 12, 1915, at Sehni Qila Pathargarh, district Bijnour (U.P.). His father, Hafiz Fateh Mohammed, was a religious priest attached to the village mosque, and given to changing his place of work every now and then. In the company of his "migratory" father Akhtar too led a nomadic existence in his childhood. After his preliminary education Akhtar went to Delhi, where his uncle, who was a school teacher, admitted him to a school-cum-orphanage called *Nuwad-ul-Islam*. Akhtar didn't go to any poetic master to learn the art of poetic composition. What inspired the poet in him was the sonorous voice of a pedestrian bard, Ishfaq, who used to sing and sell his own verses in the Jama Masjid area of Delhi. He did his B.A. in Urdu at Aligarh University, but, he left Aligarh before completing his studies, and went first to Poona and then to Bombay, where he spent a good part of his life pursuing his literary interests both as a poet and as a writer of dialogues and scripts for films. He had also visited Europe, Soviet Union and America.

Between 1943 and 1990, Akhtar published nine volumes of poetry : *Girdaab, Tareek Sayyaara, Sab Rang, Ab Joo, Yaaden, Banat-e-Lamhaat, Naya Aahang, Zameen Zameen, Sar-o-Saamaan (Complete Works)*. He won several national awards including the Sahitya Akademy Award for his book, *Yaaden*. Primarily a poet of the *nazm*, Akhtar writes a simple, natural style, with pronounced conversational rhythms, and a penchant for the inbuilt dramatic dialogue. He can be startingly fresh and unconventional in his diction. He is the poet of the fragmented modern man, caught in the dilemma of dream and reality, ideal and expediency. *Akhtar* died in Bombay on March 9, 1996, after a prolonged illness.

اختر الایمان

ایک لڑکا

دیارِ شرق کی آبادیوں کے اونچے ٹیلوں پر

کبھی آموں کے باغوں میں، کبھی کھیتوں کی مینڈوں پر

کبھی جھیلوں کے پانی میں، کبھی بستی کی گلیوں میں

کبھی کچھ نیم عریاں کم سنوں کی رنگ ریلیوں میں

سحَر دَم، جھٹپٹے کے وقت، راتوں کے اندھیرے میں

کبھی میلوں میں، ناٹک ٹولیوں میں، ان کے ڈیرے میں

کبھی ہم سن حسینوں میں بہت خوش کام و دل رفتہ

کبھی پیچاں بگولہ سا، کبھی جیوں چشم خوں بستہ

ہوا میں تیرتا، خوابوں میں بادل کی طرح اڑتا

پرندوں کی طرح شاخوں میں چھپ کر جھولتا مُڑتا

مجھے اک لڑکا، آوارہ مَنِش، آزاد سیلانی

مجھے اک لڑکا، جیسے تند چشموں کا رواں پانی

نظر آتا ہے، یوں لگتا ہے جیسے یہ بلائے جاں

مرا ہمزاد ہے، ہر گام پر، ہر موڑ پر جَولاں

اسے ہمراہ پاتا ہوں، یہ سائے کی طرح میرا

تعاقب کر رہا ہے، جیسے میں مفرور ملزم ہوں

یہ مجھ سے پوچھتا ہے اختر الایمان تم ہی ہو؟

200

Akhtar-ul-Imaan
A Boy (Ek Larka)

Vaulting o'er mounds and mounts in some Eastern town,
In furrowed fields or mango-groves merrily frolicking round,
Swimming in the brimming lakes, sauntering down the lanes,
Or with urchins, semi-nude, playing rustic games;
In the morn, in the twilight, in the darkening nights,
Watching fairs 'mid band of players, frequenting their camping
site,
Now with the beauteous dames romantically engaged,
Now with a ruffled brow, angry, bloodshot face;
Flying with the sailing clouds, floating with the breeze,
Swinging like the merry birds on the branching trees,
A restless, freedom-loving boy, by wanderlust possessed,
For ever on the move like water-fonts aburst—
This boy confronts me daily, would not let me rest.
This plague of life, I trust, is my surrogate,
Who shadows me at every step like my very shade.
"Are you Akhtar-ul-Imaan ?" repeatedly he says,
As if I were a culprit, a run-away from jail.

Dayaar-e-sharq ki aabaadion ke oonche teelon par,
Kabhi aamon ke baghon mein, kabhi kheton ke meindon par,
Kabhi jheelon ke paani mein kabhi basti ki galion mein,
Kabhi kuchh neem-uriaan kamsinon ki rang ralion mein,
Sehar dam, jhutpate ke waqt, raaton ke andhere mein,
Kabhi melon mein, naatak tolion mein, un ke dere mein,
Kabhi humsin haseenon mein bahut khush kaam-o-dil rafta,
Kabhi pechaan bagoola sa, Kabhi jeon chashm-e-khoon basta;
Hawa mein tairta, khwaabon mein badal ki tarah urta,
Parindon ki tarah shaakhon mein chhup kar jhoolta, murta.
Mujhe ik larka, aawaara manish, aazaad, sailaani,
Mujhe ik larka jaise tund chashmon ka rawan paani,
Nazar aata hai, yoon lagta hai, jaise yeh bala-e-jaan,
Mira humzaad hai, har gaam par, har mor par jaulaan,
Use hamraah paata hoon, yeh saaey ki tarah mera
Ta-aqab kar raha hai jaise main mafroor mulzim hoon,
Yeh mujh se poochhta hai. Akhtar-ul-Imaan tum hi ho ?

201

خدائے عزّ و جل کی نعمتوں کا معترف ہوں میں
مجھے اقرار ہے اس نے زمیں کو ایسے پھیلایا
کہ جیسے بستر کمخواب ہو،دیبا و مخمل ہو
مجھے اقرار ہے، یہ خیمہِ افلاک کا سایہ
اسی کی بخششیں ہیں،اس نےسورج ، چاند،تاروں کو
فضاؤں میں سنوارا اک حدِ فاصل مقرّر کی
چٹانیں چیر کر دریا نکالے، خاکِ اَسفل سے
مری تخلیق کی، مجھ کو جہاں کی پاسبانی دی
وہ حاکم قادرِ مطلق ہے،یکتا اور دانا ہے
اندھیرے کو اجالے سے جدا کرتا ہے، خود کو میں
اگر پہچانتا ہوں اس کی رحمت اور سخاوت ہے
اسی نے خسروی دی ہے لیموں کو مجھے نکبت
اسی نے یاوہ گویوں کو مرا خازن بنایا ہے
تو نگر ہرزہ کاروں کو کیا، دریوزہ گر مجھ کو
مگر جب جب کسی کے سامنے دامن پسارا ہے
یہ لڑکا پوچھتا ہے اخترالایمان تم ہی ہو؟

202

Akhtar-ul-Imaan

Praise be to Lord the Great for His boundless grace,
He made this wondrous globe, hung it in the space.
Covered the earth from end to end with a sheet of grass,
Richer than the brocade, softer that the velvet cloth;
Tc Him we owe, I accept, this sparkling, skiey dome,
Spangled with the shining stars, with sun and moon adorned.
He carved the rocks, rolled the rivers, fixed the limits of sky and earth,
Shaped me out of lowly dust, gave me guardianship of earth.
The Lord Supreme of earth and air, uniquely wise and great,
He marked the shade from sun, put them in their place.
He gave treasures to the misers, to me my dismal state,
This consciousess of self and being is His gift, His grace.
To wagging tongues He gave control of my purse and pelf,
To me He gave the begging bowl, to liars, all the wealth.
But whenever I stretch my hand before this preferred race,
"Are you Akhtar-ul-Imaan ?" the boy asks enraged.

Khuda-e-azz-o-jal ki naimton ka motrif hoon main,
Mujhe iqrar hai us ne zameen ko aise phailaaya,
Ke jaise bistar-e-kamkhwaab ho, deeba-o-makhmil ko,
Mujhe iqrar hai, yeh khaime-e-iflaak ka saya,
Usi ki bakhshashen hain, us ne sooraj, chaand, taaron ko,
Fizaaon mein sanwara, ik had-e-faasil muqarrar ki,
Chitaane cheer kar darya nikaale chaak-e-asphal se,
Miri takhleeq ki, mujh ko jahan ki paashaani di.
Woh haakim qaadir-e-mutliq hai, yakta aur dana hai,
Andhere ko ujale se juda karta hai, khood ko main
Agar pahchaanta hoon us ki rahmat aur sakhaawat hai.
Usi ne khusrawi di hai, laimoon ko, mujhe nakbat,
Usi ne yaawa goyon ko mira khaazin banaaya hai.
Tawangar harza kaaron ko kiya, daryooza gar mujh ko,
Magar jab kisi ke saamne daman pasaara hai,
Yeh larka poochhta hai, Akhtar-ul-Imaan tum hi to ?

اخترالایمان

معیشت دوسروں کے ہاتھ میں ہے، میرے قبضے میں
جز اک ذہنِ رَسا کچھ بھی نہیں، پھر بھی، مگر مجھ کو
خروشِ عمر کے اِتمام تک اِک بار اُٹھانا ہے
عناصِر منتشر ہو جانے، نبضیں ڈوب جانے تک
نوائے صبح ہو یا نالہِ شب، کچھ بھی گانا ہے
کبھی جب سوچتا ہوں اپنے بارے میں تو کہتا ہوں
کہ تو اک آبلہ ہے جس کو آخر پھوٹ جانا ہے
سَحَر کی آرزو میں شب کا دامن تھامتا ہوں جب
یہ لڑکا پوچھتا ہے اختر الایمان تم ہی ہو؟
یہ لڑکا پوچھتا ہے جب تو میں جھلّا کے کہتا ہوں
وہ آشفتہ مزاج، اندوہ پرور، اِضطراب آسا
جسے تم پوچھتے رہتے ہو، کب کا مر چکا ظالم
اسے خود اپنے ہاتھوں سے کفن دے کر فریبوں کا
اسی کی آرزوؤں کی لحد میں پھینک آیا ہوں
میں اس لڑکے سے کہتا ہوں وہ شعلہ مر چکا جس نے
کبھی چاہا تھا اک خاشاکِ عالم پھونک ڈالے گا
یہ لڑکا مسکراتا ہے، یہ آہستہ سے کہتا ہے
"یہ کذب و افترا ہے، جھوٹ ہے، دیکھو میں زندہ ہوں"

204

Akhtar-ul-Imaan

To others He gave means of life, to me a barren lot,
Nothing did He grant to me except perceptive thought.
Yet I've to bear with life, as long as it lasts,
Till the elements dissolve, the wheel grinds to halt,
Midnight dirge, or morning lay, something must engage my
heart.
When I think about myself and contemplate my fate,
I realise I'm a blister, doomed to burst one day.
But when, in the hope of day, the hand of night I seize,
"Are you Akhtar-ul-Imaan," the boy again repeats.

Vexed with his questioning, thus I cut him short :
That wild, restless, sorrow's child, about whom you ask,
That terror died long ago, I've buried him deep,
Coffined with his hopes and dreams, in his grave he sleeps.
That flame is now expunged, which once itched to burn
This world, this heap of straw, with its weeds and worms.

Softly the boy remarks, with a touch of glee,
"This is false, a blatant lie, look, I live and breathe !"

Maeeshat doosron ke haath mein hai, mere qabze mein,
Juz ik zihn-e-rasa kuchh bhi nahin, phir bhi, magar mujh ko
Kharosh-e-umr ke itmaam tak ik baar uthaana hai,
Anaasir munteshar ho jaane, nabzen doob jaane tak,
Nawa-e-subah ho ya naale-e-shab, kuchh bhi gana hai.
Kabhi jab sochta hoon apne baare mein tau kahta hoon,
Ke tu ik aabla hai jis ko aakhir phoot jaana hai.
Sehar ki aarzoo mein shab ka daman thaamta hoon jab,
Yeh larka poochhta hai, "Akhtar-ul-Imaan tum hi ho ?"

Yeh larka poochhta hai jab tau main jhilla ke kahta hoon,
Woh aashufta sar, andoh parwar, izteraab aasa,
Jise tum poochhte ho, kab ka mar chuka Zaalim,
Use khood apne haathon se kafan dekar farebon ka,
Usi ki aarzoo-onki lahd mein phaink aaya hoon.
Main is larke se kahta hoon woh shola mar chuka jis ne
Kabhi chaaha tha ik khaashaak-e-aalam phoonk dalega,

Yeh larka muskaraata hai, yeh aahista se kahta hai,
"Yeh kizab-o-iftra hai, jhoot hai, dekho main zinda hoon".

اخترالایمان

پگڈنڈی

ایک حسینہ درماندہ سی بے بس تنہا دیکھ رہی ہے

جیسے یونہی بڑھتے بڑھتے رنگِ افق پر جا جھولے گی

جیسے یونہی افتاں خیزاں جاکر تاروں کو چھولے گی

راہ کے پیچ و خم میں کوئی راہی الجھا دیکھ رہی ہے

انگڑائی لیتی، بل کھاتی، ویرانوں سے، آبادی سے

ٹکراتی، کتراتی، مڑتی، خشکی پر گرِداب بناتی

اٹھلاتی، شرماتی، ڈرتی، مستقبل کے خواب دکھاتی

سایوں میں ستاتی، مڑتی، بڑھ جاتی ہے آزادی سے

راہی کی آنکھوں میں ڈھلتی، گرتی اور سنبھل جاتی ہے

ٹھنڈی چھاؤں میں تاروں کی سیمیں خواب کا دھار ابنتی

دن کی روشن قندیلوں میں، میداں میں آوارہ بنتی

ندیوں سے، چشموں سے ملتی کوسوں دور نکل جاتی ہے

پھولوں کے اجسام کچلتی، ذرّوں کے فانوس جگاتی

درماندہ اشجار کے نیچے شاخوں کا واویلا سنتی

ہر نو وارد کے رستے میں نادیدہ اک جال سا بنتی

بڑھ جاتی ہے منزل کہہ کر کلیاں زیرِ خاک سلاتی

206

Akhtar-ul-Imaan
Footpath (Pagdandi)

A beauteous belle, helpless, weary, sits alone with vacant gaze,
As if she 'uld touch the horizon, frolic with its rainbow shades;
As if, somehow, rising, falling, she would touch the silver stars,
Finding on the winding path, a lone traveller strayed and lost.

Twisting, turning, pausing, bending, passing through the towns
and wilds,
Making whirlpools on land, threading through the countryside.
Pushing ahead, or skirting past, in pleasant, wishful dreams
absorbed,
Having had a wayside nap, she resumes her onward march.

Focussed in the traveller's eyes, stumbling, straightening up her
strides,
Shining like a silver gleam, beneath the cool, starlit night,
Wandering through the sun and shade of the plains and wilds,
Running beside springs and runnels, traversing miles on miles.

Crushing buds and blooms en route, shooting through the shining
grains,
Listening to the rattling boughs, shaken by the wind and rain,
Weaving for unwary travellers a web of puzzling roads,
Sending wayside buds to sleep, heading for the goal.

Ek haseena, darmaanda si be bas tanha dekh rahi hai,
Jaise yunhi barhte barhte rang-e-ufaq par ja jhoolegi,
Jaise yunhi uftaan khezaan ja kar taaron ko chhoo legi,
Raah ke pech-o-kham mein koi raahi uljha dekh rahi hai.

Angraai leti, bal khati, weeranon se, aabadi se,
Takraati, katraati, murti, khushki par girdaab banaati,
Ithlaati, sharmaati, darti, mustaqbil ke khwab dikhaati,
Sayon mein sustaati, murti, barh jati hai aazadi se;

Rahi ki aankhon mein dhalti, girti aur sambhal jaati hai,
Thandi chhuon mein taaron ki seemein khwab ka dhara banti,
Din ki roshan qandeelon mein, maidaan mein aawaara banti,
Nadion se, chashmoon se milti koson door nikal jaati hai.

Phoolon ke ijsaam kuchalti, zarron ke faanoos jagaati,
Darmande ashjaar ke neeche shaakhon ka waavela sunti,
Har nauwarad ke raste mein na-deeda ik jaal si bunti,
Barh jaati hai manzil kah kar, kalian zer-e-khaak sulaati.

اخترالایمان

غم دیدہ پس ماندہ راہی تاریکی میں کھو جاتے ہیں
پاؤں راہ کے رخساروں پر دھندلے نقش بنا دیتے ہیں
آنے والے اور مسافر پہلے نقش مٹا دیتے ہیں
وقت کی گرد میں دبتے دبتے ایک فسانہ ہو جاتے ہیں
راہ کے پیچ و خم میں اپنا دامن کوئی کھینچ رہا ہے
فردا کا پر پیچ دھندلکا، ماضی کی گھنگھور سیاہی
یہ خاموشی، یہ سناٹا، اس پر اپنی کور نگاہی
ایک سفر ہے تنہا راہی، جو سہنا تھا خوب سہا ہے
ایک حسینہ درماندہ سی بے بس تنہا دیکھ رہی ہے
جیون کی پگڈنڈی یونہی تاریکی میں بل کھاتی ہے
کون ستارے چھو سکتا ہے، راہ میں سانس اکھڑ جاتی ہے
راہ کے پیچ و خم میں کوئی راہی الجھا دیکھ رہی ہے
یہ سورج، یہ چاند ستارے راہیں روشن کر سکتے ہیں؟
تاریکی آغازِ سحر ہے، تاریکی انجام نہیں ہے؟
آنے والوں کی راہوں میں کوئی نور آشام نہیں ہے؟
ہم سے اتنا بن پڑتا ہے جی سکتے ہیں، مر سکتے ہیں

208

Akhtar-ul-Imaan

Weary, broken-hearted travellers get stranded in the dark,
Dimly dotted lie the footprints etched on the sinuous path,
The new bands of travellers stamp out the older marks,
And the dust of whirling time consigns them to the bin of past.

Someone tugs at my hem on the zigzag path,
Dark, dismal past behind, future knot on knot ;
Such silence, such loneliness ! on top, this failing sight,
Long journey, lone traveller, bravely did we suffer and strive !

A beauteous belle, helpless, weary, sits alone with vacant gaze,
The path of life, dark and winding, dimly lifts its hazy face,
Breath-exhausting is the climb, who can reach the stars ?
Her eyes rest on someone stranded from the path.

Can the sun and moon and stars illumine the darkening path ?
Will the night herald dawn, will it lift, the gloomy pall ?
Will the traveller of to-morrow find a dark-dispelling torch ?
We can only struggle and suffer, and submit when death recalls.

Ghum-deeda pasmaanda raahi taareeki mein kho jaate hain,
Paaon raah ke rukhsaaron par dhundle naqsh bana dete hain,
Aane waale aur musaafir pahle naqsh mita dete hain,
Waqt ki gard mein dabte dabte ek fasaana ho jaate hain.

Raah ke pech-o-kham mein apna daman koi kheinch raha hai,
Farda ka pur-pech dhundalka, maazi ki ghangor seaahi,
Yeh khaamoshi, yeh sannata, is par apni koor nigaahi,
Ek safar hai tanha raahi, jo sahna tha khoob saha hai.

Ek haseena darmaanda si be bas tanha dekh rahi hai,
Jeevan ki pagdandi yoonhi taareeki mein bal khaati hai,
Kaun sitare chhoo sakta hai, raah mein saans ukhar jaati hai,
Raah ke pech-o-khum mein koi raahi uljha dekh rahi hai.

Yeh sooraj, yeh chaand sitare raahen roshan kaı sakte hain ?
Taareeki aaghaaz-e-sehar hai, taareeki anjaam nahin hai ?
Aane waale ki raahon mein koi noor-aashaam nahin hai ?
Hum se itna ban parta hai, ji sakte hain, mar sakte hain.

اخترالایمان

شیشے کا آدمی

اٹھاؤ ہاتھ کہ دستِ دعا بلند کریں

ہماری عمر کا اک اور دن تمام ہوا

خدا کا شکر بجالایئں آج کے دن بھی

نہ کوئی واقعہ گزرا نہ ایسا کام ہوا

زباں سے کلمہِ حق راست کچھ کہا جاتا

ضمیر جاگتا اور اپنا امتحاں ہوتا

خدا کا شکر بجالایئں آج کا دن بھی

اسی طرح سے کٹا منہ اندھیرے اٹھ بیٹھے

پیالی چائے کی پی، خبریں دیکھیں ناشتہ پر

ثبوت بیٹھے بصیرت کا اپنی دیتے رہے

بخیر و خوبی پلٹ آئے جیسے شام ہوئی

اور اگلے روز کا موہوم خوف دل میں لیے

ڈرے ڈرے سے ذرا بال پڑ نہ جائے کہیں

لیے دیے یونہی بستر میں جاکے لیٹ گئے

Akhtar-ul-Imaan
The Fragile Man (Sheeshe ka Aadmi)

Let us lift our hands in prayer,
Another day is smoothly done;
Thanks to the Mighty Lord that even to-day
No event came to pass, no task was shaped;
We didn't utter a syllable true,
Lest our conscience got a jolt or our mettle put to test.
God be thanked that even to-day
Was a replica of yesterdays :
Got up early, had bed tea, scanned the morning news,
And at breakfast time our astuteness displayed,
Came back in the evening, uninjured, unscathed,
And waited for the next day, vaguely haunted by the fear
Lest our conduct to-morrow offends the public taste;
Thus complacent and confused we slip into the bed and sleep.

Uthaao haath ke dast-e-dua buland karen,
Hamaari umr ka ik aur din tamaam hua,
Khuda ka shukar baja laaen aaj ke din bhi,
Na koi waaqa guzra na aisa kaam hua,
Zabaan se kalma-e-haq raast kuchh kaha jaata,
Zameer jaagta aur apna imtehaan hota,
Khuda ka shukr baja laaen aaj ka din bhi,
Isi tarah se kata, munh andhere uth baithe,
Payaali chaae ki pi, khabren dekheen, naashta par
Saboot baithe baseerat ka apni dete rahe.
Ba-khair-o-khoobi palat aae jaise shaam hui,
Aur agle roz ka mauhoom khauf dil mein lieye,
Dare dare se zara baal par na jaae kahin,
Lieye dieye yoonhi bistar mein ja ke let gaye.

211

Ghulam Rabbaani Taaban
(1914-1993)

GHULAM RABBANI TAABAAN (1914-1993)

Ghulam Rabbani Taabaan was born on February 15, 1914 at Pitora, in Farukhabad district (U.P.). He did his Intermediate from Aligarh University, B.A. from St. Johns College, Agra, and LL.B. from Agra College, Agra. Having failed to make his mark in the legal profession he turned his attention to poetry and politics. He began his poetic career by writing humorous verse. Some of the parodies he wrote offended some of his friends. He turned to serious poetry in 1941, and soon acquired mastery in the twin fields of *nazm* and *ghazal*.

At Agra he had got interested in and initiated into communist ideology and politics. He was a member of the secret society which used to hold meetings against the British Raj. He was also an active member of the Progressive Writers' Association which he had joined under the influence of Sajjad Zaheer, a leading light of the Progressives.

Taabaan joined Maktaba Jamia, Delhi, in 1957, and worked as its manager till 1970. He stayed in Delhi for the rest of his life.

His poetical works include *Saaz-e-Larzaan, Hadis-e-Dil, Zauq-e-Safar* and *Nawa-e-Aawara*. In addition, he has translated several books from English into Urdu. He has also written critiques of several classical Urdu poets such as Quli Qutab Shah, Wali Daccany, Mir and Dard.

Taabaan was a widely travelled poet. He was also a recepient of several awards, which included Padma Shree by the Government of India, Sahitya Akademi Award, Soviet Land Nehru Award, and awards from Urdu Akademies.

غلام ربّانی تاباں

دیوالی

وقار! روح کے تاروں کو کیوں چھوا تو نے

تمہاری نظم ''دیوالی'' بہت اچھی ہے

مگر یہ رات کی گردن میں دیپ مالائیں

سیاہیوں میں اجالے کے بد نما دھبّے

غریب حبشی کو جیسے جذام ہو جائے

یہ ٹمٹماتے دیے صبح کا بدل تو نہیں

میں سوچتا ہوں کہ اس رات چین و برما میں

کسی محاذ پہ کتنے دیے جلے ہوں گے

جوان خون کی ہر بوند اک کرن بن کر

اک ایسی صبح کی تشکیل کر رہی ہو گی

ہزار صدیوں کی تاریک و تیرہ راتوں میں

بنی رہی جو انساں کے خواب کا مرکز

وہ صبح دور نہیں

اندھیری رات کے سینے سے نور کا چشمہ

ابلنے والا ہے

Ghulam Rabbani Taabaan
Dewali

Why did you touch my tender chord ?
Your "Dewali" is really nice, Waqar !
But these rows of lights on the neck of night —
White spots on sable hide—
Recall a negro leprosy-struck;
Yet these glimmering rows—
These twinkling lamps, are not a substitute for day.
I think of China and of Burma,
And their smoking battle-fronts,
Where youthful soldiers spill their blood,
To found a morning fresh and bright
To end the endless reign of night.
This dawn of hope is not now far,
Any moment it may burst
Springing like a flood of light from the breast of dark.

Waqar ! rooh ke taaron ko kyon chhooa tu ne,
Tumhaari nazm "dewali" bahut hi achhi hai,
Magar—yeh raat ki gardan mein deep maalaaen
Seaahion mein ujaale ke bad-numa dhabbe,
Gharib habshi ko jaise jazam ho jaae,
Yeh timtamaate dieye subah ka badal tau nahin.

Main sochta hoon ke is raat Cheen-o-Burma mein,
Kisi mahaaz par kitne dieye jale honge,
Jawaan khoon ki har boond ik kiran ban kar,
Ik aisi subah ki tashkeel kar rahi hogi
Hazaar sadion ki taareek-o-teera raaton mein
Bani rahi hai jo insaan ke khwab ka markiz,
Woh subah door nahin
Andheri raat ke seene se noor ka chasma
Ubalne waala hai.

غلام ربّانی تاباؔں

یہ ٹمٹماتے دیے ـــــ لکشمی کے چرنوں میں
سبھی نے حسنِ عقیدت کے پھول ڈالے ہیں
وہ جن کو لکشمی دیوی سے قربِ خاص نہیں
گھروں میں اپنے بھی دیپک جلائے بیٹھے ہیں
شکستہ جھونپڑیوں کو سجائے بیٹھے ہیں
کہ اس طرف بھی عنایت کی اک نظر ہو جائے
شکستہ جھونپڑیوں ـــــ ٹوٹے پھوٹے کھنڈروں میں
کبھی بھی لکشمی دیوی نہ مسکرائے گی
کبھی بہار نہ ان کے چمن میں آئے گی
اگر وہ خود ہی نظامِ چمن نہ بدلیں
سیاہیوں کے نمائندے ـــــ رات کے بیٹے
ہمارے فکر و تخیّل کو باندھنے کے لیے
توہمّات کی زنجیریں ڈھال لیتے ہیں
کبھی دوالی کبھی شبِ برات آتی ہے

216

Ghulam Rabbani Tabaan

These twinkling lamps — a homage deep
At Laxmi's holy feet,
Is paid by all including those
Who are from her gates debarred.
Even the poor light their huts,
Hoping that the Deity Great would bless them with Her holy
grace;
In their broken homes and hearths
Never will the Goddess smile,
Never will the spring arrive,
Unless they themselves decide to change the system and the
style.
The sons of Night, agents of the Dark,
In the superstition's trap have caught our heads and hearts,
Perpetuating in the process,
Here Dewali, there Shab-e-Raat.

Yeh timtamaate dieye-Laxmi ke charnon mein,
Sabhi ne husn-e-aqeedat ke phool daalen hain,
Woh jinko Laxmi Devi se qareeb-e-khaas nahin,
Gharon mein apne bhi deepak jalaae baithe hain,
Shikasta jhaunparion ko sajaae baithe hain,
Ke istaraf bhi inaait ki ik nazar ho jaae,
Shikasta jhaunparion—toote phoote khandron mein
Kabhi bhi Laxmi Devi na muskaraaegi
Kabhi bahaar na un ke chaman mein aaegi,
Agar woh khud hi nizaam-e-chaman na badlenge.

Seaahion ke numaainde, raat ke bete,
Hamaare fikar-o-takhayyul ko baandhne ke lieye,
Tohumaat ki zanjeeren dhaal lete hain,
Kabhi Dewali kabhi Shab-e-raat aati ahi.

غلام ربّانی تاباؔں

تاشقند

شہرِ خوباں ہے یہی شہرِ نگاراں ہے یہی
دوستو مجمعِ ترکانِ حسیس تو دیکھو

میرا ذمّہ جو کبھی سوئے فلک جائے نظر
دیکھنے والو مہ و مہرِ زمیں تو دیکھو

سادگی ہائے در و بام پہ طنزاً نہ ہنسو
ان مکانوں کے طرحدار مکیں تو دیکھو

جس پہ زندانی حالات کا کرتے ہو گماں
ان کے چہروں پہ ذرا نورِ یقیں تو دیکھو

تاج پہ سایہ فگن جیسے گھٹا ساون کی
زلف کی چھاؤں میں تابندہ جبیں تو دیکھو

دستِ محنت نے تراشے ہیں بتانِ صد رنگ
آؤ یہ رشکِ صنم خانہِ چیں تو دیکھو

جلوہِ گل سے بنا آئینہ خانہ گلشن
ذرّے ذرّے میں تب و تابِ نگیں تو دیکھو

گلعذاروں کا بہاروں کا وطن ہے تاباؔں
تم بھی دنیا کی یہ فردوسِ بریں تو دیکھو

218

Ghulam Rabbani Taabaan
Tashkand

This is the town of beauties sweet, the seat of rich delights,
Come my friends, watch these throngs of Turkish dames and
    wights.

You'll never watch the skies, I can bet, O friends,
If these moons and suns of earth could but catch your eye.

Cast not a scornful glance on these simple roofs and doors,
Pause to see the inmates wise, that within these doors reside.

Think not these simple folk are prisoners of their circumstance,
Mark how with inward faith their looks are shining dazzling
    bright.

Like the Taj overspread with floating summer clouds,
Shine their broad beauteous brows, with sable locks striped.

The hard-working hands have carved these figures multi-hued,
Come and see these works of art, rivalling Chinese sculptural
    heights.

The garden looks a crystal palace with the flush of vernal bloom,
See, how every grain is sparkling, like a diamond shining bright.

This is the land of scented spring, of gardens green and wide,
You should also come and see this earthly paradise.

Shahr-e-khoobaan hai yehi, shahr-e-nigaraan hai yehi,
Dosto majma-e-turkaan-e-haseen tau dekho.

Mera zimma jo kabhi soo-e-falak jaae nazar,
Dekhne waalo mah-o-mehr-e-zameen tau dekho.

Saadgi haae dar-o-bam pe tanzan na hanso,
In makaanon ke tarahadaar makeen tau dekho.

Jis pe zindaani-e-haalaat ka karte ho gumaan,
Unke chehron pe zara noor-e-yaqeen tau dekho.

Dast-e-mehnat ne taraashe hain butaan-e-sad rang,
Aao yeh rashk-e-sanam-khaana-e-Cheen tau dekho.

Jalwa-e-gul se bana aaeena khaana gulshan,
Zarre zarre mein tab-o-taab-e-nageen tau dekho.

Gulazaaron ka bahaaron ka watan hai, Taabaan,
Tum bhi duniya ki yeh firdaus-e-bareen tau dekho.

**Ahmad Nadeem Qasmi
(b. 1916)**

AHMED NADEEM QASMI (b. 1916)

Ahmed Nadeem Qasmi was born at Anga village in Khoshab district, Pakistan, on 20 November, 1916. He lost his father, Pir Ghulam Nabi, in early childhood, and the task of his education and upbringing was shouldered by his uncle, Pir Hyder Shah, a man well-versed in Persian and Arabic, with a marked taste for poetry. It was he who initiated Nadeem into the world of poetry and literature. He passed his B.A. in 1934 from Bahawalpur.

After the death of his uncle, Nadeem had to pass through a time of economic difficulty. Beginning with a short stint in the department of irrigation, Nadeem chose the journalistic career, and stuck to it all through his life. He worked for a number of Urdu journals such as *Tahzib-e-Naswaan, Phool,* and *Adab-e-Latif.* In addition, he edited *Savera* and *Naqoosh,* and started his own literary journal, *Fanoon.* In recognition of his abilities, he was chosen to direct the activities of *Majlis-e-Taraqqi-e-Adab,* which position he held for a long time.

Nadeem had started writing poetry quite early in his schooldays, and his first poem was published in a famous journal, *Siasat,* when he was only 15 years of age. His poetry is founded on his personal experience of life. The greatness and glory of man, the inequalities of class and caste, and the oppressive ways of the ruling elite are some of the motivating forces of his art. As he had spent his early life in rural surroundings, the impressions of rural life have also found a powerful expression in his poems. Primarily a poet of the *nazm,* Nadeem is also a master of the *ghazal.* His poetical collections include *Rim Jhim, Jalaal-o-Jamaal, Shola-e-gul, Dasht-e-Wafa,* and *Maheet.* He has also written several short stories.

221

احمد ندیم قاسمیؔ

ہوس سے عشق کو دستِ وگریباں کر دیا میں نے

زمانے کے خردمندوں کو حیراں کر دیا میں نے

قدم بوسی ہی جن بدبخت ذرّوں کا مقدّر تھی

جلا دے کر انھیں مہرِ درخشاں کر دیا میں نے

غریبوں کے گریباں کو قبأوں میں بدل ڈالا

امیروں کی قبأوں کو گریباں کر دیا میں نے

جلا کر شمعِ احساسِ تفکّر خانہِ دل میں

اندھیرے رہگزاروں میں چراغاں کر دیا میں نے

جسے تہذیبِ حاضر نے نکالا اپنی محفل سے

پھر اس جوشِ جنوں کو دین و ایماں کر دیا میں نے

غرض احساس کی قندیل کو سینے میں بھڑکا کر

پھر اس بھٹکے ہوئے انساں کو انساں کر دیا میں نے

مگر باایں ہمہ اسلاف کی تاریخ کہتی ہے

کہ اپنی خانماں سوزی کا ساماں کر دیا میں نے

Ahmed Nadeem Qasmi

I have got love and lust in a duel engaged,
All the wise of the world watch the sight amazed.

The humble grains which were born to kiss the lowly dust,
I have lent them sheen and glint, turned to suns ablaze.

The tattered collars of the poor I've changed to cloaks,
And have set the purple cloaks collar-like frayed.

Kindling reasoned thought and feeling in the hall of heart,
I've dispelled the gathering gloom of the darkened ways.

Passionate frenzy banned and barred from the modern life,
I have now restored to its rightful place.

Awakening the sensitive feel of the human heart,
I have set the folks strayed on the path straight.

But despite my worthy venture, history seems to say:
I've sown the seeds of ruin for my future state.

Hawas se ishq ko dast-o-garebaan kar diya main ne,
Zamaane ke khiradmandon ko hairaan kar diya main ne.

Qadambosi hi jin badbakht zarron ka muqaddar thi,
Jila dekar unhen mehar-e-darakhshaan kar diya main ne.

Garibon ke garebaan ko qabaaon mein badal daala,
Ameeron ki qabaaon ko garebaan kar diya main ne.

Jala kar shama-e-ahsaas-o-tafakkur khaana-e-dil mein,
Andhere rahguzaaron mein chiraghaan kar diya main ne.

Jise tahzeeb-e-haazir ne nikala apni mahfil se,
Phir is josh-e-janoon ko deen-o-imaan kar diya main ne.

Gharaz ahsaas ki qandeel ko seene mein bharka kar,
Phir is bhatke hue insaan ko insaan kar diya main ne.

Magar ba-een-hama, islaaf ki taareekh kahti hai,
Ke apni khaanmuun suzi ka samaan kar diya main ne.

223

احمد ندیم قاسمیؔ

مہذب

مجھے کل مرا ایک ساتھی ملا
جس نے یہ راؤ کھولا
کہ ۔۔۔ "اب جذبہ و شوق کی وحشتوں کے زمانے گئے"

پھر وہ آہستہ آہستہ ۔۔۔ چاروں طرف دیکھتا
مجھ سے کہنے لگا :
"اب بساطِ محبّت لپیٹو
جہاں سے بھی مل جائے دولت ۔۔۔ لپیٹو
غرض کچھ تو تہذیب سیکھو"

Ahmed Nadeem Qasmi
The Civilised

Yesterday I met a friend
Who to me this truth unveiled :
"Frantic love and fervent passion now have fallen out-of-grace !"
Then he slowly looked around
And gave me this advice :
"Your wares of love and faith — enwrap !
Wealth, with both your hands, grab !
Learn, in short, to be civilised !"

Mujhe kal mira ek saathi mila
Jis ne yeh raaz khola,
Ke — "Ab jazba-o-shauq ki wahshaton ke zamaane gaye!"
Phir woh aahista, aahista, chaaron taraf dekhta
Mujh se kahne laga :
"Ab basaat-e-mahabbat lapeto,
Jahan se bhi mil jaae daulat — sameto,
Gharz kuchh tau tahzib seekho !"

احمد ندیم قاسمی

یہ راہبر

یہ راہبر ہیں کسی کو باخبر ہونے نہیں دیں گے

گزر جائے گی شب، لیکن سحر ہونے نہیں دیں گے

مجھے محبوس رکھیں گے وہ وعدوں کی فصیلوں میں

کسی دیوار میں تعمیرِ در ہونے نہیں دیں گے

مجھے مامور رکھیں گے وہ بارش کی دعاؤں پر

مگر بوندوں سے میرا حلق تر ہونے نہیں دیں گے

مجھے محصور رکھیں گے عجب برزخ کے عالم میں

سفر کرنے نہیں دیں گے، بسر ہونے نہیں دیں گے

وہ مجھ سے کام لیں گے دشت کو گلشن بنانے کا

مگر اک گل بھی میرے زیبِ سر ہونے نہیں دیں گے

زمیں کی قوتِ روئیدگی بر حق سہی لیکن

کسی بھی شاخ کو وہ بارور ہونے نہیں دیں گے

سنیں گے نو بہ نو نغمے، مگر جب جی نہ چاہے گا

ہوا کو بھی چمن میں نغمہ گر ہونے نہیں دیں گے

ندیؔم اپنے ہنر سے دست کش ہونا ہی بہتر ہے

کہ یہ پتھر مجھے آئینہ گر ہونے نہیں دیں گے

226

Ahmed Nadeem Qasmi
These Leaders (Yeh Rahbar)

These our leaders will not let us step out in the light,
Even when the night has passed, will not let the sun arrive.

They'll keep us all encaged within the walls of promises tall,
Will not even a single inlet in the iron wall provide.

"Pray for rain day and night," so they urge us and advise,
But they do not let a drop down our palates glide.

They ensure that we remain bogged in deep suspense,
Will not let us move a step, or our fate decide.

They expect we should make the barren wastes bloom,
But even a single rose or bud is to us denied.

The soil is rich. let's concede, but this fact despite,
They won't let a single branch bloom or fructify.

They'll entertain themselves with trendy, lilting tunes,
But if they like, will not let even the wind to sigh.

You should better now, Nadeem, renounce the sacred Muse,
Amid the hail of rocks and stones, can your crystal ware survive ?

Yeh rahbar hain kisi ko baa khabar hone nahin denge,
Guzar jaaegi shab, lekin sahar hone nahin denge.

Mujhe mahboos rakhenge woh waadon ki faseelon mein,
Kisi deewar mein taamir-e-dar hone nahin denge.

Mujhe maamoor rakhenge woh baarish ki duaaon par,
Magar boondon se mera halq tar hone nahin denge.

Mujhe mahsoor rakhenge ajab barzakh ke aalam mein.
Safar karne nahin denge, basar hone nahin denge.

Woh mujh se kaam lenge dasht ko gulshan banaane ka,
Magar ik gul bhi mere zeb-e-sar hone nahin denge

Zameen ki quwwaat-e-roeedgi, bar-haq sahi, lekin,
Kisi bhi Shaakh ko woh baar-war hone nahin denge,

Sunenge nau-ha-nau naghme, magar jab ji na chaahega.
Hawa ko bhi chaman mein naghma gar hone nahin denge.

Nadeem apne hunar se dast kash hona hi behtar hai,
Ke yeh pathar mujhe aaeena gar hone nahin denge.

احمد ندیم قاسمی

آزادی کے بعد

کتنے خاکے مری امنگوں کے

بیچ کھاتے ہیں یوں ہواؤں میں

جس طرح چرخ کے تمام نجوم

یک بیک اڑ چلیں خلاؤں میں

کونپلوں سے اُگے ہیں انگارے

جن کی حدّت سے تپ رہے ہیں چمن

بُن رہے ہیں گلے سڑے پتّے

کتنی جامد حقیقتوں کے کفن

روٹیاں بوٹیوں سے تلتی ہیں

عصمتوں کی سجی دکانوں پر

پیٹ بھرنے کے بعد ناچتا ہے

خون کا ذائقہ زبانوں پر

آدمیّت پلٹ کے تکتی ہے

اپنے بچپن کے رہگزاروں کو

جیسے معزول شہر یار گئے

اپنی عظمت کی یادگاروں کے

Ahmed Nadeem Qasmi
After Independence (Azadi ke Baad)

All my dreams and wishful thoughts
Are blown apiece by wind and blast,
As if the stars, all at once,
In the hollow dark dissolve.

Shoots and tendrils sparks breathe,
And burn the garden with their heat,
The rotten leaves are set to weave,
Coffins for the truths deceased.

Flesh is bartered for the bread
In the honour-trading mart,
The taste of blood sticks to tongues,
And brimful roll the belly-pots.

Humanity casts a backward look
On the distant childhood paths,
As a sovereign long-deposed,
Spots of happy time recalls.

Kitne khaake miri umangon ke,
Pech khaate hain yoon hawaaon mein,
Jis tarah charkh ke tamaam najoom
Yak ba-yak ur chalen khilaaon mein.

Konplon se uge hain angaare,
Jin ki hiddat se tap rahe hain chaman,
Bun rahe hain gale sare patte,
Kitni jaamad haqiqaton ke kafan.

Rotian botion se tulti hain
Ismaton ke saji dukaanon par,
Pet bharne ke baad naachta hai,
Khoon ka zaaiqa zabaanon par.

Aadmeeat palat ke takti hai,
Apne bachpon ke rahguzaaron ko,
Jaise maazool shahr yaar gine,
Apni azmat ki yaadgaaron ko.

احمد ندیم قاسمیؔ

زندگی، عزمِ زندگی سے تھی
کارواں کے غبار میں گم ہے
زاہدِ کہنہ سال کی مانند
مقبروں کے شمار میں گم ہے
ایک آفاق گیر سنّاٹا
زندگی، زندگی پکارتا ہے
سٹپٹاتا ہے اپنے ہونٹوں سے
خون کی پپڑیاں اتارتا ہے
زندگی کو سنبھالنے کی مہم
کب مقدّر کے اختیار میں ہے
یہ زمیں، یہ خلا کی رقّاصہ
آدمِ نو کے انتظار میں ہے

230

Ahmed Nadeem Qasmi

Life without the will to live,
In the dust of caravan clogged,
Like a feeble, ancient priest,
Counts the graves, scans the yard.

Deadly silence, deep and wide,
Yearns for vanished life and bawls,
Scrapes the blood congealed on lips,
Grows frantic, howls and calls.

The fight to mend the course of life,
Lies beyond the pail of fate,
The earth, this dancing orb in space,
The birth of newer man awaits !

Zindagi, azm-e-zindagi se tahi,
Kaarwaan ke ghubaar mein gum hai,
Zaahid-e-kuhna saal ki maanind,
Maqbaron ke shumaar mein gum hai.

Ek afaaq gir sannaata,
Zindagi, zindagi, pukaarta hai,
Satpataata hai, apne honton se,
Khoon ki paprian utaarta hai.

Zindagi ko sambhaalne ki muhim,
Kab muqaddar ke ikhtiar mein hai,
Yeh zameen, yeh khila ki raqaasa,
Aadam-e-nau ke intezaar mein hai.

Jagan Nath Azad
(b. 1918)

JAGAN NATH AZAD (b. 1918)

Jagan Nath Azad, son of the famous Urdu poet, Tilok Chand Mehroom (1885-1966), was born on December 5, 1918, in Isa Khail, district Mianwali, Pakistan. He had his schooling at Kor Kot and Mianwali, and college education in Rawalpindi and Lahore, from where he obtained his M.A. degree in Persian in 1944. To begin with, he did some editorial work for the Urdu magazines, *Adbi Duniya* and *Jai Hind*. He also taught for a short time at D.A.V. College, Lahore. After the partition, he migrated to India and was emplóyed with the Ministry of Information and Broadcasting. In 1977 Azad joined the University of Jammu as Professor of Urdu. He is at present Professor Emeritus of the University of Jammu.

The old dictum that only a good man can be a good poet aptly applies to Azad. According to Ihtesham Hussain, "Azad has tried to find peace in turmoil, joy in despair, love in hatred, and thought in feeling". The trauma of the partition of India has left a deep impact on his mind and poetry. Many of his poems give a moving expression to his sense of loss and longing. Apart from being a poet, Azad is a distinguished prose-writer and critic, and a specialist of the poetry and philosophy of Iqbal. His works include *Be Karaan, Sitaron se Zarron Tak, Kahkashaan, Watan mein Ajnabi, Nawa-e-Pareshaan,* and *Boo-e-Rameeda.* Among his longer poems may be mentioned *"Maatam-e-Nehru", "Shaair ki Awaaz"* and *"Dilli ki Jama Masjid".*

جگن ناتھ آزاد

غالبؔ

شعر و ادب کی دنیا کیا تھی اک جذبات کی دنیا تھی

فکر و نظر کے رنگ سے خالی محسوسات کی دنیا تھی

تو نے اس خاکے میں آ کر ذوقِ خرد کا رنگ بھرا

حسنِ ازل کے سانچے میں انوارِ ابد کا رنگ بھرا

شعر کی سر حد دل سے بڑھ کر فکر و نظر تک پھیل گئی

چاند کی ضَو تاروں کی تجلّی نورِ سحر تک پھیل گئی

شعر تو کیا ہر لفظ ہے تیرا روحِ تغزل جانِ سخن

ہر اسلوبِ فکر ہے تیرا قندیلِ ایوانِ سخن

تو نے ایسے رستے کھولے شعر و سخن کی دنیا میں

آپ بہاریں کھنچ آئیں اس سرو و سمن کی دنیا میں

کہتے ہیں اشعار ترے یوں فن تفریح کا نام نہیں

فن تخیّل کی رفعت ہے فن ذکرِ شیشہ و جام نہیں

کہنہ رستوں کو اپنائے فن کی اس میں شان نہیں

رجعت کا ملبوس ہو تن پر فن کی یہ پہچان نہیں

Jagan Nath Azad
Ghalib

What was the world of poetic thought, a realm with sheer
    emotion fraught,
A world with feeling over-wrought, unleavened with serious
    thought.

You enlivened this lifeless draft with perceptions deep and sharp,
Gave to the spirit of beauty, eternal, everlasting garb.

You pushed the bounds of art to scale intellectual heights,
Brought down the moon and stars, made our mornings fresh
    and bright.

Your verse in every word represents the finer breath of art,
Your deep, reflective style is a lamp dispelling dark.

You have opened avenues new in the world of poetic art,
New springs have come to bless the garden-beds and flowerpots.

"Art is not an idle plaything," thus your verse exhorts,
"Not the tale of cup and ale, but the highest reach of thought.

"To re-tread the trodden path is not the hallmark of art,
Nor to dress a hackneyed thought in a trendy, modern garb."

Shair-o adab ki duniya kya thi, ik jazbaat ki duniya thi,
Fikar-o-nazar ke rang se khali, mahsoosaat ki duniya thi.

Tu ne is khaake mein aa kar zauq-e-khirad ka rang bhara,
Husn-e-azal ke saanche mein anwaar-e-abad ka rang bhara.

Shair ki sarhad dil se barh kar fikar-o-nazar tak phail gai,
Chaand ki zau, taaron ki tajalli noor-e-sehar tak phail gai.

Shair tau kya, har lafz hai tera rooh-e-taghazzul, jaan-e-sakhun,
Har asloob-e-fikar hai tera qandeel-e-aiwaan-e-sakhun.

Tu ne aise raste khole shair-o-sakhun ki duniya mein,
Aap bahaaren khinch aaeen is sarv-o-saman ki duniya mein.

Kahte hain ishaar tire yun fun tafrih ka naam nahin,
Fun takhayyul ki rafat hai, fun zikar-e-sheesha-o-jaam nahin.

Kuhna raston ko apnaaey, fun ki is mein shaan nahin,
Raj-at ka malboos ho tan par, fun ki yeh pahchaan nahin.

جگن ناتھ آزادؔ

تو نے بتایا فن جدّت ہے فکر و نظر کا اوج ہے فن
طوفانوں کی روح میں جو رقصندہ ہو وہ موج ہے فن
جن پہ چلے فنکار پرانے تو نے وہ رستے چھوڑ دیئے
شعر میں جتنے بھی تقلید کے بت تھے تو نے توڑ دیئے
تو وہ اہلِ نظر تھا جس کو دینِ بزرگاں بھا نہ سکا
خضر وہ رہبر اک دنیا کا تیری منزل پا نہ سکا
تیری نازک بات میں بھی فنکار، کوئی ابہام نہیں
اس تخریب کے بھونڈے دور میں تیرا فن ناکام نہیں
وہ تیرا اسلوبِ بیاں وہ فکر کی گرمی کیا کہیے
غرقِ فلسفہ وہ تیری گفتار کی نرمی کیا کہیے
تیرا فن پیغامِ بقا ہے موت کا یہ پیغام نہیں
فکر و عمل کا جام ہے تیرا خوابِ فنا کا جام نہیں

236

Jagan Nath Azad

Art is perception fresh, seasoned with passionate thought,
It is the vibrant ocean wave in the heart of tempest lodged.

You rebelled against convention, invented novel ways of thought,
You refused to imitate the poetic masters of the past.

Your deep, discerning mind is not content with antique lore,
Even Khizar, the fabled guide, couldn't comprehend your goal.

Your subtle mode of speech eschews all false conceit,
Even in this debunking age, you make a strong appeal.

Ah, your enviable style, and your soul-stirring thought !
On top of it, your rich content, couched in accents slow and
soft !

Invigorating is your Muse, a call for fuller life,
It urges us to think and act, and overcome the wish to die.

Tu ne batayaa fun jaddat hai, fikar-o-nazar ka auj hai fun,
Toofaanon ki rooh mein jo raqsanda ho woh mauj hai fun.

Jin par chale funkaar puraane, tu ne woh raste chhor diye,
Shair mein jitne bhi taqleed ke but the, tu ne tor diye.

Tu woh ahle-e-nazar tha jisko deen-e-bazurgaan bha na saka,
Khizar, woh rahbar ik duniya ka, teri manzil paa na saka.

Teri naazuk baat mein bhi, funkar, koi abhaam nahin.
Is takhreeb ke bhaunde daur mein, tera fun nakaam nahin.

Woh tera asloob-e-bayaan, woh fikar ki garmi kya kahieye,
Gharq-e-phalsafa woh teri guftaar ki narmi kya kahieye.

Tera fun paighaam-e-baqa hai, maut ka yeh paighaam nahin,
Fikar-o-amal ka jaam hai tera, khwab-e-fana ka jaam nahin.

237

جگن ناتھ آزاد

کل رات کو

کامراں یوں تھا مرا بختِ جواں کل رات کو
جھک رہا تھا یرے دَر پہ آسماں کل رات کو

حسن جب تھا عشق کے گھر میہماں کل رات کو
اٹھ چکا تھا ہر حجابِ درمیاں کل رات کو

کاش بن جاتی حیاتِ جاوداں کل رات کو
کس قدر محبوب تھی عمرِ رواں کل رات کو

دِل اگر تنہا مرا تیر و کماں کی زد پہ تھا
دِل کی زد پر بھی رہے تیر و کماں کل رات کو

بن رہی تھیں حلقہ میری زیست کے گرداب کا
کچھ سنہری کچھ رو پہلی چوڑیاں کل رات کو

رک گئی تھیں یوں زمین و آسماں کی گردشیں
نیم شب پر شام ہی کا تھا گماں کل رات کو

کیا خبر کیوں حسن کی فرمائشوں کے باوجود
عشق نے چھیڑی نہ اپنی داستاں کل رات کو

صبح پھر لانے کو ہے لمبی جدائی کا پیام
یہ بھی اک آواز آئی ناگہاں کل رات کو

238

Jagan Nath Azad
Yesternight

Yesternight my lucky star was shining dazzling bright,
The sky was kneeling at my door, descending from Elysian
  heights.

Beauty was a welcome guest at the house of love,
Every veil betwixt the two had suddenly vaporised.

How I wish this passing night could somehow be eternalised,
Lovely seemed the life ephemeral; Oh, I wished to hold it tight.

If my heart was the target of her bow and dart,
Her darts too couldn't escape my heart's congregated might.

Yesternight my very breath, as it rose and fell,
Was encaged in clinking bangles, glancing gold and white.

The earth and sky, yesternight, their motion did suspend,
It seemed like the early eve, far advanced though was night.

Know not why, though beauty prompted, love didn't respond
Didn't tell its tale of love, didn't relate its plight.

"Be prepared for parting now, the dawn approacheth nigh."
Unawares came the voice, and broke the spell of night.

Kaamraan yoon tha mira bakht-e-jawan kal raat ko,
Jhuk raha tha mere dar pe aasmaan kal raat ko;

Husn jab tha ishq ke ghar maihmaan kal raat ko,
Uth chuka tha har hijab-e-darmiaan kal raat ko.

Kaash ban jaati hayaat-e-jaaawedaan kal rat ko,
Kis qadar mahboob thi umr-e-rawan kal raat ko.

Dil agar tanha mira teer-o-kamaan ki zad pe tha,
Dil ki zad par bhi rahe teer-o-kaman kal raat ko.

Ban rahin thin halqa meri zeest ke girdaab ka,
Kuchh sunahri, kuchh rupahli choorian kul raat ko.

Ruk gaeen thin yoon zameen-o-aasmaan ki gardishen,
Neem shab par shaam hi ka tha gumaan kal raat ko.

Kya khabar kyon husn ki farmaaishon ke ba-wajood,
Ishq ne chheri na apni daastaan kal raat ko.

Subah phir laane ko hai lambi judaai ka payaam,
Yeh bhi ik aawaaz aai nagahaan kal raat ko.

جگن ناتھ آزادؔ

خواب کی طرح سے ہے یاد

خواب کی طرح سے ہے یاد کہ تم آئے تھے

جس طرح دامنِ مشرق میں سحر ہوتی ہے

ذرّے ذرّے کو تجلّی کی خبر ہوتی ہے

اور جب نور کا سیلاب گزر جاتا ہے

رات بھر ایک اندھیرے میں بسر ہوتی ہے

کچھ اسی طرح سے ہے یاد کہ تم آئے تھے

جیسے گلشن میں دبے پاؤں بہار آتی ہے

پتّی پتّی کے لیے لے کے نکھار آتی ہے

اور پھر وقت وہ آتا ہے کہ ہر موجِ صبا

اپنے دامن میں لیے گرد و غبار آتی ہے

کچھ اسی طرح سے ہے یاد کہ تُم آئے تھے

جس طرح محوِ سفر ہو کوئی ویرانے میں

اور رستے میں کہیں کوئی خیاباں آجائے

چند لمحوں میں خیاباں کے گزر جانے پر

سامنے پھر وہی دنیائے بیاباں آجائے

کچھ اسی طرح سے ہے یاد کہ تم آئے تھے

240

Jagan Nath Azad
You Came Like A Dream

You came like a dream, I trow;

When the dawn springs from East,
Every grain begins to glow,
But when the surging light recedes,
Dark sweeps across the globe;
This is how you came, I trow.

As the vernal breezes blow,
Life stirs in bud and rose,
But when the time of fall arrives,
Dusty winds despoil the grove.
This is how you came, I trow.

As a traveller in the wilds,
Comes upon a blooming grove,
Soon it endeth, and he finds,
Again by wilderness enclosed.
This is how you came, I trow.

Khwab ki tarah se hai yaad ke tum aae the

Jis tarah daaman-e-mashriq mein sehar hoti hai,
Zarre zarre ko tajalli ki khabar hoti hai,
Aur jab noor ka sailaab guzar jaata hai,
Raat bhar ek andhere mein basar hoti hai.
Kuchh isi tarah se hai yaad ke tum aae the.

Jaise gulshan mein dabe paaon bahaar aati hai,
Patti patti ke lieye le ke nikhaar aati hai,
Aur phir waqt woh aata hai ke har mauj-e-saba,
Apne daaman mein lieye gard-o-ghubaar aati hai.
Kuchh isi tarah se hai yaad ke tum aae the.

Jis tarah mahw-e-safar ho koi weeraane mein,
Aur raste mein kahin koi khayabaan aa jaae,
Chand lamhon mein khayabaan ke guzar jaane par,
Saamne phir wohi duniya-e-bayabaan aa jaae.
Kuchh isi tarah se hai yaad ke tum aae the.

Kaifi Azmi
(b. 1918)

KAIFI AZMI (b. 1923)

Kaifi Azmi was born at Mijwan in Azam Garh district (U.P.). His father, Sayed Fateh Hussain Rizwi, was a tehsildar. He was a religious man, religious to the extent of being superstitious. He would attribute the death of his four daughters in infancy to the wrath of God, kindled by his impious act of giving Western education to his elder sons. To make amends for his sin he decided that his youngest child, Kaifi (whose full name is Athar Hussain Kaifi) be given Islamic education in a religious school. Consequently, Kaifi was admitted to *Sultan-ul- Madaras* at Lucknow, a place which was not to the liking of the budding revolutionary. Because of his anti-estalishment activity Kaifi was expelled from the school, and he had to complete his education through self-study at home. He passed several examinations in Urdu, Arabic and Persian from Lucknow and Allahabad Universities.

Like Ali Sardar Jafri, his elder contemporary, Kaifi is a pioneering poet of the Progressive Movement in Urdu. Sajjad Zaheer describes him as the "red rose" of Urdu poetry. His poetical works comprise *Jhankaar, Aakhir-e-Shab,* and *Aawara Sijde.* Many poems of these volumes are included in his poetical collection, *Sarmaaya.* Kaifi was awarded Padma Shree for *Aawara Sijde,* which award he later returned in protest against the Government of India's Urdu policy.

Though he has also written *ghazals,* Kaifi is primarily a poet of the *nazm.* It is remarkable that inspite of his life-long commitment to a political ideology, Kaifi has maintained his link with the well-springs of love and lyricism, as is evidenced in his poems, *Ek Lamha* and *Tasawwur.*

It may be mentioned as a footnote that Kaifi is the father of the famous actress, Shabana Azmi.

243

کیفیؔ اعظمی

تصوّر

یہ کس طرح یاد آ رہی ہو، یہ خواب کیسا دکھا رہی ہو

کہ جیسے سچ مچ نگاہ کے سامنے کھڑی مسکرا رہی ہو

یہ جسم نازک، یہ نرم باہیں، حسین گردن، سڈول بازو

شگفتہ چہرہ، سلونی رنگت، گھنیرا جوڑا، سیاہ گیسو

نشیلی آنکھیں، رسیلی چتون، دراز پلکیں، مہین ابرو

تمام شوخی، تمام بجلی، تمام مستی، تمام جادو

ہزاروں جادو جگا رہی ہو یہ

یہ خواب کیسا دکھا رہی ہو

گلابی لب، مسکراتے عارض، جبیں کشادہ، بلند قامت

نگاہوں میں بجلیوں کی جھل مل، اداؤں میں شبنمی لطافت

دھڑکتا سینہ، مہکتی سانسیں، نوامیں رس، انکھڑیوں میں امرت

ہمہ حلاوت، ہمہ ملاحت، ہمہ ترنّم، ہمہ نزاکت

لچک لچک گنگنا رہی ہو

یہ خواب کیسا دکھا رہی ہو

244

Kaifi Azmi
Imagination (Tasawwur)

How you flash across my mind, conjuring up a pleasant dream.
There you stand, as if real, with your smiling face agleam.

Graceful neck and rounded arms, slender frame, exquisitely
   shaped,
Sable locks, knotted bun, lovely hue and blooming face,

Drunken eyes, attractive brow, long eyelashes flashing rays,
Lightning-filled, mischief-raising, intoxicating, magic gaze !

What a vision you create,
With your wonder-working face !

Tall stature, ample brow, rosy lips and smiling face,
Lightning-like the eyes sparkle, dewy soft is every grace.

Heaving bosom, fragrant breath, honeyed voice, ambrosial gaze,
Sweet and saucy, all together, melody mixed with gentle grace.

There you stand and hum a tune, as your body undulates,
What a vision before my eyes, doth your lovely shape create !

Yeh kis tarah yaad aa rahi ho, yeh khwab kaisa dikha rahi ho,
Ke jaise sach much nigah ke saamne khari muskra rahi ho,

Yeh jism naazuk, yeh narm baahen, haseen gardan, sadol baazu,
Shagufta chehra, saloni rangat, ghanera joora, seaah gaisu !

Nasheeli aankhen, raseeli chitwan, daraaz palken, maheen abroo,
Tamam shokhi, tamam bijli, tamam masti, tamam jaadoo !

Hazaaron jaadoo jaga rahi ho,
Yeh khwab kaisa dikha rahi ho.

Gulabi lab, muskarate aaraz, jabeen kushada, buland qamat,
Nigah mein bijlion ki jhilmil, adaaon mein shabnami litafat.

Dharakta seena, mehkti saansen, nawa mein ras, ankhrion mein amrit,
Hama halawat, hama malahat, hama tarahhum, hama nazakat !

Luchuk lachak gunguna rahi ho,
Yeh khwab kaisa dikha rahi ho !

کیفیؔ اعظمی

تو کیا مجھے تم جلا ہی لو گی، گلے سے اپنے لگا ہی لو گی

جو پھول جوڑے سے گر پڑا ہے، تڑپ کے اس کو اٹھا ہی لو گی

بھڑکتے شعلوں، کڑکتی بجلی سے میر اخر من بچا ہی لو گی

گھنیری زلفوں کی چھاؤں میں مسکرا کے مجھ کو چھپا ہی لو گی

کہ آج تک آزما رہی ہو

یہ خواب کیسا دکھا رہی ہو

نہیں محبّت کی کوئی قیمت جو کوئی قیمت ادا کرو گی

وفا کی فرصت نہ دے گی دینا، ہزار عزمِ وفا کرو گی

مجھے بھلنے دو رنجؔ و غم سے سہارے کب تک دیا کرو گی

جنوں کو اتنا نہ گد گداؤ، پکڑ لوں دامن تو کیا کرو گی

قریب بڑھتی ہی آ رہی ہو

یہ خواب کیسا دکھا رہی ہو

Kaifi Azmi

Will you then ignite my spark, will you hug me to your heart ?
Will you pick up with a start, the flower fallen from your locks ?
Will you really save my stores from the raging thunder-blast,
Will you hide me in the shade of your rich and sable locks ?
Perhaps you merely test my faith,
What a dream you create !

Love is something beyond price, how will then you compensate ?
You may make a thousand pledges, the world will surely shake
    your faith,
Withdraw your kind compassion, let me live with griefs and
    aches,
Tickle thee not my frenzic passion, lest I fold thee in embrace !
Nearer every minute you grow,
What a vision you invoke !

Tau kya mujhe tum jila hi logi, gale se apne laga hi logi,
Jo phool joore se gir para hai, tarap ke us ko utha hi logi

Bharakte sholon, karakti bijli se mera khirman bacha hi logi,
Ghaneri Zulfon ki chhaaon mein muskara ke mujh ko chhupa hi logi,

Ke aaj tak aazmarahi ho,
Yeh khwab kaise dikha rahi ho !

Nahin mahabbat ki koi qeemat, jo koi qeemat ada karogi,
Wafa ki fursat na degi duniya, hazaar azm-e-wafa karogi;

Mujhe bahlne do ranj-o-ghum se, sahare kab tak diya karogi,
Janoon ko itna na gudgudaao, pakar loon daaman tau kya karogi ?

Qarib barhti hi aa rahi ho,
Yeh khwab kaisa dikha rahi ho !

کیفیؔ اعظمی

ایک لمحہ

جب بھی چوم لیتا ہوں ان حسین آنکھوں کو

سو چراغ اندھیرے میں جھلملانے لگتے ہیں

خشک خشک ہونٹوں میں جیسے دل کھنچ آتا ہے

دل میں کتنے آئینے تھرتھرانے لگتے ہیں

پھول کیا، شگوفے کیا، چاند کیا، ستارے کیا

سب رقیب قدموں پہ سر جھکانے لگتے ہیں

ذہن جاگ اٹھتا ہے روح جاگ اٹھتی ہے

نقش آدمیت کے جگمگانے لگتے ہیں

لو نکلنے لگتی ہے مندروں کے سینے میں

دیوتا فضاؤں میں مسکرانے لگتے ہیں

رقص کرنے لگتی ہیں مورتیں اجنتا کی

مدّتوں کے لب بستہ غار گانے لگتے ہیں

پھول کھلنے لگتے ہیں اجڑے اجڑے گلشن میں

تشنہ تشنہ گیتی پر ابر چھانے لگتے ہیں

لمحہ بھر کو یہ دنیا ظلم چھوڑ دیتی ہے

لمحہ بھر کو سب پتھر مسکرانے لگتے ہیں

248

Kaifi Azmi
One Moment (Ek Lamha)

When I kiss those lovely eyes,
A hundred tapers begin to glow,
The famished lips come alive,
The gleaming heart reflects a rose,
Buds and blossoms, moon and stars,
Like humbled rivals bend and bow;
The soul uplifts, reason awakes;
Marks of glory crown the brow;
Shrines emit a sacred light
The gods smile and bless the globe;
Ajanta's figures begin to dance,
The muted caves with music roar,
Faded gardens spring to life,
The rain quells the thirst below;
For one moment the earth reforms,
And even the stones acquire a glow.

Jab bhi choom leta hoon in haseen aankhon ko,
Sau chirag andhere mein jhilmalaane lagte hain,
Khushk khushk honton mein jaise dil khinch aata hai,
Dil mein kitne aaeene thartharaane lagte hain,
Phool kya, shigofe kya, chaand kya, sitaare kya,
Sab raqib qadmon par sar jhukane lagte hain;
Zehan jaag uthta hai, rooh jaag uthti hai,
Naqsh aadmeet ke jagmagane lagte hain;
Lau nikalne lagti hai mandiron ke seene se,
Devta fizzaon mein muskarane lagte hain,
Raqs karne lagti hain moorten Ajanta ki,
Mudatton ke lab-basta ghaar gaane lagte hain,
Phool khilne lagte hain ujre ujre gulshan mein,
Tishna tishna geeti par abr chaane lagte hain,
Lamha bhar ko yeh duniya zulm chhor det hai,
Lamha bhar ko sab paththar muskarane lagte hain.

اب تم آغوشِ تصوّر میں بھی آیا نہ کرو

مجھ سے بکھرے ہوئے گیسو نہیں دیکھے جاتے

سرخ آنکھوں کی قسم ، کانپتی پلکوں کی قسم

تھرتھراتے ہوئے آنسو نہیں دیکھے جاتے

اب تم آغوشِ تصوّر میں بھی آیا نہ کرو

چھوٹ جانے دو جو دامانِ وفا چھوٹ گیا

کیوں یہ لغزیدہ خرامی یہ پشیماں نظری

تم نے توڑا نہیں رشتہِ دل ٹوٹ گیا

اب تم آغوشِ تصوّر میں بھی آیا نہ کرو

میری آہوں سے یہ رخسار نہ کملا جائیں

ڈھونڈتی ہوگی تمھیں رس میں نہائی ہوئی رات

جاؤ کلیاں نہ کہیں سیج کی مرجھا جائیں

اب تم آغوشِ تصوّر میں بھی آیا نہ کرو

میں اس اجڑے ہوئے پہلو میں بٹھالوں نہ کہیں

لبِ شیریں کا نمک عارضِ نمکیں کی مٹھاس

اپنے ترسے ہوئے ہونٹوں میں چرالوں نہ کہیں

250

Kaifi Azmi
Don't Visit Me Now, My Love

Don't visit me now, my love, even in my dreams and thoughts,
I can't bear to see your hair dishevelled, defiled,
I swear by your quivering lashes, by your ruddy eyes,
How can I see your tears trembling all the while ?
Don't visit me now, my love, even in my dreams and thoughts,
It matters not if we have from the path of love strayed,
Why regret in vain, my dear, why this penitent gaze ?
Yours is not the fault at all, if broken lie the bonds of faith.
Don't visit me now, my love even in my dreams and thoughts
Lest your cheeks lose their colour confronted with my sighs.
Lest the flowers on your bed exhaust their breath and die,
Go now, it waits for you, the honey-drenched night !
Don't visit me now, my dear, even in my dreams and thoughts,
Lest I should enfold you in my yearning lap,
Lest my famished lips steal the honey of your salted cheeks,
Lest I kiss your luscious lips and drain them of their sap.

Ab tum aaghosh-e-tasawwur mein bhi aaya na karo,
Mujh se bikhre hur gaisu nahin dekhe jaate,
Surkh aankhon ki qasam, kaanpti palkon ki qasam,
Thartharaate hue aansoo nahin dekhe jaate.
Ab tum aaghosh-e-tasawwur mein bhi aaya na karo,
Chhoot jaane do jo damaan-e-wafa chhoot gaya,
Kyon yeh laghzeeda kharaami, yeh pashemaan nazri,
Tum ne tora nahin, rishta-e-dil toot gaya.
Ab tum aaghosh-e-tasawwur mein bhi aaya na karo,
Meri aahon se yeh rukhsaar na kumla jaaen,
Dhoondati hogi tumhen ras mein nahaai hui raat,
Jaao, kalian na kahin sej ki murjha jaaen.
Ab tum aaghosh-e-tasawwur mein bhi aaya na karo,
Main is ujre hue pahloo mein bitha loon na kahin,
Lab-e-sheerein ka namak, aaraz-e-numkeen ki mithaas,
Apne tarse hue honton mein chura loon na kahin.

Qateel Shifai
(b. 1919)

QATEEL SHIFAI (b. 1919)

Qateel Shifai, whose real name is Aurang Zeb Khan, was born at Hari Pur in Hazara district (Pakistan), on December 24, 1919. Because of adverse circumstances at home, Qateel's education didn't go beyond High School. After unsuccessfully trying to make his living through small business ventures, he joined the film world and settled down as a song writer at Lahore, earning thereby both money and fame. Poetry came to him quite naturally. There was no poet among his ancestors, no tradition of poetry in his family. At first he used to take his compositions to Shifa Khanpuri—from whom he derives his poetic name, "Shifai"—for correction and advice. Later he also sought guidance from Ahmed Nadeem Qasmi who was his friend and neighbour. But he depended, by and large, on his own instinctive taste and talent, and on constant practice in writing.

Qateel is essentially a lyrical poet, lyrical and musical even in his *nazms* and narrative poems. He is a specialist of romantic songs and lyrics, of "geet", marked for its lilt and melody. Ahmed Nadeem Qasmi, in his Introduction to Qateel's poetical collection, *Hariaali*, has placed him with the distinguished "geet" writers of his time, with men like Hafeez, Saghir, Inderjeet Sharma, and Taaseer. Farigh Bukhari calls him the king of melody, which he creates with a sensitive selection of words, and their artistic arrangement.

Qateel's famous collections include *Guftgoo, Aamokhta, Pairahan, Gajar, Hariaali* and *Jaltarang*.

قتیل شفائی

بازار

جوانی، حسن، غمزے، عہد، پیماں، قہقہے، نغمے

رسیلے ہونٹ، شرمیلی نگاہیں، مرمریں باہیں

یہاں ہر چیز بکتی ہے

خریدارو!

بتاؤ کیا خریدو گے؟

بھرے بازو، گٹھیلے جسم، چوڑے آہنی سینے

بلکتے پیٹ، روتی غیر تیں، سہمی ہوئی آہیں

یہاں ہر چیز بکتی ہے

خریدارو!

بتاؤ کیا خریدو گے؟

زبانیں، دل، ارادے، فیصلے، جاں بازیاں، نعرے

یہ آئے دن کے ہنگامے، یہ رنگا رنگ تقریریں

یہاں ہر چیز بکتی ہے

خریدارو!

بتاؤ کیا خریدو گے؟

Qateel Shifai
Bazaar

Youth, beauty, glances, guffaws, pledges, promises, songs,
Juicy lips, coy looks, marble wrists and arms,
Everything is here for sale,
What will you, O buyers,
Take ?

Rounded arms, solid bodies, broad steely chests,
Crying bellies, humbled brows, sighs deep-suppressed,
Everything is here for sale,
What will you, O buyers,
Take ?

Decisions, slogans, sacrifices, resolutions, hearts and tongues,
The daily outbursts of riots, multi-shaded eloquence,
Everything is here for sale,
What will you, O buyers,
Take ?

Jawani, husn, ghumze, ahd, paimaan, qahqahe, naghme,
Raseele hont, sharmeeli nigaahen, marmareen baanhen,
Yahaan har cheez bikti hai !
Kharidaaro !
Bataao kya kharidoge ?

Bhare baazoo, gatheele jism, chaure aahni seene,
Bilakte pet, roti ghairaten, sahmi hui aahen,
Yahaan har cheez bikti hai !
Kharidaaro !
Bataao kya kharidoge ?

Zabaanen, dil, irrade, faisle, jaan baaziaan, naare,
Yeh aae din ke hangaame, yeh ranga rang taqreeren,
Yahaan har cheez bikti hai !
Kharidaaro !
Bataao kya kharidoge ?

قتیلؔ شفائی

صحافت، شاعری، تنقید، علم و فن، کتب خانے

قلم کے معجزے، فکر و نظر کی شوخ تصویریں،

یہاں ہر چیز بکتی ہے

خریدارو!

بتاؤ کیا خریدو گے؟

اذانیں، سنکھ، حجرے، پاٹھ شالے، ڈاڑھیاں، قشقے،

یہ لمبی لمبی تسبیحیں، یہ موٹی موٹی مالائیں،

یہاں ہر چیز بکتی ہے

خریدارو!

بتاؤ کیا خریدو گے؟

علی الاعلان ہوتے ہیں یہاں سودے ضمیروں کے

یہ وہ بازار ہے جس میں فرشتے آ کے بک جائیں

یہاں ہر چیز بکتی ہے

خریدارو!

بتاؤ کیا خریدو گے؟

256

Qateel Shifai

Poems, critiques, books and knowledge, hints on culture, science
    and art,
Miracles of pen and page, vignettes of skilful thought,
Everything is here for sale,
What will you, O buyers,
Take ?

Prayers, conchs, cells and schools, beards, sacred marks,
Long-stringed rosaries, beads, loud and large,
Everything is here for sale,
What will you, O buyers,
Take ?

Consciences are put to auction in this public mart,
"Tis the place where angels too can be sold and bought,
Everything is here for sale,
What will you, O buyers,
Take ?

Sahaafat, shaairy, tanqeed, ilem-o-fun, kutab khaane,
Qalam ke mojze, fikar-o-nazar ki shokh tasweeren,
Yahaan har cheez bikti hai !
Kharidaaro !
Bataao kya kharidoge ?

Azaanen, sankh, hujre, paath shaale, daarhiaan, qashqe,
Yeh lambi lambi tasbeehen, yeh moti moti maalaaen,
Yahaan har cheez bikti hai !
Kharidaaro !
Bataao kya kharidoge ?

Ali-ul-ilaan hote hain yahaan saude zameeron ke,
Yeh woh bazaar hai jis mein farishte aake bik jaaen,
Yahaan har cheez bikti hai !
Kharidaaro !
Battao kya kharidoge ?

قتیل شفائی

نگارِ سیمیں

سینہ ہے کہ بلّور کی شفّاف صراحی

باہیں ہیں کہ برسات کے مہکے ہوئے نالے

رفتار ہے یا صبح کا گاتا ہوا جھونکا

زلفیں ہیں کہ اڑتے ہوئے پُر پیچ بگولے

یہ قد جو کھنک جائے تو کانسی کا کٹورا

یہ آنکھ جو اٹھے تو ستاروں کو بھی چھولے

اے رقص کے انداز میں چلتی ہوئی دیوی

آ میں تجھے آنکھوں کے شوالے میں سجالوں

آ وقت کے صحراؤں میں بھٹکی ہوئی دیوی

آ میں تجھے راہوں کے دھندلکے سے بچالوں

آ حرص کے شعلوں میں جھلستی ہوئی رانی

آ میں تجھے بھیگی ہوئی پلکوں میں چھپالوں

یہ رات یہ حالات یہ تاریک اجالے

ایسے میں ترے جسم کو چین نہ آسکے گا

اِک روز پگھل کر کسی آغوش میں کھو جا

ہر رات کا جلنا تجھے راس نہ آسکے گا

258

Qateel Shifai
Gleaming Beauty (Nigaar-e-Seemein)

Is this the breast or crystal clear shaped into a flask,
Are these your arms or rainy runnels scattering scent unasked ?
Is it your gait or morning breeze in murmuring whiffs discharged,
Are these your locks or swirling gusts blowing thick and fast ?
The stately stature, touched and teased, would tinkle like a bowl
    of bronze,
The downcast eyes, if upraised, would touch the shining stars.

O goddess poised on dancing feet,
Let me enshrine you in my eyes,
O ascetic strayed in deserts dark,
Let me flood your path with light.
O queen consumed by fire of lusts,
Hide thee in my tearful eyes.

This night, this state of life, these lights spreading dark,
Where can you find repose in this state distraught ?
Better melt down at once into someone's arms,
Burning inch by inch at night would do you deadly harm.

Seena hai ke billaur ki shaffaf suraahi,
Baanhen hain ke barsaat ke mahke hue naale,
Raftaar hai ya subah ka gaata hua jhonka,
Zulfen hain ke urte hue purpech bagole,
Yeh qad jo khanak jaae tau kaansi ka katora,
Yeh aankh jo uth jaae tau sitaaron ko bhi chhoo le.

Ai raqs ke andaaz mein chalti hui devi,
Aa main tujhe aankhon ke shivaale mein sajaloon,
Ai waqt ke sahraaon mein bhatki hui jogan,
Aa main tujhe raahon ke dhundalke se bacha loon,
Ai hiras ke sholon mein jhulasti hui raani,
Aa main tujhe bheegi hui palkon mein chhipa loon.

Yeh raat, yeh huluut, yeh taareek ujaale,
Aise mein tire jism ko chain aa na sakega,
Ik roz pighal kar kisi aaghosh mein kho ja,
Har raat ka jalna tujhe raas aa na sakega.

Sahir Ludhianvi
(1922-1980)

ABDUL HAIE SAHIR LUDHIANVI (1922-1980)

Sahir was the son of a rich landlord who was known for his love of pleasure and luxury. He had married several times, but had only one male issue—Sahir—to perpetuate his race. After he fell out with Sahir's mother, the landord father went to the court to claim guardianship of his son. But Sahir preferred to stay with his mother, foregoing a life of luxury in favour of a more contented and independent life. Sahir had his education at Government College, Ludhiana. As a mark of respect for the poet, a street in Ludhiana has been named Sahir Ludhianvi Road.

Though Sahir gave ample evidence of his poetic abilities right in his college days, he really shot into fame with the publication, in 1943, of his poetical collection, *Talkhiaan*. Two poems of this volume, "Taj Mahal" and "Chakley," became immediately popular. Apart from the enlightened, radical vision which informs his poetry, Sahir wins our admiration through his simple, unaffected style, which, without breaking with the tradition of 'qafia' and 'radif', seems fresh and forceful. Whether he writes *nazms*, *ghazals*, or songs, he articulates his thoughts with bold sincerity and clarity.

Goaded by economic necessity, Sahir went to Bombay and started writing film songs. He made a signal contribution towards improving the quality of these songs, which were later published under the title, *Gaata Jaae Banjaara*. Mention must also be made of his long poem, *Parchhaaian*, which is an anti-war document. However, despite his success as a writer of the film songs, the public had to wait in vain for another collection as authentic and as artistic as *Talkhiaan*. The insistent note of pain and pathos heard in his poetry may be attributed both to the general and personal frustration. Sahir was a lonely man who remained unmarried all his life. He died in 1980 at the age of 58.

ساحر لدھیانوی

اسی دوراہے پر

اب نہ ان اونچے مکانوں میں قدم رکھوں گا

میں نے اک بار یہ پہلے بھی قسم کھائی تھی

اپنی نادار محبّت کی شکستوں کے طفیل

زندگی پہلے بھی شرمائی تھی جھجھلائی تھی

اور یہ عہد کیا تھا کہ بہ ایں حالِ تباہ

اب کبھی پیار بھرے گیت نہیں گاؤں گا

کسی چلمن نے پکارا بھی تو بڑھ جاؤں گا

کوئی دروازہ کھلا بھی تو پلٹ آؤں گا

پھر ترے کانپتے ہونٹوں کی فسوں کار ہنسی

جال بننے لگی بنتی رہی ،بنتی ہی رہی

میں کھنچا تجھ سے مگر تو مری راہوں کے لیے

پھول چنتی رہی چنتی رہی چنتی ہی رہی

262

Sahir Ludhianvi
At This Crossing (Isi Daurahe Par)

I will never step again inside these mansions tall,
Earlier too I had made the self-same resolve;

When my poor love disdained,
Had made me shiver in shock and shame.

And I had pledged that in this plight,
I won't sing of love or of happy life,

If someone calls, I won't reply,
If a door is found ajar, I'll pass it by.

But your tremulous lips asmile,
Wove a web to snare my life,

I tried and tried to avoid your bowers,
But you paved my path with flowers;

Ab na in oonche makaanon mein qadam rakhoonga,
Main ne ik baar yeh pehle bhi qasam khaai thi,

Apni nadaar mahabbat ki shikaston ke tufail,
Zindagi pehle bhi sharmaai thi, jhunjlaai thi;

Aur yeh ahd kiya tha ke ba-een-haal-e-tabaah,
Ab kabhi payaar bhare geet nahin gaaoonga,

Kisi chilman ne pukara bhi tau barh jaaoonga,
Koi darwaaza khula bhi tau palat aaoonga.

Par tire kaanpte honton ki fasoonkaar hansi,
Jaal bun-ne lagi, bunti rahi, bunti hi rahi;

Main khincha tujh se magar tu miri raahon ke lieye,
Phool chunti hi rahi, chunti hi rahi.

ساحرؔ لدھیانوی

برف برسائی مرے ذہن و تصوّر نے مگر
دل میں اک شعلۂ بے نام سا لہرا ہی گیا
تیری چپ چاپ نگاہوں کو سلگتے پا کر
میری بیزار طبیعت کو بھی پیار آ ہی گیا
اپنی بدلی ہوئی نظروں کے تقاضے نہ چھپا
میں اس انداز کا مفہوم سمجھ سکتا ہوں
تیرے زرکار دریچوں کی بلندی کی قسم
اپنے اقدام کا مفہوم سمجھ سکتا ہوں
اب نہ ان اونچے مکانوں میں قدم رکھوں گا
میں نے اک بار یہ پہلے بھی قسم کھائی تھی
اسی سرمایہ و افلاس کے دوراہے پر
زندگی پہلے بھی شرمائی تھی جھنجھلائی تھی

264

Sahir Ludhianvi

Despite my reason's icy blast,
A little flame did seize my heart,

Seeing your quietly smouldering eyes,
I couldn't help but yield and fall.

Do not your changed intentions hide,
I can see through your disguise,

By your golden doors I swear,
I have at last my fate realised.

I will never step again inside these mansions tall,
Earlier too I had made the self-same resolve,

When at this crossing of wealth and want,
My life was put to shame and shock.

Baraf barsaai mire zehan-o-tasawwur ne magar,
Dil mein ik shola-e-be naam sa lahra hi gaya,

Teri chup chaap nigaahon ko sulagte pa kar,
Meri bezaar tabiat ko bhi pyaar aa hi gaya.

Apni badli hui nazron ke taqaaze na chhupa,
Main is andaaz ka mafhoom samajh sakta hoon,

Tere zarkaar dareechon ki bulandi ki qasam,
Apne iqdaam ka maqsoom samajh sakta hoon.

Ab na in oonche makaanon mein qadam rakhoonga,
Main ne ik baar yeh pahle bhi qasam khaai thi,

Isi sarmaaya-o-iflaas ke daurahe par,
Zindagi pahle bhi sharmaai thi, jhunjalaai thi.

ساحؔر لدھیانوی

فنکار

میں نے جو گیت ترے پیار کی خاطر لکھے

آج ان گیتوں کو بازار میں لے آیا ہوں

آج دکان پہ نیلام اٹھے گا اِن کا

تو نے جن گیتوں پہ رکھی تھی محبت کی اساس

آج چاندی کی ترازو میں تلے گی ہر چیز

میرے افکار مری شاعری میرا احساس

جو تری ذات سے منسوب تھے ان گیتوں کو

مفلسی جنس بنانے پہ اتر آئی ہے

بھوک تیرے رخِ رنگیں کے فسانوں کے عوض

چند اشیائے ضرورت کی تمنّائی ہے

دیکھ اس عرصہ گہہِ محنت و سرمایہ میں

میرے نغمے بھی مرے پاس نہیں رہ سکتے

تیرے جلوے کسی زردار کی میراث سہی

تیرے خاکے بھی مرے پاس نہیں رہ سکتے

آج ان گیتوں کو بازار میں لے آیا ہوں

میں نے جو گیت ترے پیار کی خاطر لکھے

Sahir Ludhianvi
The Artist (Fankaar)

The songs that I had written for you,
I have, my love, now put on sale;
The songs nurtured by your love,
Will now be auctioned or retailed,
My thoughts and feelings, and my art,
Will now be weighed in silver scales.

The songs rooted in your love,
Want has turned to "goods for sale",
Hunger-pressed I have to sell,
For basic needs my amorous tales.

In this world of toil and wealth,
Even my songs are not my own,
Your charms belong to someone else,
Your images too, lo, I disown.

I have, my love, put on sale,
The songs which your love exhale.

Main ne jo geet tire payaar ki khaatir likhe,
Aaj un geeton ko bazaar mein le aaya hoon

Aaj dukaan pe neelaam uthe ga unka,
Tu ne jin geeton pe rakhi thi mahabbat ki asaas,
Aaj chaandi ke taraazoo mein tulegi har cheez,
Mere ifkaar, miri shaairy, mera ahsaas.

Jo tiri zaat se mansoob the un geeton ko,
Muflisi jins banaane par utar aai hai,
Bhook, tere rukh-e-rangeen ke fasaanon ke iwaz,
Chand ishia-e-zaroory ki tamannaai hai.

Dekh is arsa gah-e-mehnat-o-surmaaya mein,
Mere naghme bhi mire paas nahin rah sakte,
Tere jalwe kisi zardaar ki meeraas sahi,
Tere khaake bhi mire paas nahin rah sakte.

Aaj un geeton ko bazaar mein le aaya hoon,
Main ne jo geet tire payaar ki khaatir likhe.

ساحرؔ لدھیانوی

اے شریف انسان

خون اپنا ہو یا پرایا ہو
نسلِ آدم کا خون ہے آخر
جنگ مشرق میں ہو کہ مغرب میں
امنِ عالم کا خون ہے آخر
بم گھروں پہ گریں کہ سرحد پر
روحِ تعمیر زخم کھاتی ہے
کھیت اپنے جلیں کہ اوروں کے
زیست فاقوں سے تلملاتی ہے
ٹینک آگے بڑھیں کہ پیچھے ہٹیں
کوکھ دھرتی کی بانجھ ہوتی ہے
فتح کا جشن ہو کہ ہار کا سوگ
زندگی میّتوں پہ روتی ہے
جنگ تو خود ہی ایک مسئلہ ہے
جنگ کیا مسئلوں کا حل دے گی
آگ اور خون آج بخشے گی
بھوک اور احتیاج کل دے گی

268

Sahir Ludhianvi
O, Gentlemen !

It may be ours or others' blood,
It's the blood of human race;
The war may rage in East or West,
It's the earth that runs to waste.

Bombs may fall on homes or fronts,
The spirit of life is crushed and mauled,
Whichever fields are bombed or burnt,
Life itself doth suffer and starve.

The tanks may roll on or retreat,
It's the womb of earth that bleeds,
Triumphal chant or sorrowing dirge,
Life the loss of life beweeps.

War is a riddle in itself,
Can it any riddle resolve ?
It comes carrying fire and blood,
Leaves behind the dogs of war.

Khoon apna ho ya parayaa ho,
Nasl-e-aadam ka khoon hai aakhir;
Jang mashriq mein ho ke maghrib mein,
Aman-e-aalam ka khoon hai, aakhir.

Bom gharon pe giren ke sarhad par,
Rooh-e-taameer zakhm khaati hai,
Khet apne jalen ke auron ke,
Zeest faaqon se tilmalaati hai.

Tank aage barhen ke peechhe haten,
Kokh dharti ki baanjh hoti hai,
Fateh ka jashan ho ke haar ka sog,
Zindagi mayyaton pe roti hai.

Jang tau khood hi ek masla hai,
Jang kya maslon ka hal degi !
Aag aur khoon aaj bakhshegi,
Bhook aur ihtiaaj kal degi.

ساحرؔ لدھیانوی

اس لیے اے شریف انسانوں
جنگ ٹلتی رہے تو بہتر ہے
آپ اور ہم سبھی کے آنگن میں
شمع جلتی رہے تو بہتر ہے
برتری کے ثبوت کی خاطر
خون بہانا ہی کیا ضروری ہے
گھر کی تاریکیاں مٹانے کو
گھر جلانا ہی کیا ضروری ہے
جنگ کے اور بھی تو میداں ہیں
صرف میدانِ کشت و خوں ہی نہیں
حاصلِ زندگی خرد بھی ہے
حاصلِ زندی جنوں ہی نہیں
آؤ ہم لوگ عصرِ نو کے لیے
اِک نئی طرزِ فکر عام کریں
امن اور جنگ ساتھ ساتھ چلیں
ایسی جنگوں کا اہتمام کریں

270

Sahir Ludhianvi

Therefore, O men of gentle birth !
Beware ! Avoid the course of war,
Keep the lamp of life alit,
In every home and every hearth.

Must you shed innocent blood,
To demonstrate how great you are ?
Must you burn the house itself,
To dispel the deepening dark ?

There are many wars to fight,
Besides the one that kills and maims,
Frenzy isn't the whole of life,
Wisdom, too, should hold its reins.

Let's for the coming race,
Devise a system terror-free,
Invent a new type of war,
Consistent with the joys of peace.

Is lieye, ai sharif insaanon,
Jang talti rahe tau behtar hai,
Aap aur hum sabhi ke aangan mein,
Shama jalti rahe tau behtar hai.

Bartari ke saboot ki khaatir,
Khoon bahaana hi kya zaroori hai,
Ghar ki taareekiyan mitaane ko,
Ghar jalaana hi kya zaroori hai ?

Jang ke aur bhi tau maidaan hain,
Siraf maidaan-e-kushat-o-khoon hi nahin,
Haasil-e-zindagi khirad bhi hai,
Haasil-e-zindagi janoon hi nahin.

Aao hum log asr-e-nau ke lieye,
Ik nai tarz-e-fikar aam karen,
Aman aur jang saath saath chalen,
Aisi jangaon ka ahtemaam karen.

271

Nasir Kaazmi
(1925-1972)

NASIR KAAZMI (1925-1972)

Nasir Kaazmi was born at Ambala in East Punjab, in 1925. After the creation of Pakistan in 1947 he moved to Lahore where he stayed till his death in 1972. It was in Lahore that he developed and displayed his poetic genius, and earned the reputation of being a front-ranking poet. He also worked as editor of the Urdu journals, *Auraq-e-Nau* and *Hamayun*, and enjoyed a good position in the world of letters, not only in Pakistan, but also in India and abroad. He has left behind him three collections of *ghazals*, "Barg-e-Nai", 1954, "Dewan", 1957, and "Pehli Baarish", published posthumously in 1975.

As a poet Nasir Kaazmi was influenced by Firaq Gorakhpuri among the moderns, and through him, by Mir Taqi Mir, the classical master of the ghazal. He shows this influence in the simplicity and musicality of his language, in the choice of shorter measures for his *ghazals*, and in his controlled expression of melancholic thought and feeling. He has no fondness for the heavy, stylised diction, or for the stereotyped images and allusions. Consequently, he has become a great favourite with the *ghazal* singers in both parts of the Indian subcontinent. His *ghazals* give an effective expression to the twentieth century sense of world-weariness and disillusion. Both in his mood and mode of writing he is a lyricist *par excellence*, who can cast a spell on his readers by virtue of his sincerity, sweetness, and melancholia. Apparently artless and simple, Nasir Kaazmi makes skilful use of paradox and ambiguity to interpret the contraries of life.

ناصر کاظمی

☆

میں نے جب لکھنا سیکھا تھا

پہلے تیرا نام لکھا تھا

میں وہ صبرِ صمیم ہوں جس نے

بارِ امانت سر پہ لیا تھا

میں وہ اسمِ عظیم ہوں جس کو

جنّ و ملک نے سجدہ کیا تھا

تو نے کیوں میرا ہاتھ نہ پکڑا

میں جب رستے میں بھٹکا تھا

جو پایا ہے وہ تیرا ہے

جو کھویا تھا وہ بھی تیرا تھا

تجھ بن ساری عمر گزاری

لوگ کہیں گے تو میرا تھا

پہلی بارش بھیجنے والے

میں ترے درشن کا پیاسا تھا

274

Nasir Kaamzi
Ghazal

When I was learning to write,
At first your name I had inscribed.

I'm the undeterred courage,
Who chose the onerous trust of life.

I'm that respected name,
Whom jinns and seraphs deify.

Why didn't you hold my hand,
When I had strayed aside ?

What I got, came from you,
What I lost, you had supplied.

"You were mine," the people say,
Without you, yet, I lived my life.

O ye, the cause of maiden rain,
I was thirsting for your sight.

Main ne jab likhna seekha tha,
Pahle tera naam likha tha.

Main woh sabar-e-sameem hoon jis ne,
Baar-e-amaanat sar pe liya tha.

Main woh ism-e-azeem hoon jisko,
Jinn-o-malik ne sajda kiya tha.

Jo paaya hai woh tera hai,
Jo khoya woh bhi tera tha.

Tujh bin saari umr guzaari,
Log kahenge tu mera tha.

Pahli baarish bhejne waale,
Main tere darshan ka payaasa tha.

275

دِل میں اور تو کیا رکھا ہے

تیرا درد چھپا رکھا ہے

اتنے دکھوں کی تیز ہوا میں

دل کا دیپ جلا رکھا ہے

دُھوپ سے چہروں نے دنیا میں

کیا اندھیر مچا رکھا ہے

اس نگری کے کچھ لوگوں نے

دکھ کا نام دوا رکھا ہے

وعدۂ یار کی بات نہ چھیڑو

یہ دھوکا بھی کھا رکھا ہے

بھول بھی جاؤ بیتی باتیں

اِن باتوں میں کیا رکھا ہے

چپ چپ کیوں رہتے ہو ناصرؔ

یہ کیا روگ لگا رکھا ہے

276

Nasir Kaazmi

What else is there in my heart,
But your sorrow firmly locked.

I keep my inner lamp alight,
In the sorrow's blinding blast.

The sunny beauties of this world,
Have wrought a havoc, deadly dark.

Pain is given the name of potion,
By some denizens of this part.

Mention not the friend's promise,
I too was beguiled a lot.

What avails remembering them,
Forget about the things of past.

Nasir, what keeps you mum ?
What is it that ails your heart !

Dil mein aur tau kya rakha hai,
Tera dard chhipa rakha hai.

Itne dukhon ki tez hawa mein,
Dil ka deep jala rakha hai.

Dhoop se chehron ne duniya mein,
Kya andher macha rakha hai.

Is nagri ke kuchh logon ne,
Dukh ka naam dawa rakha hai.

Waada-e-yaar ki baat na chhero,
Yeh dhoka bhi kha rakha hai.

Bhool bhi jaao beeti baaten,
In baaton mein kya rakha hai.

Chup chup kyon rathe ho, Nasir,
Yeh kya rog laga rakha hai !

جب ذرا تیز ہوا ہوتی ہے

کیسی سنسان فضا ہوتی ہے

ہم نے دیکھے ہیں وہ سنّاٹے

جب ہر اک سانس صدا ہوتی ہے

دل کا یہ حال ہُوا تیرے بعد

جیسے ویران سَرا ہوتی ہے

رونا آتا ہے ہمیں بھی لیکن

اس میں توہینِ وفا ہوتی ہے

گلشنِ فکر کی منہ بند کلی

شبِ مہتاب میں وا ہوتی ہے

حادثہ ہے کہ خزاں سے پہلے

بوئے گل گل سے جدا ہوتی ہے

اک نیا دور جنم لیتا ہے

ایک تہذیب فنا ہوتی ہے

جب کوئی غم نہیں ہوتا ناصرؔ

بے کلی دل کی سوا ہوتی ہے

Nasir Kaazmi

When the wind becomes a gale,
What a silence then prevails !

We have known those silences,
When every breath becomes a wail.

In your absence the heart seems,
An empty inn, a barren waste !

We can also weep and wail,
But it denigrates our faith.

The folded bud of fledgling thought,
Beneath the moon unfolds its face.

What a chance, before the fall,
The rose is by its scent betrayed !

A new age takes its birth,
A civilisation passes away.

When no more of grief is there, Nasir,
Evermore the heart bewails !

Jab zara tez hawa hoti hai,
Kaisi sunsaan faza hoti hai.

Hum ne dekhe hain woh sannaate bhi,
Jab har ik saans sada hoti hai.

Dil ka yeh haal hua tere baad,
Jaise weeraan sara hoti hai.

Rona aata hai hamen bhi lekin,
Ismein tauheen-e-wafa hoti hai.

Gulshan-e-fikar ki munh band kali,
Shab-e-mahtaab mein wa hoti hai.

Haadisa hai ke khizaan se pehle,
Boo-e-gul gul se juda hoti hai.

Ik naya daur janam leta hai,
Ek tehzeeb fana hoti hai.

Jab koi ghum nahin hota, Nasir,
Be kali dil ki siwa hoti hai.

دلِ میں اِک لہر سی اٹھی ہے ابھی

کوئی تازہ ہوا چلی ہے ابھی

شور برپا ہے خانۂ دل میں

کوئی دیوار سی گری ہے ابھی

بھری دنیا میں جی نہیں لگتا

جانے کسی چیز کی کمی ہے ابھی

تُو شریکِ سخن نہیں ہے تو کیا

ہم سخن تیری خامشی ہے ابھی

یاد کے بے نشاں جزیروں سے

تیری آواز آ رہی ہے ابھی

شہر کی بے چراغ گلیوں میں

زندگی تجھ کو ڈھونڈتی ہے ابھی

سو گئے لوگ اس حویلی کے

ایک کھڑکی مگر کھلی ہے ابھی

تم تو یارو ابھی سے اٹھ بیٹھے

شہر میں رات جاگتی ہے ابھی

وقت اچھا بھی آئے گا ناصر

غم نہ کر زندگی پڑی ہے ابھی

Nasir Kaazmi

A wave-like something stirs my heart,
A fresh breeze is blowing across.

There is loud uproar within,
Perhaps a wall has fallen apart.

What could it be that I lack,
The bustling world attracts me not.

What matters if you do not talk,
Your silence speaks on your behalf.

From the memory's nameless isles,
Comes your voice, rich and soft.

In the city's lightless lanes,
Life is looking for your prop.

The inmates of the house have slept,
Yet a casement lies ajar.

You dear, have woken early,
The night in town is young and hot.

Nasir, better days will come,
You still have time, grieve ye not.

Dil mein ik lahar si uthi hai abhi,
Koi taaza hawa chali hai abhi.

Shor barpa hai khana-e-dil mein,
Koi deewar si giri hai abhi.

Bhari duniya mein ji nahin lagta,
Jaane kis cheez ki kami hai abhi.

Tu shareeke-sakhun nahin hai tau kya,
Hum sakhun teri khaamshi hai abhi.

Yaad ke be nishaan jazeeron se,
Teri aawaaz aa rahi hai abhi.

Sahr ki be chiragh galion mein,
Zindagi tujhko dhoondati hai abhi.

So gaye log is haveli ke,
Ek khirki magar khuli hai abhi.

Tum tau yaaro abhi se uth baithe,
Shahr mein raat jaagti hai abhi.

Waqt achha bhi aaega, Nasir,
Ghum na kar, zindagi pari hai abhi.

Balraj Komal
(b. 1928)

BALRAJ KOMAL (b. 1928)

Born in a village near Sialkot (Pakistan) on September 25, 1928, Balraj Komal migrated to India after the partition, and settled in Kalkaji, a township in South Delhi. He did his M.A. in English from Punjab University, and served for a long time as a teacher of English and as an Education Officer in the Directorate of Education, Delhi.

In spite of his preoccupation with teaching and administrative responsibilities, Balraj spared no effort in cultivating his poetic and literary talents. He began his literary career with the publication of his poem, *Akeli* in 1948, and has by now over a dozen books to his credit, the famous ones being, *Meri Nazmen* (1954), *Rishta-e-Dil* (1963), *Safar Mudaam Safar* I1969), *Nizad-e-Sang* (1975), *Parindon Bhara Aasmaan* (1984), and *Agla Warq* (1996).

A man of refined sensibility, Balraj is counted among the front ranking poets of the present age. He is also a perceptive critic, a scholar and a translator. Having been a student of English literature, he is particulary influenced by the 20th century writers like T.S. Eliot and Yeats. He is a representative of the new Urdu poetry which dispenses with the convention of "radif" and "qafia", and prefers, instead, the natural, conversational rhythms of blank verse or "free-verse". A specialist of the *nazm* Balraj makes effective use of symbolic imagery which, quite often, is easily accessible to an average, intelligent reader.

Balraj was awarded the Sahitya Akademi Award in 1984 for his collection of poems, *Parindon Bhara Aasmaan*.

بلراج کومل

خوشبو

ترے لمسِ دستِ حسیں کی

دل آویز خوشبو

تری انگلیوں سے

مری انگلیوں میں گزرتی ہوئی جب

ہتھیلی میں اتری تو میں نے

اسے دستِ تشنہ

میں کچھ اس طرح سے سمیٹا

کہ محفوظ کر لوں گا شاید ابد تک

میں اپنے لیے، صرف اپنے لیے

تیرا حسنِ شگفتہ، جمالِ درخشاں

گماں سے حسیں خواب تک، میں

نے محسوس تجھ کو کیا، پاؤں سے سر تلک ہو گیا میں منور

284

Balraj Komal
Fragrance (Khushboo)

When your hand's
Fragrant feel
Flowing from your fingers soft,
Filtering through my fingers,
Rested on my palm,
I clutched it in my eager grasp,
Hoping it will live and last
To become my sole preserve,
And your beauty beaming bright,
Shall for ever with me abide.
From fitful doubt to wishful dream,
From head to heel I gauged your being and felt suffused with light.

Tire lams-e-dast-e-haseen ki
Dil-aawez khushboo
Tiri ungalion se
Miri ungalion mein guzarti hui jab
Hatheli mein utri tau main ne
Ise dast-e-tishna
Mein kuchh is tarah se sameta
Ke mahfooz karloonga shaaid abad tak
Main apne lieye, siraf apne lieye
Tera husn-e-shagufta, jamaal-e-darakhshaan.
Gumaan se haseen khwaab tak, main
Ne mahsoos tujhko kiya, paaon se sar talak ho gaya main munawar

بلراج کومل

کفِ آرزو کھولتا ہوں

تجھے آج آزاد کرتا ہوں بوئے فروزاں

ہواؤں میں نیلی فضاؤں میں اڑتی پھر و آسمانوں کو چھولو

ستاروں پہ اترو

عناصر کو باہوں میں لے لو

کہ خوشبو ہو تم، رنگ ہو، روشنی ہو

سرِ موسمِ گل

سنورتی ہوئی، کیفِ جشن ادا میں

نئی زندگی ہو

Balraj Komal

Lo, I open out my palm
And set you free, O scented gleam !
Spread your wings in the sky, float across the blue inane,
Perch on stars or embrace
The elements of the sky and space,
For you are scented hue and light,
Herald of the vernal tide;
You represent the spring in bloom,
And a freshening wave of life !

Kaf-e-aarzoo kholta hoon
Tujhe aaj aazaad karta hoon boo-e-farozaan
Hawaaon mein neeli fazaaon mein urti phiro
Aasmaanon ko chhoo lo,
Sitaaron pe utro
Anaasar ko baahon mein le lo,
Ke khushboo ho tum, rang ho, roshni ho
Sar-e-mausam-e-gul
Sanwarti hui, kaif-e-jashan-e-ada mein
Nai zindagi ho.

بلراج کومل

صبا کے ہاتھ پیلے ہو گئے

صبا کے ہاتھ پیلے ہو گئے

میں ساعتِ سرشار میں

لاکھوں دعائیں

خوبصورت آرزوئیں

پیش کرتا ہوں

صبا ممنون ہے

لیکن زباں سے

کچھ نہیں کہتی

صبا اب روز و شب

دیوار و در تن پر سجاتی ہے

اب آنچل چھت کا سر پر اوڑھتی ہے

لمسِ فرشِ مرمریں سے

پاؤں کی تزئین کرتی ہے

وہ کہساروں، شگفتہ وادیوں، جھرنوں

چمکتے، نیلگوں، آکاش کے نغمے نہیں گاتی

صبا اب لالہ و گل کی طرف شاید نہیں آتی

Balraj Komal
Saba is Now a Wedded Bride

Saba is now a wedded bride.
At this felicitous hour
A thousand prayers and gentle throughts
Gush out from my heart.

Saba feels obliged,
But her lips
Are sealed.

Saba now adorns her body
Day and night with doors and walls,
Covers her head beneath the roof,
Scrubs her feet
On marble floors.
Of mountains, vales and rills,
Of azure sky and sparkling stars,
No more doth she sing.
Saba, maybe, no more frequents the flowery dales and hills.

Saba ke haath peele ho gaye
Main saait-e-sarshaar mein
Laakhon duaaen
Khoobsoorat aarzooen
Pesh karta hoon.

Saba mamnoon hai
Lekin zabaan se
Kuchh nahin kahti.
Saba ab roz-o-shab

Dewaar-o-dar tan par sajaati hai,
Ab aanchal chhat ka sar par orhti hai,
Lams-e-farsh-e-marmareen se
Paaon ki tazayyan karti hai
Woh kuhsaaron, shagufta waadion, jharnon,
Chamakte, neelgoon aakaash ke
Naghme nahin gaati
Saba ab lala-o-gul ki taraf shaaid nahin aati.

بلراج کومل

صبا شبنم ادا، تصویرِ پابستہ
درِ روزن میں آویزاں
حسیں نازک بدن
روشن مؤثر ساحلوں پر اب نہیں بہتی
صبا لب کھولتی ہے مسکراتی ہے
صبا سرگوشیوں میں
اب کسی سے کچھ نہیں کہتی

Balraj Komal

Saba of the dewy grace, a painted picture fixed and nailed,
Put up in the window frame,
A slender beauteous shape,
No longer doth freely flow
Along the open, sunlit shores,
Saba moves her lips and smiles,
But no more in whispers soft,
In anyone confides !

Saba shabnam ada, tasweer-e-pa basta,
Dar-e-rauzan mein aawezaan
Haseen naazuk badan
Roshan munawwar saahilon par ab nahin bahti,
Saba lab kholti hai, muskaraati hai,
Saba sargoshion mein
Ab kisi se kuchh nahin kahti.

بلراج کومل

سرکس کا گھوڑا

سپید اور بھورا

بدن کا چھریرا

وہ نٹ کھٹ بچھیرا

خرید آگیا گاؤں کے ایک میلے میں

لایا گیا ہنٹروں چابکوں کی پُر اسرار دنیا میں

سیکھے وہ انمول دلچسپ کرتب

اڑے چیختے پھیلتے دائروں میں

پھلانگیں سلگتی، بھیانک تکونیں

اٹھا کر پیٹھ پر رقص کرتے ہوئے بندروں کو

اشاروں کی آواز سن کے وہ لیکے

ہنسے ہنہنائے

تماشائیوں کو لبھائے رجھائے،

292

Balraj Komal
The Circus Horse

White and brown
Stout and strong
That fitful foal
From village fair bought
To the baffling world of goad and lash brought
In the screaming, widening rings trained,
Tamed and taught sundry tricks :
Jumping burning pits and cones,
Carrying dancing apes on back,
Dancing to the master's tune,
Neighing aloud
To entertain the crowds alaugh.

Saped aur bhoora
Badan ka chhareera,
Woh nat khat bachhera,
Kharida gaya gaon ke ik mele mein,
Laaya gaya hunteron chaabkon ki pur-asraar duniya mein;
Seekhe woh anmol dilchasp kartab
Ure cheekhte phailte daairon mein,
Phalaange sulagti, bhayaanak tikonen
Uthakar chale peeth par raqs karte hue bandaron ko,
Isharon ki aawaaz sunkar woh lapke,
Hanse, hinhinaae
Tamaashaaion ko lubhaae, rijhaae.

293

بلراج کومل

وہ سرکس کا گھوڑا

پریشان شہروں میں کرتب دکھاتا، تماشائیوں کے دلوں کو لبھاتا

تحیر ہنسی قہقہوں تالیوں کی فضاؤں میں برسوں چھلانگیں لگاتا

اسی گاؤں کے ایک میلے میں پہنچا

خرید آگیا تھا، جہاں سے وہ بچپن میں لیکن وہاں اب

وہاں کون تھا؟ اس کو پہچاننے والا کوئی نہیں تھا

Balraj Komal

That circus horse,
Wandering from town to town,
Enthralling the watcher's hearts,
Showing feats amid applause
Of clappings, tittering and guffaws,
Chanced to reach the village fair,
From where he was bought.
But none was there who knew him, none who recognised.

Woh circus ka ghora
Pareshaan shahron mein kartab dikhata, tamaashaaion ke dilon
Ko lubhata,
Tahayyur, hansi, qahqahon, taalion ki fazaaon mein barson
Chaalaangen lagata,
Isi gaon ke ik mele mein pahuncha,
Kharida gaya tha jahan se woh bachpan mein lekin wahan ab
Wahan kaun tha ? Us ko pahchaanane wala koi nahin tha.

Munir Niazi
(b. 1928)

MUNIR NIAZI (b. 1928)

Munir Niazi was born on April 19, 1928, at Khanpur, district Hoshiarpur (India). He had his schooling at Khanpur and Montgomery (now called Sahiwal), and college education in Bahawalpur, Lahore and Jullundhar. After the partition of India, he migrated to Pakistan, and settled, first in Montgomery, and finally in Lahore. In Montgomery he had started his own publishing house, *Arzhang Publishers*, and had also started his weekly journal called *Saat Rang*. In fact, the seven-coloured rainbow holds for Munir, as it does for D.H. Lawrence in his novel, "The Rainbow", a special appeal for its inherent symbolism of universal peace and love.

Munir has been associated for long with several literary societies and conference in the capacity of an adviser and organiser. He is by now a distinguished name in the world of letters, loved and admired on both sides of the Indian subcontinent. His poems have been widely circulated and translated into Chinese, Arabic, Persian, French and English. He has travelled extensively in America, Canada and Norway. He has produced fifteen books of Urdu poetry, and four books of Punjabi poetry. Some of his famous publications include *Tez Hawa aur Tanha Phool, Jangal mein Dhanak, Dushman ke Darmiaan Shaam, Mah-e-Munir, Chhe Rangeen Darwaaze, Aaghaaz-e-Zamistan mein Dobara,* and *Pehli Baat hi Akhri Thi.* In recognition of his literary achievement, he was honoured with "The Pride of Performance" by the Government of Pakistan. In his younger days Munir was a daring, handsome lad—a sportsman, a swimmer, a horse rider, a rifle shooter, and finally a sailor in the British India Navy which, however, he had deserted while on duty.

منیر نیازی

پہلی بات ہی آخری تھی

پہلی بات ہی آخری تھی

اس سے آگے بڑھی نہیں

ڈری ہوئی کوئی بیل تھی جیسے

پورے گھر پر چڑھی نہیں

ڈر ہی کیا تھا کہہ دینے میں

کھل کر بات جو دِل میں تھی

اس پاس کوئی اور نہیں تھا

شام تھی نئی محبّت کی

ایک جھجک سی ساتھ رہی کیوں

قرب کی ساعتِ حیراں میں

حد سے آگے بڑھنے کی

پھیل کے اس تک جانے کی

اس کے گھر پر چڑھنے کی

298

Munir Niazi
The First Thing Was The Last Thing
(Pahli Baat hi Akhri Thi)

The first thing was the last thing;
It didn't advance at all,
Like a creeper stunted, shrivelled,
It failed to climb the house and hall.
Where was the harm in speaking out
What at heart I longed to say ?
None else was within earshot,
Love was in its nascent stage.
Why then did I hesitate
To get close and intimate ?
Why didn't I break convention,
Why didn't extend my hands
And clamber over her roof and walls ?

Pahli baat hi aakhiri thi,
Us se aage barhi nahin,
Dari hui koi bel thi jaise
Poore ghar pe charhi nahin.
Dar hi kya tha kah dene mein
Khul kar baat jo dil mein thi,
Aas paas koi aur nahin tha,
Shaam thi nai mahabbat ki;
Ek jhijak si saath rahi kyon,
Qurb ki saait-e-hairaan mein
Had se aage barhne ki
Phail ke us tak jaane ki
Us ke ghar par charhne ki.

منیّر نیازی

پت جھڑ

وہ دِن بھی آنے والا ہے
جب تیری اِن کالی آنکھوں میں ہر جذبہ مٹ جائے گا
تیرے بال جنہیں دیکھیں ــــ تو
ساون کی گھنگھور گھٹائیں، آنکھوں میں لہراتی ہیں
ہونٹ رسیلے
دھیان میں لاکھوں پھولوں کی مہکار جگائیں
وہ دِن دور نہیں جب اِن پر
پت جھڑ کی رت چھا جائے گی
اور اِس پت جھڑ کے موسم کی
کسی اکیلی شام کی چپ میں
گئے دِنوں کی یاد آئے گی
جیسے کوئی کسی جنگل میں گیت سہانے گاتا ہے
تجھ کو پاس بلاتا ہے

Munir Niazi
The Fall (Pat Jhar)

That time is fast approaching,
When your black, beauteous eyes will be dead to all emotion.

Your hair that recall
Saawan's sable rainy clouds surging in the skiey dome,

Your luscious lips which exhale
Fragrance of a million blooms—
Will fall a prey to autumn gale,
In the not-too-distant day.

And in the silence deep
Of the autumn's lonely eve,
Memory of the bygone days,
Will ring like music soft and sweet;
As if someone in the forest sings for you and calls !

Woh din bhi aane waala hai,
Jab teri in kaali aankhon mein har jazba mit jaaega,

Tere baal, jinhen dekhen tau—
Saawan ki ghangor ghataaen aankhon mein lahraati hain,

Hont raseele
Dhayaan mein laakhon phoolon ki mahkaar jagaaen
Woh din door nahin jab in par
Pat jhar ki rut chha jaaegi,

Aur us pat jhar ke mausim ki
Kisi akeli shaam ki chup mein
Gaye dinon ki yaad aaegi
Jaise koi kisi jungle mein geet suhaane gaata hai.
—Tujh ko paas bulaata hai.

منیرؔ نیازی

☆

ڈر کے کسی سے چھپ جاتا ہے جیسے سانپ خزانے میں
زر کے زور سے زندہ ہیں سب خاک کے اس ویرانے میں

جیسے رسم ادا کرتے ہوں شہروں کی آبادی میں
صبح کو گھر سے دور نکل کر شام کو واپس آنے میں
نیلے رنگ میں ڈوبی آنکھیں کھلی پڑی تھیں سبزے پر
عکس پڑا تھا آسمان کا شاید اس پیمانے میں
دبی ہوئی ہے زیرِ زمیں اِک دہشت گنگ صداؤں کی
بجلی سی کہیں لرز رہی ہے کسی چھپے تہہ خانے میں
دل کچھ اور بھی سرد ہوا ہے شامِ شہر کی رونق سے
کتنی ضیا بے سود گئی ہے شیشے کے لفظ جلانے میں
میں تو منیرؔ آئینے میں خود کو تک کر حیران ہوا
یہ چہرہ کچھ اور طرح تھا پہلے کسی زمانے میں

302

Munir Niazi
Ghazal

As a snake, struck with fear, slinks into the treasure trove,
Denizens of this barren heath seek refuge in their gold.

As if to perform a ritual, people of this bustling town,
Quit their places every morn, and at eve homeward roll.

A pair of eyes bathed in blue lay unfolded on the green,
Seemed as if the azure sky lay reflected in their bowls.

The whirlwind of suppressed voices lies beneath the earth
subdued,
Flash and thunder, bound and chained, in some cavern fret and
roar.

The city come alive at night chills my heart all the more,
What a huge waste of light in lighting up these neon boards !

When I looked into the mirror, oh, I felt surprised,
This is not the face I saw, Munir, in the days of yore.

Dar ke kisi se chhup jaata hai jaise saanp khazaane mein,
Zar ke zor se zinda hain sab khaak ke is weeraane mein.

Jaise rasm ada karte hon shahron ki aabaadi mein,
Subah ko ghar se door nikal kar shaam ko waapis aane mein.

Neele rang mein doobi aankhen khuli pari thin sabze par,
Aks para tha aasmaan ka shaaid is paimaane mein.

Dabi hui hai zer-e-zameen ik dahshat gung sadaaon ki,
Bijli si kahin larz rahi hai kisi chhupe tah khaane mein.

Dil kuchh aur bhi sard hua hai sham-e-shahr ki raunaq se,
Kitni zia be sood gai hai sheeshe ke lafz jalaane mein.

Main tau Munir aaeene mein khud ka tak kar hairaan hua,
Yeh chehra kuchh aur tarah tha pahle kisi zamaane mein.

Ahmed Faraaz
(b. 1934)

AHMED FARAAZ (b. 1934)

Ahmed Faraaz was born in Kohat and educated at Islamia College, Peshawar. He is a front-ranking poet of Pakistan, a romantic rebel who, despite being a bureaucrat, has the courage to castigate oppression and injustice, defend democracy against dictatorship, and suffer persecution for the cause of love and liberty. He is an optimist asserting, like Shelley the British romantic, that "every night brings its own stars" (*Har raat sataare saath laati hai*). He can write with equal ease both the poetry of protest, and romantic lyrics of the type, *Ranjish hi sahi...*. He is admired both in Pakistan and India. He was honoured with the Firaq Award by the Government of India in 1987.

Ahmed Faraaz has held several positions of responsibility in the government institutions of Pakistan. In 1971 he was appointed the Resident Director of the National Centre, Peshawar. In 1975 he moved to the Ministry of Information, and in 1977 he was made the Project Director of the Pakistan Academy of Letters. He has also headed the National Book Foundation of Pakistan.

Among his poetical works may be mentioned *Tanha Tanha, Nayaaft, Pas-Andaaz Mausam, Dard Ashob, Shab Khoon, Mere Khwab Reza Reza,* and *Janaan Janaan.* His poems have been translated into several languages.

احمد فراز

رنجش ہی سہی دل ہی دکھانے کے لیے آ

آ پھر سے مجھے چھوڑ کے جانے کے لیے آ

کچھ تو مرے پندارِ محبت کا بھرم رکھ

تُو بھی تو کبھی مجھ کو منانے کے لیے آ

پہلے سے مراسم نہ سہی پھر بھی کبھی تو

رسم و رہِ دنیا ہی نبھانے کے لیے آ

کس کس کو بتائیں گے جُدائی کا سبب ہم

تُو مجھ سے خفا ہے تو زمانے کے لیے آ

اِک عمر سے ہوں لذّتِ گریہ سے بھی محروم

اَے راحتِ جاں مجھ کو رُلانے کے لیے آ

اب تک دلِ خوش فہم کو تجھ سے ہیں امیدیں

یہ آخری شمعیں بھی بجھانے کے لیے آ

Ahmed Faraaz

Even if you bear a grudge, come at least to tease my heart,
Prithee, visit me once again, come, if even to depart.

Prick not my pride of love, show a little regard,
You should also come sometime to assuage my heart.

Gone are the courtesies of yore, even then sometime,
Come at least for custom sake, to keep a nice facade.

Whom all to tell the cause of rift, how to answer all,
Accepted, you are cross with me, come for the world at large.

For long I have been denied even the luxury of tears,
Come at least to make me weep, O, my joy of heart !

Even now this gullible heart has pinned its hopes on you,
Blow out these last glimmering tapers, come, extinguish all !

Ranjish hi sahi, dil hi dukhaane ke lieye aa,
Aa phir se mujhe chhor ke jaane ke lieye aa.

Kuchh tau mire pindaar-e-mahabbat ka bharam rakh,
Tu bhi kabhi mujhko manaane ke lieye aa.

Pahle se maraasam na sahi, phir bhi kabhi tau,
Rasm-o-rah-e-duniya hi nibhaane ke lieye aa.

Kis kis ko bataaenge judaai ka sabab hum,
Tu mujh se khafa hai tau zamaane ke lieye aa.

Ik umr se hoon lazzat-e-giriya se bhi mahroom,
Ai raahat-e-jaan, mujhko rulaane ke lieye aa.

Ab tak dil-e-khush fahm ko tujh se hain umeedein,
Yeh aakhri shammein bhi bujhaane ke lieye aa.

احمد فراز

ہم پیار سکھانے والے ہیں

تم اپنے عقیدوں کے نیزے نیزے

ہر دِل میں اتارے جاتے ہو

ہم لوگ محبّت والے ہیں

تم خنجر کیوں لہراتے ہو

اس شہر میں نغمے بہنے دو

بستی میں ہمیں بھی رہنے دو

ہم پالنہار ہیں پھولوں کے

ہم خوشبو کے رکھوالے ہیں

تم کس کا لہو پینے آئے

ہم پیار سکھانے والے ہیں

اس شہر میں پھر کیا دیکھو گے

جب حرف یہاں مر جائے گا

جب تیغ پہ لے کٹ جائے گی

جب شعر سفر کر جائے گا

Ahmed Faraaz
We Preach The Creed of Love
(Hum Pyar Sikhane Waale Hain)

Why ram ye down our hearts
Bayonets of your sharp beliefs ?
We are simple loving folks
Sheathe your sword, let us be.

Let this town be music-steeped,
Let us also live and breathe !

We preserve the blooms and buds,
Fragrance of the wind and breeze,
You are bent on shedding blood,
"Love for all", is what we preach.

What will then be left to see,
When the word is put to sleep,
When you slay the melody sweet,
And the Muse is made to flee ?

Tum apne aqeedon ke neze neze
Har dil mein utaare jaate ho
Hum log mahabbat waale hain
Tum khanjar kyon lahraate ho

Is shahr mein naghme bahne do
Basti mein hamen bhi rahne do.

Hum palanhaar hain phoolon ke
Hum khushboo ke rakhwaale hain,
Tum kis ka lahoo peene aae,
Hum pyaar sikhane waale hain.

Is shahr mein phir kya dekhoge
Jab harf yahaan mar jaaega,
Jab tegh pe lai kat jaaegi,
Jab shair safar kar jaaega.

احمد فراز

جب قتل ہوا سر سازوں کا

جب کال پڑا آوازوں کا

جب شہر کھنڈر بن جائے گا

پھر کس پر سنگ اٹھاؤ گے

اپنے چہرے آئینوں میں

جب دیکھو گے ڈر جاؤ گے

Ahmed Faraaz

When lyre strings broken lie,
And not a single voice is nigh,
When everywhere the ruins stretch,
Whom will then you stone to death ?
Your own image in the glass,
Will give you scares, make you start !

Jab qatal hua sur saazon ka,
Jab kaal para aawazon ka,
Jab shahr khandar ban jaaega,
Phir kis par sang uthaoge,
Apne chehre aaeenon mein,
Jab dekhoge dar jaaoge.

احمد فراز

☆

سارا شہر بلکتا ہے

پھر بھی کیسا سکتا ہے

ہر کوئی تصویر نما

دور خلا میں تکتا ہے

گلیوں میں بارود کی بو

یا پھر خون مہکتا ہے

سب کے بازو نخ بستہ

سب کا جسم دہکتا ہے

ایک سفر وہ ہے جس میں

پاؤں نہیں دل تھکتا ہے

تیرا بچھڑنا جانِ غزل

شہرِ غزل کا مقطع ہے

Ahmed Faraaz

The whole city weeps and wails,
What a silence yet prevails !

Everyone is a painted picture,
Staring vacant into space.

The streets reek with smoking bullets,
Or the smell of blood exhale.

Every arm is cold and numb,
Yet the bodies are ablaze.

There is a journey in which the heart,
And not the feet suffers travail.

Leaving you, O, life of lyric,
Completes the edifice of my wail.

Saara shahr bilakta hai,
Phir bhi kaisa sakta hai.

Har koi tasweer numa,
Door khila mein takta hai.

Galion mein baarood ki boo,
Ya phir khoon mahkta hai.

Sab ke bazoo yakh basta,
Sab ka jism dahakta hai.

Ek safar woh hai jis mein,
Paaon nahin dil thakta hai.

Tera bichharna, jaan-e-ghazal,
Shahr-e-ghazal ka maqta hai.

313

احمد فرازؔ

دوسری ہجرت

پھر مرے مکّہ سے پیغمبر

ہجرت کر کے چلا گیا ہے

اور اب پھر سے

کعبہ کے رَم خوردہ بت

اصنامِ طلائی

اپنی اپنی مسند پر آ بیٹھے ہیں

سچ کا لہو

ان کے قدموں میں

عنّابی قالین کی صورت بچھا ہوا ہے

کمخوابی خیموں کے اندر

بزمِ حریفاں پھر سجتی ہے

کِذب و ریا کی دَف بجتی ہے

Ahmed Faraaz
The Second Flight (Doosri Hijrat)

The Prophet has once again,
Migrated from my Mecca.
Once again
The fugitive idols,
The golden-robed gods of Kaaba,
Have to their seats returned.

The blood flowing from truth slain
At their feet lies spread,
Like a carpet, purple-red.

Inside their velvet tents
The rivals festive sessions hold,
Deceit and cunning trumpets blow.

Phir mire Mecca se paighamber
Hijrat karke chala gaya hai
Aur ab phir se
Kaaba ke rum-khurda but
Isnaame-e-tilaai
Apni apni masnid par aa baithe hain.

Sach ka lahu
Unke qadmon mein
Unnaabi qaaleen ki soorat bichha hua hai

Kamkhwabi khaimon ke andar
Bazm-e-harifaan phir sajti hai
Kizab-o-ria ki daf bajti hai.

تھکا گیا ہے مسلسل سفر اداسی کا
اور اب بھی ہے مرے شانے پہ سر اداسی کا

وہ کون کیمیا گر تھا کہ جو بکھیر گیا
ترے گلاب سے چہرے پہ زر اداسی کا

مرے وجود کے خلوت کدے میں کوئی تو تھا
جو رکھ گیا ہے دیا طاق پر اداسی کا

میں تجھ سے کیسے کہوں یارِ مہرباں میرے
کہ تو علاج نہیں مری ہر اداسی کا

یہ اب جو آگ کا دریا مرے وجود میں ہے
یہی تو پہلے پہل تھا شرر اداسی کا

نہ جانے آج کہاں کھو گیا ستارۂ شام
وہ میرا دوست مرا ہمسفر اداسی کا

فراز دیدہِ پُر آب میں نہ ڈھونڈ اسے
کہ دل کی تہہ میں کہیں ہے گہر اداسی کا

Ahmed Faraaz

Ceaseless travel, sad and weary, has tired me out complete,
Even now depression sits pressing down my shoulder seat.

Who was the alchemist who has thus splashed,
The yellow dust of gold on your rosy cheeks ?

Someone surely must be there hidden inside my lonely being,
Who has left inside my heart a dolorous lamp, shaded deep.

O, my friend, kind and dear, how should I explain,
You are not a cure for sorrows that my vitals eat.

The flood of fire that has now overwhelmed my restless being,
Is the spark that had once glimmered pale and weak.

I do not know where to-day the evening star is lost —
The sharer of my lonesome voyage, comrade of my tedious
    beats.

Do not look for it Faraaz, in your overflowing eyes,
Perhaps the gem of sorrow lies hidden in your cavern deep.

Thaka gaya hai musalsal safar udaasi ka,
Aur ab bhi hai mire shaane pe sar udaasi ka.

Woh kaun keemiaa gar tha ke jo bakher gaya,
Tire gulab se chehre pe zar udaasi ka.

Mire wajood ke khilwat kade mein koi tau tha,
Jo rakh gaya hai diya taaq par udaasi ka.

Main tujh se kaise kahun yaar-e-mehrbaan mere,
Ke tu ilaaj nahin meri har udaasi ka.

Yeh ab jo aag ka darya mire wajood mein hai,
Yehi tau pehle pahl tha sharar udaasi ka.

Na jaane aaj kahan kho gaya sitaara-e-shaam,
Woh mera dost mira humsafar udaasi ka.

Faraaz, deeda-e-pur aab mein na dhoond use,
Ke dil ki tah mein kahin hai guhar udaasi ka.

317

Makhmoor Saeedi
(b. 1938)

MAKHMOOR SAEEDI (b. 1938)

Makhmoor Saeedi was born in Tonk (Rajasthan) on December 31, 1938. His father, Ahmed Khan Nazish, and his grandfather were accredited Urdu poets, and it is from them that he seems to have inherited his poetic taste. Makhmoor received his schooling in Tonk, and higher education at Agra University. He wrote his first poem in the year 1948, when he was only ten years of age. Among the early influences on his poetic development may be mentioned Dr. Mohammed Iqbal, Akhtar Sheeraani, and Josh Malihabadi.

Makhmoor is a versatile writer who has displayed his talent not only in the field of poetry, but also in the areas of literary criticism, journalism, and translation. He is at present working as Assistant Editor of *Aiwan-e-Urdu* and *Umang*. He has several poetical collections to his credit, including *Sabrang, Seah bar Safed, Awaaz ke Jism, Wahid Mutakallam,* and *Aate Jaate.* The poems in this anthology have been culled from his latest book, *Deewar-o-Dar ke Darmiaan.*

Makhmoor is a poet of love and beauty, but of love that is real and earthy, an affair as much of the heart and soul as of hands, eyes, ears and lips. Being a creature of the modern age, he has his share of world-weariness, and a sense of alienation. Man, he feels is a lonely wayfarer in the crowd.

Makhmoor can acquit himself equally well both in the conventional mode of rhymed verse, and in blank verse and free-verse. In addition to writing *ghazals* and *nazms,* he has written *rubaies, qitas, dohas* and *geets.*

319

مخمور سعیدی

یادیں خوابوں کی دشمن ہیں

یادیں

بھولے بسرے کل کی یادیں

اِک اِک گزرے پل کی یادیں

'آج' میں 'کل' کے رنگ کچھ اتنے گہرے بھر دیں

حال کو اکثر ماضی کر دیں

بیت چکا جو ۔۔۔ اس کی جگ مگ دھند میں کھو کر

رہ جائے 'موجود' اچانک 'غائب' ہو کر

آنکھ سے اوجھل اِک اِک منظر

اپنی جھلک کچھ یوں دکھلائے

سامنے آنکھوں کے اب کیا ہے؟ نظر نہ آئے

یادیں ۔۔۔ کل کی یادیں

اِک اِک پل کی یادیں

دیدہ و دل پر جادو جانے کیسا کر دیں

320

Makhmoor Saeedi
Memories Are The Foe of Dreams
(Yaaden Khwabon Ki Dushman Hain)

Memories !..........................
Memories of long-forgotten days,
Of every moment that has slipped, of hours gone away,
Which inject into "to-day" the colours fast of yesterday,
Convert the present into past,
Flush it in its rosy rays,
Banish present out of sight,
Dissipate what meets our gaze;
Conjure up the vanished gleam,
And confound the living scenes,
Leave our sense of sight amazed.

Memories of yesterdays !
Of every moment flown away,
What a spell they exercise, on our hearts as well as eyes !

Yadeen...............

Bhoole bisre kal ki yaaden,
Ik ik guzre pal ki yaaden,
Aaj mein kal ke rang kuchh itne gahre bhar den,
Haal ko aksar maazi kar den,
Beet chuka jo-us ki jag mag dhund mein kho kar,
Rah jaae "maujood" achanak "gaaib" ho kar,
Aankh se ojhal ik ik manzir,
Apni jhalak kuchh yoon dikhlaae,
Saamne aankhon ke ab kya hai, nazar na aae.

Yaaden, kal ki yaaden,
Ik ik pal ki yaaden
Deeda-o-dil par jaadoo jaane kaisa kar den.

مخمورؔ سعیدی

بھیڑ میں اکثر تنہا کر دیں
آج جو اپنے ہیں، ہو جائیں بے گانے سے
جانے پہچانے چہرے سب انجانے سے
زندہ حقائق افسانے سے

یادیں ۔۔۔۔ خوابوں کی دشمن ہیں
تازہ رشتوں کی الجھن ہیں
آنے والے کل کی جانب
بڑھتے قدموں کو یوں روکیں
جیسے پرانے ملنے والے
دوست نیا تم کوئی بنانا چاہو تو ۔۔۔۔ ٹوکیں

Makhmoor Saeedi

Make us lonely in the crowd,
Turn our present friends to strangers,
Alienate familiar sights,
Make reality legend-like,
Memories are the foe of dreams,
New links they don't esteem,
Hold us back when we try,
To launch upon a forward drive,
As an old friend may thwart,
The growth of new friendly ties.

Bheer mein aksar tanha kar den
Aaj jo apne, ho jaaen begaane se,
Jaane pahchaane chehre sab anjaane se
Zinda haqaaiq afsaane se !

Yaaden—khwabon ki dushman hain
Taaza rishton ki uljhan hain
Aane waale kal ki jaanib—
Barhte qadmon ko yoon rokein
Jaise puraane milne waale
Dost naye tum koi banaana chaaho tau—tokein.

☆ مخمورؔ سعیدی

پَر تو دھنک میں کس کا، گھٹاؤں میں کون ہے؟
موسم کی دِل نواز اداؤں میں کون ہے؟
چاروں طرف کھلے ہوئے پھولوں میں کس کا رنگ؟
مہکی ہوئی چمن کی فضاؤں میں کون ہے؟
تیغِ ستم سے کٹتی زبانوں پہ کس کا نام؟
سہمے ہوئے دِلوں کی دعاؤں میں کون ہے؟
سورج، ستارے، چاند، سبھی آئینہ بکف
شام و سحر کے چہرہ نماؤں میں کون ہے؟
کِس کے فروغ سے ہے معانی کی آب و تاب؟
لفظوں کی بے چراغ گھٹاؤں میں کون ہے؟
فِکر و نظر کا خواب، تو لفظ و بیاں کی آس
خاموشیوں میں کون، صداؤں میں کون ہے؟
مجرم تو کائناتِ ظہورِ انا کا میں
لپٹا ہوا انا کی رداؤں میں کون ہے؟
مخمورؔ اِس سفر میں اسے ساتھ لے کے چل
کب سے بھٹک رہا ہے، خلاؤں میں، کون ہے؟

324

Makhmoor Saeedi

Whose glow informs the rainbow, who in clouds resides,
Who inspires the gladsome weather and its playful tides ?

Who has lent glint and gloss to the vernal buds and blooms,
Who has filled the garden air with fragrance rarified ?

Whose name the tongues repeat when with tyrant't sword oppressed,
Whom do they pray for help, the hearts petrified ?

Holding mirror in hand they stand—the sun and moon and stars,
Who inspires these self-exhibitors, rulers of the day and night ?

Who imparts strength and richness to the meanings deep ambushed,
Who in dark, wordy caverns, hides his visage burning bright ?

Flight of fancy, reach of mind, the hope to find the word to match,
Who inhabits the heart of silence, or in sound and stir resides ?

I'm the sinner accused of suffering from the egotistic pride,
But who sits enwrapped in ego, who behind its veil doth hide ?

Take him, too, along with you in your voyage, Makhmoor,
Someone has been roaming wild in the dreary voids of life.

Partau dhanak mein kiska, ghataaon mein kaun hai,
Mausim ki dil nawaaz adaaon mein kaun hai ?

Chaaron taraf khile hue phoolon mein kis ka rang,
Mahki hui chaman ki fazaaon mein kaun hai.

Tegh-e-sitam se kat-ti zabaanon pe kiska naam,
Sahme hue dilon ki duaaon mein kaun hai ?

Sooraj, sitaare, chaand, sabhi aaeena ba-kaf,
Lafzon ki be chiragh gufaaon mein kaun hai ?

Kis ke farogh se hai maani ki aab-o-aab,
Shaam-o-sahar ke chehra numaaon mein kaun hai?

Fikar o nazar ka khwab, tau lafaz-o-bayaan ki uus,
Khaamoshion mein kaun, sadaaon mein kaun hai ?

Mujrim tau kaainaat-e-zahoor-e-ana ka main,
Lipta hua ana ki ridaaon mein kaun hai ?

Makhmoor is safar mein use saath le ke chal,
Kab se bhatak raha hai khilaaon mein, kaun hai ?

Nida Fazli
(b. 1938)

NIDA FAZLI (b. 1938)

Nida Fazli (full name : Muqtada Hasan Fazli), son of Murtaza Hasan Baaidi, was born in Delhi on October 12, 1938. A university-educated poet possessing a B.A. degree, Nida has been engaged for a long time in writing songs for the Indian cinema, which has given him fame and money. But Nida is not a mere film-song writer producing poems and tunes to order; he is a genuine poet with a modern sensibility, and an ability to build poetry out of his own conviction and observations.

The poems included in this anthology contain sufficient evidence of his sensitivity and modernity, and his concern with the relatively less explored regions of the human mind. These poems deal with the problem of the breakdown of communication in personal relationships, the problem of loneliness and alienation, and the dilemma of wearing or not wearing one's heart on the sleeve—all of which are typically modern concerns. These poems are also modern in their style, for they reject the traditional lyrical style, and adopt, instead, a more speech-like manner and the free-verse form that is more suited to the thoughtful, analytical and dramatic needs of the speaker. "I like Nida's poetry from the core of my heart", says Firaq Gorakhpuri. "In his hands poetry becomes pure poetry breaking the confines of the ancient and the modern."

Nida's publications include *Lafzon ka Pul* (a poetical collection, *Mulaqaaten* (character-sketches), and *Mor Nautch* (collected works) published in 1978.

ندا فاضلی
لفظوں کا پُل

مسجد کا گنبد سونا ہے

مندر کی گھنٹی خاموش

جز دانوں میں لپٹے

سارے آدرشوں کو

دیمک کب کی چاٹ چکی ہے

رنگ

گلابی

نیلے

پیلے

کہیں نہیں ہیں

تم اس جانب

میں اس جانب

بیچ میں میلوں گہرا اغار _____ لفظوں کا پُل ٹوٹ چکا ہے

تم بھی تنہا _____ میں بھی تنہا

Nida Fazli
The Bridge of Words (Lafzon Ka Pul)

The dome of mosque is silence-steeped,
Silent too the temple gong;
The ideals lying securely shelved,
Have since been eaten by the ants.
Colours :
Pink
Blue
Yellow,
Are nowhere in sight;
You, on that end,
I, on this,
Betwixt, a cavern deep and wide.
Broken lies the bridge of words,
Both are lonely,
You and I.

Masjid ka gumbad soona hai
Mandir ki ghanti khaamosh,
Juzdaanon mein lipte
Saare aadarshon ko
Deemak kab ki chaat chuki hai;
Rang
Gulaabi
Neele
Peele,
Kahin nahin hain
Tum us jaanib
Main is jaanib
Beech mein meelon gahra ghaar
Lafzon ka pul toot chuka hai,
Tum bhi tanha
Main bhi tanha.

ندا فاضلی

فضا خاموش ہے

بہت سے کام ہیں :

بنجر زمین پر گھاس پھیلا دیں

درختوں کو اگائیں، ڈالیوں پر پھول مہکا دیں

پہاڑوں کو قرینے سے لگائیں، چاند لٹکائیں

خلاؤں کے سروں پر نیلگوں آکاش پھیلا دیں

ستاروں کو کریں روشن، ہواؤں کو گتی دے دیں

پُھدکتے پتھروں کو پنکھ دے کر نغمگی دے دیں

لبوں کو مسکراہٹ انکھڑیوں کو روشنی دے دیں

سڑک پر ڈولتی پر چھائیوں کو زندگی دے دیں

فضا خاموش ہے !

تم آؤ تو تخلیق ہو دنیا

میں اتنے سارے کاموں کو اکیلا کر نہیں سکتا !

Nida Fazli
The Air is Motionless and Still (Faza Khaamosh Hai)

Many a task remains to do ....!
To cover the barren land with grass,
To grow the plants and make them bloom,
Re-arrange the mountains wild and deck them with the moon,
Fill the gaps with azure sky,
Lend speed and light to air and stars,
Invest the vaulting stones with wings,
Illume the lips with smiles, re-kindle the vision,
Instil into the wandering shades a new spirit of life.

The air is motionless and still......
Only when you come can I the world reform,
All alone I cannot so many tasks perform.

Bahut se kaam hain............!

Banjar zameen par ghaas phaila den
Darakhton ko mahkaaen, daalion par phool mahka den,
Pahaaron ko qareene se lagaaen, chaand latkaaen,
Khilaaon ke siron par neelgoon aakaash phaila den,
Sitaaron ko karen roshan, hawaaon ko gati de den,
Phudakte paththron ko pankh de kar naghmagi de den,
Labon ko muskraahat, ankhrion ko roshni de den,
Sarak par dolti parchhaaion ko zindagi de den.

Faza khaamish hai.................!
Tum aao tau takhleeq ho duniya,
Main itne saare kaamon ko akela kar nahin sakta.

331

ندا فاضلی

نقابیں

نیلی، پیلی، ہری، گلابی
میں نے سب رنگین نقابیں
اپنی جیبوں میں بھر لی ہیں
اب میرا چہرہ ننگا ہے
بالکل ننگا
اب میرے ساتھی ہی مجھ پر
پگ پگ پتھر پھینک رہے ہیں
شاید وہ
میرے چہرے میں اپنے چہرے دیکھ رہے ہیں

پیدائش

بند کمرہ
جھٹپٹا سا اندھیرا
اور
دیواروں سے ٹکراتا
میں
منتظر ہوں اپنی پیدائش کے دن کا
اپنی ماں کے پیٹ سے نکلا ہوں جب سے
میں خود اپنے پیٹ کے اندر پڑا ہوں

332

Nida Fazli
Masks (Niqaaben)

Pink, blue, green and yellow,
All the colourful masks
I have in my pockets shoved.
Now my face is naked,
Utterly unmasked.
Now my friends at every step
Are casting stones at me.
Their own faces in my face,
They perhaps now see.

Neeli, peeli, hari, gulaabi,
Main ne sab rangeen niqaaben
Apni jebon mein bhar li hain
Ab mera chehra nanga hai
Bilkul nanga
Ab mere saathi hi mujh par
Pag pag paththar phaink rahe hain
Shaaid woh
Mere chehre mein apne chehre dekh rahe hain.

Birth (Paidaaish)

A closed room,
Dimly-lighted,
And
I
Foundering against its walls,
The hour of my birth await.
Since I got released from my mother's womb,
In my own belly-pit I lie entombed

Band kamra
Chhutpatata sa andhera
Aur
Deewaaron se takraata hua
Main
Muntezir hoon apni paidaaish ke din ka
Apni maan ke pet se nikla hoon jab se
Main khud apne pet ke andar para hoon.

Kishwar Naheed
(b. 1940)

KISHWAR NAHEED (b. 1940)

Kishwar Naheed is an outstanding poetess of Pakistan. A bold and intelligent woman, she holds an M.A. degree in Economics, which she had obtained from Punjab University, Lahore in 1961. She is also a prolific writer. Five volumes of her poetry were published from Pakistan, and two from India. Several of her poems have been published in foreign countries. She has also written eight books for children, and has won the prestigious UNESCO award for children's literature. Among her famous translated works is the translation of Simon de Beauvoir's *Second Sex* She has done a good deal of editorial work, and has been associated with Pakistani journals such as *Pak Jamhooriat,* and *Adab-e-Lateef.* Her love of children is only matched by her concern for women, whose welfare and emancipation have always been dear to her heart. Her long poem, "Asin Burian We Loko !" is a moving comment on the plight of women in the present ritual-ridden and male-dominated society.

Kishwar Naheed's poetical works include *Lab-e-Goya, Be Naam Musafat, Nazmen, Galiaan, Dhoop, Darwaaze,* and *Malaamton Ke Darmiaan,* all of which were later collected under the title, *Fitna Saamaani-e-Dil* (1985). Her poetry generally speaking, is symbolic, suggestive, and thoughtful.

Kishwar Naheed has described her story in her prose autobiography, *Buri Aurat ki Katha* (The Story of a Bad Woman), which, in fact, is the story of all women in the present society, where "goodness is brushed aside, and meanness flaunted with pride."

کشور ناہیدؔ

سلاسل

رشتہٴ جان ہے

فقط سانس کی زنجیر کا نام

رشتہٴ دِل ہے

فقط آنکھ کی تحریر کا نام

رشتہٴ خوں ہے

فقط اپنی ہی تصویر کا نام

رشتہٴ غم ہے

فقط حلقہٴ دِ لگیر کا نام

یہ امڈتی ہوئی موجوں سے

لپٹتا ہوا کف

یہ ہواؤں سے گلے ملتے ہوئے

خاک کے ذرّے

یہ ہر اِک راہ پہ

شاخوں سے الگ ہو کے   سراسیمہ بکھرتے پتّے

Kishwar Naheed
Chains (Salasal)

Thread of life is but the name
Of the chain of breath.

Link of heart is nothing but
The heiroglyphics of the glance.

What we call the bond of blood,
Is but our own reflex.

Bond of sorrow is the noose
Tightening round our neck and breast.

The surf struggling to enfurl
The waves breaking on the shore;

The grains of dust trying hard
The flying winds to enfold:

The withered leaves
Shook from trees,
Lying scattered on the roads;

Rishta-e-jaan hai
Faqt saans ki zanjeer ka naam.

Rishta-e-dil hai
Faqt aankh ki tahreer ka naam,

Rishta-e-khoon hai
Faqt apni hi tasweer ka naam,

Rishta-e-ghum hai
Faqt halqa-e-dilgeer ka naam.

Yeh umadti hui maujon se
Lipat-ta hua kaf,

Yeh hawaaon se gale milte hue
Khaak ke zarre,

Yeh har ik rah pe
Shaakhon se alag ho ke,
Saraseema bikhre patte.

کشور ناہیدؔ

جبر کی سل پہ

کچلتے جذبے

یہ مری خواہشِ نایافت کی

تحریریں ہیں

یہ ترے جذبہِ امید کی

زنجیریں ہیں

Kishwar Naheed

Budding passions lying crushed
Beneath a heavy stone —

These are but the symbols of
My unrealised dreams,

These too the chains of hope
Woven with your kindly beams.

Jabar ki sil pe
Kuchalte jazbe—

Yeh miri khwahish-e-na yaafat ki
Tahreeren hain,

Yeh tire jazba-e-umeed ki
Zanjeeren hain.

☆

اہلِ دِل، آؤ سنو تو ہم بھی افسانہ کہیں

کچھ دہانِ زخم کھولیں، جورِ جانانہ کہیں

پھر پلٹ آئیں لٹاکر ہم متاعِ زندگی

پھر نظر کو دشت و صحرا دِل کو ویرانہ کہیں

ہم تو چڑھ کر دار پر بھی عشق کے گائیں گے گیت

لوگ ہم کو شوق سے چاہیں تو دیوانہ کہیں

ہم وفا پیشہ، وفا خوگر، وفا کے مدّعی

زندگی کو تیری بے مہری کا نذرانہ کہیں

ہنس کے پی لیں خونِ دِل اور ہنس کے ہی ناہیدؔ ہم

آنسوؤں کو مے کہیں، آنکھوں کو پیمانہ کہیں

Kishwar Naheed

Come ye, O, feeling hearts, we'll also tell our tale,
Give a tongue to our wounds, talk about his cruel ways.

Let's return woebegone, having squandered away our life,
Sow a desert in our eyes, in our heart a barren waste.

We'll sing the songs of love even in the gallows' face,
Let the people, if they like, call us manics, passion-crazed.

We the acolytes of faith, steadfast in our vows and ways,
Let's call this life, O cruel, an offering at your altar gate.

Smiling we'll drink our blood, smiling, O Naheed,
We'll compare the eyes to goblets, tears, to the flowing ale.

Ahl-e-dil, aao, suno tau hum bhi afsana kahen,
Kuchh dahaan-e-zakhm kholen, jaur-e-janaana kahen.

Phir palat aaen luta kar hum mitaa-e-zindagi,
Phir nazar ko dasht-o-sahra, dil ko weerana kahen.

Hum tau charh kar daar par bhi ishq ke gaaenge geet,
Log hum ko shauq se chaahen tau deewaana kahen.

Hum wafa pesha, wafa khoongar, wafa ke muddaee,
Zindagi ko teri be mihri ko nazraana kahen.

Hans ke pi len khoon-e-dil aur hans ke hi Naheed hum,
Aansuon ko mai kahen, aankhon ko paimana kahen.

☆

بیمار ہیں تو اب دمِ عیسیٰ کہاں سے آئے
اس دِل میں دردِ شوق و تمنّا کہاں سے آئے

بے کار شرحِ لفظ و معانی سے فائدہ
جب تو نہیں تو شہر میں تجھ سا کہاں سے آئے

ہر چشم، سنگِ کذب و عداوت سے سرخ ہے
اب آدمی کو زندگی کرنا کہاں سے آئے

وحشت ہوس کی چاٹ گئی خاک جسم کو
بے در گھروں میں شکل کا سایہ کہاں سے آئے

جڑ سے اکھڑ گئے تو بدلتی رُتوں سے کیا
بے آب آئینوں میں سراپا کہاں سے آئے

سایوں پہ اعتماد سے اکتا گیا ہے جی
طوفاں میں زندگی کا بھروسہ کہاں سے آئے

غم کے تھپیڑے لے گئے ناگن سے لمبے بال
راتوں میں جنگلوں کا وہ سایہ کہاں سے آئے

ناہیؔد فیشنوں نے چھپائے ہیں عیب بھی
چشمے نہ ہوں تو آنکھ کا پردہ کہاں سے آئے

Kishwar Naheed

Now that we are taken ill, where to find the breath of Christ ?
Who'll kindle love and longing in his heart, passion-dry ?

It boots not to interpret the words and their intent,
When you aren't in the town, where can we find your like ?

Every eye has gone red, stoned by the lies and spite,
How can man in this age learn the art to live his life ?

The wild lust has licked away the body's crust of dust,
How can a door-less house allow a shade to creep inside ?

Changing seasons make no difference to a plant, rootless, dry,
Can a mirror, bared of gloss, reflect your face, clear and bright ?

Placing too much faith in shadows has drained my living will,
Where to pluck the heart required to cope up with the storms
    of life ?

Shocks and griefs have shorn away the long, serpentining locks,
Where to find a shady grove in the deepening night ?

Fashions Naheed, can camouflage even our flaws and faults,
Thanks to the tinted glasses, we can now screen our eyes.

Beemaar hain tau ab dam-e-Isaa kahan se aae,
Us dil mein dard-e-shauq-o-tamanna kahan se aae ?

Bekaar shara-e-lafz-o-maani se fayda.
Jab tu nahin tau shahar mein tujh sa kahan se aae ?

Har chashm sang-e-kizb-o-adaawat se surkh hai,
Ab aadmi ko zindagi karna kahan se aae ?

Wahshat hawas ki chaat gai khaak-e-jism ko,
Be dar gharon mein shakl ka saya kahan se aae ?

Jar se ukhar gaye tau badalti ruton se kya,
Be aab aaeenon mein saraapa kahan se aae ?

Sayon pe aitmaad se ukta gaya hai ji,
Toofan mein zindagi ka bharosa kahan se aae ?

Ghum ke thapere le gaye naagin se lambe baal,
Raaton mein janglon ka woh saya kahan se aae ?

Naheed faishinon ne chhupaae hain aib bhi,
Chashme na hon tau aankh ka parda kahan se aae ?

کشور ناہیدؔ

رات آتی ہے

دو بستر

ایک ہی کمرے میں ایک چھت کے سائے میں

ایک پہ بہتا نیند کا ساغر

ایک پہ بے خوابی کا صحرا

ایک پہ نرم ہوا کے جھونکے

ایک پہ لُو سے گرم تھپیڑے

دو بستر

ایک پہ تکیے کی آغوش کا گھِرا بادل

ایک پہ شکنیں، اُمڈے دریا جیسی

ایک پہ خواب کی دیوانی اور دِکھے ہونٹ

ایک پہ آنکھ کی ویرانی اور سوکھے ہونٹ

دو بستر

بیچ میں ساحل

اور نہ صحرا

پھر بھی ڈونگا لمبا پینڈا

344

Kishwar Naheed
The Night Cometh (Raat Aati Hai)

Two beds
In one room, one roof beneath,
Here a flowing river of sleep,
There, a dreamless desert, bleak;
One, lapped by gentle breeze,
The other, by burning winds besieged.

Two beds—
One, crowned with a pillow soft,
The other, river-like, ruffled and tossed;
Here sweet dreaming lips agleam,
There looks and lips so famished seem.
Two beds—two bodies turning sides;
A river into the sea enlarged,
A rock spurting fiery sparks.

Two beds—
No shore betwixt,
No desert wide,
Yet a long and deep divide !

Do bistar
Ek hi kamre mein ek chhat ke saye mein
Ek pe bahta neend ka saagar,
Ek pe be khwabi ka sahra,
El pe narm hawa ke jhaunke,
Ek pe loo se garm thapere.

Do bistar
Ek pe takieye ki aaghosh ka gahra badal,
Ek pe shiknen umde darya jaisi,
Ek pe khwab ki deewali aur dahke hont
Ek pe aankh ki weerani aur sookhe hont.
Do bistar
Ek pe karwat, darya mile samundar mein,
Ek pe karwat, nikle aag ke jaise paththar mein.

Do bistar
Beech na saahil
Aur na sahra,
Phir bhi doonga, lamba painda.

Parveen Shakir
(1952-1994)

PARVEEN SHAAKIR (1952-1994)

Parveen Shaakir's life was cut short by a road accident at the young age of 42. She has left behind her four collections of poetry, *Khushboo, Sad Barg, Khud Kalaami* and *Inkaar*, which have enough of quality and durability to perpetuate her poetic fame. Like her contemporary Kishwar Naheed, Parveen was a versatile woman, who besides being a poet, was a journalist, a teacher, and a civil servant.

She was also a regular writer of a column in the Pakistani paper, *Jang*. Her poetry is built round her own experience of life as an Eastern woman, fretting under the tyranny of custom and convention, and watching the surrounding scene of injustice and hypocrisy which she couldn't change. She writes in her preface to *Sad barg* : "I was born in a family where to think and reason was a crime. Unlike the other girls of my kind, I refused to wear blinkers on my eyes. I insisted on seeing clearly and seeing whole. I suffered in consequence".

Despite their best efforts, her tormentors failed to blow out her inner flame. This is evidenced in her poetic volumes whose very names, such as *Khushboo* and *Sad Barg*, are indicative of the poet's capacity to build a song out of suffering, and create a cosmos out of the prevailing chaos. Parveen Shakir can handle both the traditional *ghazal* and the modern *nazm* with equal facility. Without rejecting the romantic mode of the *ghazal*, she can adapt it to the needs of her modern sensibility, or invest it, in the manner of John Donne, with bold, original imagery. In recognition of her talent and achievement she was honoued with "Adam Jee Award", and given the title of "Pride of Performance" by the Pakistan Government.

347

پروین شاکر

☆

کچھ تو ہوا بھی سرد تھی، کچھ تھا ترا خیال بھی
دل کو خوشی کے ساتھ ساتھ ہوتا رہا ملال بھی

بات وہ آدھی رات کی، رات وہ پورے چاند کی
چاند بھی عین چیت کا اس پہ ترا جمال بھی

سب سے نظر بچا کے وہ مجھ کو کچھ ایسے دیکھتا
ایک دفعہ تو رک گئی گردشِ ماہ و سال بھی

دل تو چمک سکے گا کیا، پھر بھی ترش کے دیکھ لیں
شیشہ گرانِ شہر کے ہاتھ کا یہ کمال بھی

اس کو نہ پا سکے تھے جب دل کا عجیب حال تھا
اب جو پلٹ کے دیکھیے، بات تھی کچھ محال بھی

میری طلب تھا ایک شخص وہ جو نہیں ملا تو پھر
ہاتھ دعا سے یوں گرا، بھول گیا سوال بھی

گاہ قریبِ شاہ رگ، گاہ بعیدِ وہم و خواب
اس کی رفاقتوں میں رات ہجر بھی تھا وصال بھی

اس کے ہی بازوؤں میں اور اس کو ہی سوچتے رہے
جسم کی خواہشوں پہ تھے روح کے اور جال بھی

348

Parveen Shaakir

I was closeted with your thought, cold was the air that blew,
I could feel a whiff of joy, tinged with a saddening hue.

It is the tale of deep midnight, when the moon was full and bright,
It was the month of Chet besides, and your beauty full in view.

When avoiding public gaze he cast on me a furtive glance,
For once at least, the sun and stars stared motionless and mute.

Who can re-burnish this heart, but let me try and get it chiselled,
Let me test the glazier's skill, his handiwork review.

When I failed to reach his hand, strange was my inward plight,
But in retrospect I feel, difficult was my target too.

A single being was my quest, him when I failed to get,
Down dropped my praying hands, I forgot to beg and sue.

Now near the jugular vein, now beyond the reach of thought,
In his company I could feel now close, now far-removed.

Though in his arms enwrapped, I was in his thought engrossed.
Promptings of the sensual self were by spiritual self subdued.

Kuchh tau hawa bhi sard thi, kuchh tha tira khayaal bhi,
Dil ko khushi ke saath saath hota raha malaal bhi.

Baat woh aadhi raat ki, raat woh poore chaand ki,
Chaand bhi ain Chet ka, us pe tira jamaal bhi.

Sab se nazar bacha ke woh mujhko aise dekhta,
Ek dafa tau ruk gai, gardish-e-maah-o-saal bhi.

Dil tau chamak sakega kya, phir bhi tarash ke dekh lein,
Sheesha garaan-e-shahr ke haath ka yeh kamaal bhi.

Us ko na paa sake the jab, dil ka ajeeb haal tha,
Ab jo palat ke dekhieye, baat thi kuchh mahaal bhi.

Meri talab tha ek shakhs, woh jo nahin mila tau phir,
Haath dua se yoon gira, bhool gaya sawaal bhi.

Gaah qareeb-e-shaah rug, gaah baeed-e-wahm-o-khwab,
Us ki rafaaqton mein raat, hijar bhi tha, wisaal bhi.

Us ke hi baazuon mein aur us ko hi sochte rahe,
Jism ki khwaahishon pe the rooh ke aur jaal bhi.

پروین شاکر

☆

دشت و دریا سے گزرنا ہو کہ گھر میں رہنا
اب تو ہر حال میں ہے ہم کو سفر میں رہنا

فیصلے سارے اسی کے ہیں ہماری بابت
اختیار اپنا بس اتنا کہ خبر میں رہنا

کوئی خاطر نہ مدارات نہ تقریبِ وصال
ہم تو بس چاہتے ہیں تیری نظر میں رہنا

میں تو ہر چہرے میں اب تک وہی چہرہ دیکھوں
اس کو ہر روز تماشائے دگر میں رہنا

وہی تنہائی، وہی دھوپ، وہی بے ستمی
گھر میں رہنا بھی ہوا، رہگزر میں رہنا

ٹوٹنا یوں تو مقدر ہے، مگر کچھ لمحے
پھول کی طرح میسر ہو شجر میں رہنا

ہر ملاقات کے بعد اجنبیت اور بڑھی
اس کو آئینے ہمیں زعمِ ہنر میں رہنا

کوئی سیفو ہو کہ میرا ہو کہ پروین، اسے
راس آتا ہی نہیں چاند نگر میں رہنا

350

Parveen Shaakir

Whether we wade through rivers and forests, or at home stay,
Travel is our destiny, whatever be the state.

It is he who takes decisions about our life and fate,
We are only kept informed of all his dictates.

No favour, no special treat, nor a plea for union sweet,
We only want day and night to live beneath your gaze.

I still find the face beloved in every face I see,
But a new face, every day, doth his heart engage.

The same seclusion and indifference, the same scorching sun,
Staying at home is no better than wandering far away.

Though to fall is our fate, but for a little space,
Flower-like on the branch, we would like to sway.

We feel ever more estranged after every meet,
There she sits, beauty drunk, here am I, talent-crazed.

Be it Sappho, be it Mira, or be it Parveen,
If planted on the moon, would wither away and fade.

Dasht-o-darya se guzarna ho, ke ghar mein rahna,
Ab tau har haal mein hai hum ko safar mein rahna.

Faisle saare usi ke hain hamari baabat,
Ikhtiaar apna bas itna ke khabar mein rahna.

Koi khaatir, na madaraat, na taqreeb-e-wisaal,
Hum tau bas chaahte hain teri nazar mein rahna.

Main tau har chehre mein ab tak wohi chehra dekhoon,
Us ko har roz tamaashaa-e-digar mein rahna.

Wohi tanhaai, wohi dhoop, wohi be-sitami,
Ghar mein rahna bhi hua rahguzar mein rahna.

Tootna yoon tau muqaddar hai, magar kuchh lamhe,
Phool ki tarah muyassar ho shajar mein rahna.

Har mulaqaat ke baad ajnabiat aur barhi,
Us ko aaeene, hamen zom-e-hunar mein rahna.

Koi Sappho ke Mira ho, ke Parveen, use
Raas aata hi nahin Chaand Nagar mein rahna.

پروین شاکر

☆

پھیلا دیے خود ہاتھ طلبگار کے آگے
دیکھا نہیں کچھ ہم نے خریدار کے آگے

شہزادے! مری نیند کو تو کاٹ چکا ہے
ٹھہرا نہ یہ جنگل تری تلوار کے آگے

کیا جاں کے خسارے کی تمنّا ہو کہ اب عِشق
بڑھتا ہی نہیں درہم و دینار کے آگے

وہ ایڑ لگی رخشِ زمانہ کو کہ اب تو
اسوار سراسیمہ ہے رہوار کے آگے

یا قوس رکھے یا وہ ہمیں دائرہ کردے
نقطے کی طرح ہیں کسی پرکار کے آگے

جاں اپنی ہے اور آبرو نسلوں کی کمائی
سر کون بچاتا پھرے دستار کے آگے

گھمسان کا رن جیت کے لب بستہ کھڑی ہوں میں
پشت سے آئے ہوئے اک وار کے آگے

352

Parveen Shaakir

We at once seized the offer whoever did make,
Sold ourself to the buyer without settling the rate.

You have, O prince, at one stroke, slashed off my sleep,
The brunt of your mortal sword this forest couldn't brave.

Who'll wish to stake his life for the sake of love,
The bargain now doesn't cross the "cash and carry" stage.

The steed of life is spurred so hard by the maddening times,
The rider sitting astride the horse, feels stunned and mazed.

He may turn us to a circle, or leave us as a broken arc,
We are like a helpless point before compasses laid.

Life belongs to us alone, honour is our heritage,
Who'll care to save his head and lose the turban in its place ?

Having won a mortal combat, we feel unnerved,
The sudden thrust from behind, has left us dumb and dazed.

Phaila dieye khud haath talabgaar ke aage,
Dekha nahin kuchh hum ne kharidaar ke aage.

Shahzaade, miri neend ko tu kaat chuka hai,
Thahra na yeh jungle tiri talwaar ke aage.

Kya jaan ke khasaare ki tamanna ho ke ab ishq.
Barhta hi nahin darham-o-deenar ke aage.

Woh aer lagi rakhsh-e-zamaane ko, ke ab tau,
Aswaar saraseema hai rahwaar ke aage.

Ya qaus rakhe ya woh hamen daaira kar de,
Nuqte ki tarah hain kisi parkaar ke aage.

Jaan apni hai aur aabroo naslon ki kamaai,
Sar kaun bachaata phire dastaar ke aage.

Ghumsaan ka run jeet ke lab-basta khari hoon,
Main pusht se aae hue ik waar ke aage.

پروین شاکِر

خود کلامی

یوں لگتا ہے

جیسے میرے گرد و پیش کے لوگ

اِک اور ہی بولی بولتے ہیں

وہ ویو لینتھ

جس پر میرا اور ان کا رابطہ قائم تھا

کسی اور سمّے میں چلی گئی

یا میری لغت متروک ہوئی

یا ان کا محاورہ اور ہوا

مرے لفظ مجھے جس رستے پر لے جاتے ہیں

اس رستے کے معنی کے لیے

ان کی فرہنگ جدا ہے

میں لفظوں کی تقدیس کی خاطر چپ ہوں

اور میری ساری گفتگو

دیوار سے یا تنہائی سے یا اپنے سایے سے ممکن ہے

Parveen Shaakir
Self-Communion (Khud Kalaami)

It seems as if
My neighbouring folks
Speak a different tongue.
The wave-length

Which kept us interlinked,
Has quit this planet long ago.
Perhaps my lexicon is old,
Or their idiom new and bold.

The path that my words prescribe
Needs a different key
To unlock its import.

To preserve the sanctity of my words I sit tongue-tied;
I only talk to the walls, to myself, or my shade.

Yoon lagta hai
Jaise mere gird-o-pesh ke log
Ik aur hi boli bolte hain
Woh wave-length
Jis par mera aur unka raabta qaayam tha
Kisi aur kurre mein chali gai
Ya meri lugt matrook hui
Ya unka mahaawra aur hua
Mire lafz mujhe jis raste par le jaate hain

Us raste ke maani ke lieye
Un ki farhang juda hai
Main lafzon ki taqdees ki khaatir chup hoon

Aur meri saari gufatgoo
Deewaar se ya tanhaai se ya apne saye se mumkin hai.

پروین شاکر

مجھے ڈر اس پل سے لگتا ہے

جب خود میں سکڑتے سکڑتے

میں اپنے آپ سے باتیں کرنے والی

(رابطہ رکھنے والی)

فریکوینسی بھی بھلا دوں

اور اک دن

"مے ڈے، مے ڈے" کرتی رہ جاؤں

Parveen Shaakir

I am afraid the time may come
When getting more and more withdrawn,
I may lose the frequency,
The self-communing faculty,
(The link that joins me with me).
And I may sit and shout one day,
(Without knowing what I say) "May Day, May Day !"

Mujhe dar us pal se lagta hai
Jab khud mein sukar-te sukar-te
Main apne aap se baaten karne waali
(Raabta rakhne waali)
Frequency bhi bhula doon,
Aur ik din
"May Day, May Day" karti rah jaaoon.